MODERN HUMANITIES RESEARCH ASSOCIATION
CRITICAL TEXTS
VOLUME 40

ALFONSO X, THE LEARNED

CANTIGAS DE SANTA MARIA

AN ANTHOLOGY

Modern Humanities Research Association
2015

Alfonso X, the Learned

Cantigas de Santa Maria

Edited by
Stephen Parkinson

Published by

The Modern Humanities Research Association,
Salisbury House
Station Road
Cambridge CB1 2LA
United Kingdom

First published 2015

ISBN 978-1-78188-023-4

Copies may be ordered from www.criticaltexts.mhra.org.uk

CONTENTS

PREFACE

The present edition is the first output of a new complete critical edition undertaken by the Centre for the Study of the *Cantigas de Santa Maria* of Oxford University. It will eventually be integrated into a new full edition of the text and the music, in collaboration with Professor Manuel Pedro Ferreira of the Universidade Nova, Lisbon.

The selection of poems has been governed by criteria of narrative, linguistic and metrical interest and of representativity of the different genres, rather than by devotional and historical content. As a result, some of the better known versions of 'international' miracles and of tales of *cristianos, moros y judíos* have not been included, and the number of *cantigas de loor* has been limited. For reasons of space few of the lengthier poems have been included.

The structure of the anthology mirrors the organisation of the compilations of the *Cantigas de Santa Maria* (described in section 3.3 of the Introduction). It opens with a prologue, introducing a central body of forty *Cantigas de Santa Maria*, organised in blocks of ten with each tenth poem a lyric *cantiga de loor*. The sequence is closed by the epilogue, followed by a small appendix of festal and paraliturgical poems. Each poem is laid out on a complete number of pages, with text, translations and apparatus harmoniously combined, in an analogue of the layout of text, music and illustrations in the illustrated manuscripts T and F (see p. 2).

The production of the texts for this edition is funded by British Academy Research Development Award 100062, building on work for the *Cantigas de Santa Maria* Database funded by the Leverhulme Trust, the Modern Humanities Research Association, Oxford University, and the British Academy Small Grants Scheme. Various research assistants have contributed to this project since its inception in 2003: Deirdre Jackson, Alison Campbell and Roberto Ceolin, and most recently David Barnett, who has been responsible for the formatting and preparation of the texts and critical apparatus for publication, and whose sharp editorial eye has much improved the Introduction. I am grateful to Manuel Pedro Ferreira for advice on text-music relations and the identification of the Feasts of the Virgin, and to Laura Fernández for discussions of manuscript issues.

In this anthology the poems are identified by the short titles assigned in the *Cantigas de Santa Maria* Database. For general reference purposes we use the *cantiga* numbers established by Mettmann's editions (Mettmann 1959–72, 1986–89). A completely new line numbering system has been adopted, in which strophes are numbered and line numbers are assigned inside each strophe. Original translations have been provided for all poems, drawing on and expanding an archive of performable translations produced for medieval music groups from the 1970s onwards. Wherever possible, the translations have been displayed on separate pages from text and apparatus, to allow the *Anthology* to function as a monolingual teaching text.

Full documentation of every *cantiga* will be found on the *Cantigas de Santa Maria* Database <csm.mml.ox.ac.uk>.

This edition is dedicated to the memory of my parents,
Marie and John Parkinson

INTRODUCTION

1. Alfonso X and the *Cantigas de Santa Maria*

The collection of poems in praise of the Blessed Virgin Mary known as the *Cantigas de Santa Maria* (*CSM*) occupies a very special position in medieval Hispanic literature and culture, and in the works produced at the court of King Alfonso X of Castile and León.[1]

The traditional title of the collection requires some explanation, to avoid the many misunderstandings arising from its (mis)interpretation and (mis)translation. The term *cantiga* is one of a pair of terms — *cantar* and *cantiga* — used to denote lyric poetry in medieval Iberia. Both *cantar* and *cantiga* imply that such texts would be performed to music, usually by a paid performer (Castilian *juglar*, Galician-Portuguese *jogral*), as was the norm for courtly poetry throughout Iberia: the term *poema* is never used for this type of work, and there is no concept of lyric poetry not intended for musical performance.[2] The music for a *cantar* could be specially composed for (or together with) the poem, or could be adapted from existing song or dance music. The modern term *cantiga* (modern Galician *cántiga*) has none of the liturgical associations of the related term *cântico* or English *canticle*.[3] No English version of the title has established itself, and the poems are well known to musical audiences as '(the) Cantigas'. By comparison with other *cancioneiros*, perhaps the most appropriate label for the collection would in fact be *The Songbook of the Blessed Virgin*.[4]

There has to be some doubt as to whether Alfonso himself referred to his collection as the *Cantigas de Santa Maria*. In his second will and testament (of January 1284) the king made arrangements for 'los libros de los cantares de Santa Maria' to be deposited in the church where he was laid to rest.[5] The nearest thing we have to a title page — the poem placed at the beginning of the earliest manuscript, often wrongly labelled as a prologue — refers to the contents as *cantares e sões*, and is echoed by the epilogal *Petiçon* ('Petition') which asks the Virgin to accept his offering of *cantares*. The term *cantiga* is nevertheless firmly embedded in the compilations (see section 3.1).

Alfonso X, King of Castile and León from 1252 until his death in 1284, was by any standards a cultural giant. Under his patronage and direction were produced major works of history (*Cronica General*, *Cronica de España*), scientific works translated from Arabic sources (*Libro conplido en los iudizios de las estrellas*, *Libro de saber de astrologia*, *Lapidario*), chess (*Libro de axedrez*), and the legal code of the *Siete Partidas*, earning him the posthumous epithet of El Sabio (The Learned).[6] His acute sense of posterity led to these works being preserved in luxurious manuscripts produced by a highly organised system of *scriptoria*.[7] He is credited with the foundation of the Spanish University and with the systematic importation of Arabic science into Europe. His court was a magnet for scholars and poets from all over Europe. Individually, he has a place in the Galician-Portuguese lyric as a poet of considerable skill, as evidenced by a body of satirical poetry (*cantigas de escarnho*) and debate poetry (*tençōes*) of extreme ingenuity and metrical sophistication combined with a ferocity born of deep frustration.[8]

---

[1] The collection will be referred to as the *Cantigas de Santa Maria* or *CSM*. Individual poems are identified by their number in the Anthology (in square brackets), as well as by their number in the complete collection (following Mettmann 1986–89) and where relevant by their number in an individual manuscript.

[2] Inside Castilian narrative and didactic poetry there is a bifurcation between the epic *cantar de gesta*, sung to simple and stereotypical melodies, and the form which modern critics have labelled *mester de clerecia* which was intended for non-musical reading or recitation.

[3] Miranda (2010) suggests that the term *cantiga* may have been first used in the *CSM*, with some liturgical connotations, before being generalised to the secular lyric. The term *trova(s)* 'verses' is much less used than the verb *trovar* and the noun *trovador*.

[4] Kathleen Kulp-Hill (2000) translates the collection as *Songs of Holy Mary*. J. E. Keller (1958), refers to them as *canticles*. Montoya (1991) labels the *CSM* a *cancioneiro marial*, emphasising the parallelism with the secular lyric.

[5] Martínez (2003: 617–18) transcribes the will.

[6] Procter 1951.

[7] Guerrero Lovillo 1949, Montoya and Domínguez 1999, Fernández 2013b.

[8] Alfonso's reign was marked by many personal and political setbacks, not least the premature death of his son Fernando de la Cerda, his failure to secure nomination as Holy Roman Emperor, and the continual opposition of his surviving sons, which led to his deposition in 1282.

The *Cantigas de Santa Maria* represent the extension or diversion of this poetic activity into the devotional sphere, reflecting the king's very special devotion to the Mother of God: the manuscripts which preserve them are among the finest products of the Alfonsine scriptorium. Of all the works commissioned by Alfonso X they most clearly bridge the gap between authorship and patronage, as Alfonso undoubtedly wrote some of the verses, and it has been recently suggested that he may also have composed music for his own verses.[9]

The rather simplistic view of early historians by which Alfonso's satirical poetry belongs to his ill-spent youth and the *CSM* to a devout middle age has been revised but not reversed by historical studies attributing a significant number of satirical poems to Alfonso's early life as *infante* and assigning the main compilations of the *CSM*, if not their composition, to the last years of his reign (Oliveira 2010). The presence of one of the *cantigas* (40) alongside a vaguely devotional poem of praise in the secular lyric tradition shows that the link between his troubadour and devotional verse was known to the compilers of the medieval *cancioneiros*. He was also known to the Catalan Cerverí de Girona, who visited the Castilian Court in 1269 and addresses Alfonso directly in his *Canço de Madona Santa Maria*: 'Reys castelas, tota res mor e fina, mas non o fay la domn' on vos chantatz' [King of Castile, all things die and end, but not the lady of whom you sing].[10]

Four contemporary manuscripts of the *CSM* have survived.[11] The smallest, MS 10069 of the Biblioteca Nacional de Madrid, known as the Toledo manuscript and referred to by the siglum **To**, originally located in Toledo Cathedral library, represents the earliest stage of the project, a nucleus of 100 *cantigas* with prologues and epilogues, and three appended clusters, one of songs for the main feast days of the Blessed Virgin Mary, one for general feast days, and a third of additional *cantigas* not included in the central compilation. The largest, located in the Escorial library (Real Biblioteca del Monasterio de San Lorenzo de el Escorial, MS B.i.2), known as E or the *códice de los músicos*, contains the title poem, the Prologue, four hundred *cantigas de Santa Maria*, and two epilogues.[12] It also contains a separate booklet of twelve *cantigas de Festas de Santa Maria*, bound at the beginning of the volume but probably originally separate. The remaining two manuscripts, known collectively as the *códice(s) de las historias*, form a two-volume sequence which if finished would have contained 400 poems.

An additional principle of organisation comes into play in the *códice(s) de las historias*. As part of their large scale decorative plan, the fifth *cantiga* of every group of ten was more extensively illustrated, on two pages — rather than just one — arranged as a double page spread on consecutive *verso* and *recto* sides.[13] The main criterion for inclusion in this category was narrative complexity: the *miragre* needed to have enough episodes or stages to warrant twelve separate miniature panels. The first volume, held with E in the Escorial Library (Real Biblioteca del Monasterio de San Lorenzo de el Escorial MS T.i.1), known as the *códice rico* (siglum T), was in all probability completed but is currently missing the beginning of its table of contents and its last five poems, as well as two poems excised from the complete volume; the second, Banco Rari 20 of the Biblioteca Nazionale Centrale, Florence, known as the Florence manuscript (siglum F), was never completed, containing a set of disordered quires with just over 100 texts and a large number of complete and incomplete pages of illustrations. The illustrative programme of the *códice(s) de las historias* entails a much higher level of page design integrating text and music. In **To** and E the opening refrain and strophe of each *cantiga* are set to their music, with the text placed directly under musical staves, and the complete *cantiga* usually flowing over several pages; in T and F the text and music of each *cantiga* is carefully fitted onto a complete page or pages, with a larger portion of the text, and occasionally the whole *cantiga*, underlaid to its music.[14] Only T has the musical notation inserted; F has fully ruled blank staves above the text.

Over the full set of manuscripts we find a total of 419 *cantigas de Santa Maria*, of several different types: 43 *cantigas de loor*, lyrics in praise of the Blessed Virgin Mary; 16 *cantigas de Festas* and seasonal songs, two prologues

[9] Ferreira (2007) finds melodic similarities between a number of songs for which textual authorship is well supported.

[10] Fernández 2013a: 91. These references to poetic activity do not necessarily imply the existence of specific compilations.

[11] Fernández 2009, 2013a, 2013b.

[12] This name reflects the presence of illuminated pictures of musicians accompanying each *cantiga de loor*.

[13] These are now called *quints* (Parkinson 2000a) or *cantigas quinales* (Fernández 2013: 97).

[14] See Parkinson 2000b, Ferreira 1998 for the methods and implications of this principle.

and two epilogues; and 357 narratives of miracles of the Virgin (see section 3 for a full explanation of these genres and their interrelation). There is in addition a versified title, without music. Each compilation arranges its *cantigas* in groups of ten, nine narrative *miragres* followed by a *loor*; each has a different combination and order of *cantigas*, so that Alfonso's apparent ultimate intention of a central collection of 400 *cantigas* made up of 41 *loores* and 359 *miragres* is not perfectly realised in any one of them.

Linguistically and poetically the *Cantigas de Santa Maria* are part of the Galician-Portuguese lyric tradition, standing alongside the body of over 1600 poems composed in Galician and Portuguese by poets from all the Christian kingdoms of the Centre and West of the Iberian peninsula, from the late 12th century to the middle of the 14th.[15] The *CSM* show a number of Galician orthographic traits (notably the consistent use of <ll> and <nn> for the palatal consonants represented by <nh> and <lh> in the official Portuguese script of the late 13th century) beside the coexistence of regional and chronological variants found in much greater quantities in the secular lyric. They differ primarily from the secular lyric in their extensive use of the *zajal* form (see section 7.2) and in the uniform preservation of their music.

The composition of the *Cantigas*, and the collection of miracle stories destined to berecounted in the narrative poems which form the bulk of the corpus, undoubtedly occupied much of Alfonso's reign. The process of collection of miracle stories may well have started in the 1260s, with the archive progressively expanded with local miracle stories up to the production of the main compilations in the final years of Alfonso's reign, 1280–84.[16] The project remained unfinished at his death in 1284.

2. Impact and Publication History

For a lyric corpus of such quality and importance, the *CSM* had remarkably little impact on Hispanic culture until the 20th century. Despite the king's reputation as a writer of Marian songs, there is no direct or indirect contemporary evidence of performance, citation or imitation of the *Cantigas* in the Galician-Portuguese lyric, and much of the history of the manuscripts remains obscure. Alfonso's will stipulated that the *libros de los cantares de Santa Maria* should be deposited in the church of his last resting place, and that they should be performed on feast days of the Virgin. The will seems to have been respected, to the extent that T, F and E were initially deposited in the Royal Chapel of Seville Cathedral, from where T and F were soon returned to the royal collections, under Sancho IV (r. 1284–95) or Alfonso XI (r. 1313–50). T and F remained together until the accession of Queen Isabel (1474), who gave F to her loyal steward Andrés Cabrera, after which it passed into the book trade to end up, like the main copy of the secular lyric, in the hands of Italian bibliophiles. E remained in Seville until Philip II (r. 1556–98) requisitioned it for his private library, from where it passed to the Escorial library, where both E and T are recorded in an inventory of 1576.[17] **To** is first documented in Toledo Cathedral in 1727, and entered the Biblioteca Nacional in 1869: there is no documentary trace of its presumed exemplar.

There is no record of performances using the Seville manuscripts, even of the liturgically orientated *festas*.[18] The Toledo manuscript has marginal annotations indicating the feast days on which its festal *cantigas* should be sung, but once again there is no direct evidence of use. Indeed, very little notice seems to have been taken of the *Cantigas* between Alfonso's death and the 18th century, when the Jesuit father Andrés Marcos Burriel (1719–62) commissioned a copy of the Toledo manuscript, made by the calligrapher Santiago y Palomares (Boynton 2011). In the late 19th century the Real Academia Española finally commissioned a full edition of the texts, under the direction of the Marqués de Valmar, with a musical edition by Julián Ribera added as vol. 3 in 1922. The Academy edition remained the standard textual edition until 1959, when the German scholar Walter Mettmann published the first volume of his first edition, under the Portuguese imprint of the University of Coimbra (Mettmann

[15] Tavani 1969, 2002, Jensen 1978.

[16] Fernández 2009.

[17] Fernández 2009 traces the provenance and movements of the manuscripts .

[18] The *festas* may well have been kept apart from the main body of *CSM*, as a separate *livro de cantares*, until E was rebound in the 17th century.

1959–72).[19] In 1986–89 Mettmann published a revised version of his edition in a simpler format, retaining the same numbering and making superficial changes to the texts. Meanwhile the Catalan scholar Higinio Anglés had produced a monumental musical edition, based on the Valmar text, in 1943, followed by commentary in 1958 and a facsimile of E, the presumed *codex princeps*, in 1964 (Anglés 1943–64). As a result of Anglés's work, the *CSM* finally entered the modern repertory of medieval song, where they were eagerly taken up despite the absence of textual editions fit for the purpose of performance.[20]

3. Contents and Organisation

3.1 Genres

The *CSM* fall into a small number of categories or subgenres, which are relevant both for comparison between them and the secular lyric tradition and for the internal organisation of the manuscript compilations.

The main division is between *cantigas de loor* and *miragres*. The *cantigas de loor* are lyric poems celebrating the person of the Virgin Mary, and focusing on her name, qualities and epithets, and on episodes from her life. The *miragres* are narrative tales of miracles performed by or through the Virgin Mary. Both of these labels are to some extent modern creations, based on explanatory rubrics in which *cantiga* or *cantar* is used as a generic term for songs, and *miragre* and *loor* as descriptive categories of content:

> Pois que el rei fez cen cantares de miragres e de loores de Santa Maria e ouve feita sa pitiçon teve por ben de fazer outras cinco cantigas das sas festas do ano (To f. 136r).
>
> [After the king composed a hundred songs about miracles and in praise of Holy Mary, and had made his petition, he saw fit to compose a further five songs about her feast days.]

The rubrics preceding each poem use standard formats for indicating content, implying the label *cantiga* through the use of feminine gender to refer to individual pieces: for *cantigas de loor*, the basic format is *Esta ... é de loor de Santa Maria*; for miragres *Esta é como....*[21] In a real sense all the poems are 'de loor de Santa Maria' in that every miracle is a cause for devotional praise, and the whole collection is an act of devotion.[22] No additional label is used in rubrics for the *miragres*. The poems celebrating feast days appear labelled as *Cantigas das Festas de Jesucristo* and *Cantigas das Festas de Santa Maria.*

Allied to this difference of content is a difference of metrical and musical practice. The *miragres* are highly standardized in their metrics, using the *zéjel* or proto-*virelai* form (section 7) to create narrative poems of highly variable length (from 4 to 50 strophes). The *cantigas de loor* use a wide variety of strophic forms, ranging from parallelistic poems similar to the secular *cantiga de amigo* (e.g. *cantiga* 160, Anthology [4]) through *cantigas de meestria* typical of the courtly *cantiga de amor* (*Prologue*, *cantiga* 1 [1]) to highly complex strophic forms reminiscent of the Occitan *canso* (*cantiga* 340 [45]). They include most of the *cantigas* which have no refrain or a refrain which does not match the *zéjel* form, and they are typically limited to six or fewer strophes.

The organisation of all compilations of the *CSM* involves a structured alternation of *loores* and *miragres*: the very first *cantiga* is *de loor*, after which every tenth item is a *loor*, and the intervening items are *miragres*. This not only creates a rosary-like structure but also makes the compilation structure analogous to the internal

---

[19] An edition of 34 *cantigas* by Manuel Rodrigues Lapa (1933) was influential in raising issues of layout and metrical structure but did not diverge from Valmar in textual matters.

[20] Fidalgo (2003) edits the text of the *cantigas de loor*; Schaffer (2010) is a transcription and edition of To; Cunningham (2000) is a musical edition of the *cantigas de loor* with texts based primarily on Mettmann.

[21] The modern title appears only twice, associated with the literal Prologue to the collection, in the table of contents of E, *Este e o prologo das cantigas de Santa Maria* [This is the prologue of the Songs of Holy Mary], and following the same poem in T, *aqui se acaba o prologo das cantigas de Santa Maria* [Here ends the Prologue of the Songs of Holy Mary].

[22] This is captured in the rubric to the *Petiçon* (To f. 133v): *Esta e la pitiçon que fez el rei don Afonso a Santa Maria por galardon destos cen cantares que ouve feitos dos seus miragres a loor dela* [This is the petition of King Alfonso to Holy Mary, asking for his reward for the hundred songs he composed on her miracles, in praise of her].

structure of the *zéjel* in which the regular repetition of the refrain establishes the moral of the poem as a constant.[23]

Closely related to the *cantigas de loor* are the *cantigas de festas*, poems dedicated to feast days, both major feasts of the Catholic church and the five feasts of the Virgin (Nativity 8 September; Annunciation 25 March; Purification/Candlemas 2 February; Assumption/Dormition 15 August; Expectation 18 December). There is considerable overlap between these groups: three *loores* were reused as festal *cantigas* in E[24] and several other *loores* deal with feast days or standard religious topoi (*cantiga* 1 [1] on the Seven Joys of the Virgin, *cantiga* 408 (**To** 50) on the Seven Sorrows).

A final class of poems related to *loores* are the poems which frame the complete compilations as prologues and epilogues. The opening Prologue and the epilogal *Petiçon* [41] are metrically distinctive and numerologically significant, the former being a refrainless *cantiga de meestria* in seven strophes and the latter an emblematic poem of 100 lines in ten ten-line monorhymed strophes (mirroring the ten groups of ten poems of which the first compilation of 100 poems was constructed). One unclassifiable poem which seems to have been lost in the compilation process is *Ben vennas Maio* (406 [43]) a maytime song in which the king welcomes May with a series of satirical requests to the Virgin: despite the association between May and Mary (partly through the numerology of five, celebrated in *cantiga* 70 [20] and the prologue to the *Festas*) this song appears as no 1 of the **To** appendix, but does not reappear: it could not be used as a festal *cantiga* as there is no Marian feast in May, it could not be a *loor* as it reflects the folk tradition of *maias*, and it could not be a *miragre* as it has no narrative.[25] Similarly the five *Festas de Jesucristo* appended to **To** (a song on the Creation, followed by songs for Easter, Epiphany, the Assumption, and Pentecost) are not incorporated into the full compilations.

3.2 *Text and Paratext*

The presentation of the poems in the compilations involves a complex page layout integrating of a number of textual and paratextual elements. (Not all manuscripts show the complete set of paratexts, as interrupted production, physical loss of folios and cropping of leaves have taken their toll.) In the case of the narrative *cantigas* the paratextual elements constitute parallel narratives.

Each poem is provided with a rubric (or epigraph) summarizing its content, which is copied into the tables of contents preceding the complete manuscripts.[26] In most of the manuscripts each *cantiga* is also assigned a number, which is either incorporated in the rubric (in **To**, **E Festas**) or placed in a running head (E, T).[27] In **To** each of the appended clusters of poems (the five *Festas de Santa Maria*, the five *Festas de Jesucristo*, and the appendix of sixteen additional *cantigas*) is introduced by a narrative rubric.

In the layout programme of the ornate *códices de las historias*, T and F, each poem is matched with one or two full-page illustrative miniatures, typically divided into six panels, providing a graphic narrative. Sadly, many of the poems created in the final stages of the project, and those discarded during the evolution of the collections, were never illustrated. The panels of the miniatures are themselves provided with narrative captions or legends, which act as a bridge between the images and the text.

---

[23] Nepaulsingh (1986: 19, 33–36) seems to have been the first of many critics to develop the links between the *Cantigas*, the medieval rosary and the *rosarium* (a type of 50-stanza poem to the Virgin), citing iconographical evidence for a rosary constructed in sequences of ten beads. (The object illustrated in panel d of the miniature for *cantiga* 172 (T f. 189v) is, however, more likely to be an 18-stone necklace than a poorly depicted rosary.)

[24] *Cantiga* 340 also appears as no 2 of the *Festas de Santa Maria* (*FSM*); *cantiga* 210, a *loor* on the Annunciation, is repeated as no. 6 of the *FSM*, and the litany appearing as the final *loor* of the **To** collections is reused as *FSM* 12.

[25] Schaffer 2001.

[26] Schaffer 1992 shows that subtle differences in the form of rubrics show an evolution from those highlighting the agency of the Blessed Virgin, in the initial compilation, to a greater focus on the beneficiary in the newer poems incorporated in T and F, and back to an emphasis on Holy Mary in the final one hundred poems of E.

[27] The cantigas of F are unnumbered, and have been assigned numbers by modern editors according to their order in the manuscript. The folios of F have been cropped so it is not possible to know whether the headers containing the numbers were completed.

The miniatures of the *códice de las historias* are themselves a major corpus of iconography, depicting a vast range of 13th-century artefacts, characters, places, and activities, and deploying many subtle techniques of graphic narrative. They stand in a complex relationship to the texts, which they not only visualise but also interpret, modify and supplement. In some cases the miniatures draw on narrative content from hagiographical sources which the composers of the textual narrative did not know or chose not to use (e.g. the presence of a hermit in *cantiga* 7 [3]). The captions further complicate this relationship, being summaries of the images but incorporating references to the texts themselves. Most poems end with an act of recognition, repentance or collective praise, which typically provides the final panel of the miniature. In T a later hand has inserted extensive Castilian prose summaries in the margins beneath the miniatures of *cantigas* 2–25, but these must be considered additions rather than an integral part of the compilations.

The relationship between text and image and text and paratext is a complex one, but in almost every case the paratext is derivative and represents scribes' or artists' often faulty understanding of the text: it can rarely be used with authority to resolve issues arising from the text.

3.3 *Manuscripts and Compilations*

The four manuscripts of the *CSM* (described in 1 above) do not stand in a simple genealogical relation one to another, as none can be said to be a copy or a descendant of any of the others. Instead they represent three different *compilations*, in which an evolving archive of *cantigas*, probably stored as individual sheets or rolls, was presented in different combinations, orders and decorative schemes.

The earliest compilation, and arguably the earliest manuscript, is **To**. It contains what is assumed to be the initial compilation ordered by Alfonso, of 100 poems (11 *de loor*, 89 *de miragre*, organised in tens) with a prologue and an epilogue, and a versified preface or title page. Both the preface and the epilogue refer explicitly to the number of 100 *cantigas*.[28] **To** contains a number of additional clusters (copied in sequence, rather than being bound as separate booklets), containing five *Festas de Santa Maria*, five *Festas de Jesucristo*, and sixteen additional *cantigas* of various types, with a separate number sequence.[29] Opinion is divided on whether the manuscript is the original first compilation, a copy contemporaneous with the first compilation, or a copy executed outside the royal scriptorium at a later date. The musical notation uses a different notational system from the other manuscripts, arguably earlier and more primitive; the texts have been amended, not always for the better, by collation with the readings of T/E, and have a number of marginal annotations providing *inter alia* instructions for the liturgical use of the festal *cantigas*.

T, F and E represent the mature development of the project, with T/F implementing it in its most elaborate presentational form. It is not possible to tell whether the expansion of the corpus from one hundred to four hundred was a single change of policy or a progressive expansion first to two hundred and finally to four hundred, or whether the king's collection policy drove compilation or vice versa. It is clear, however, that the **To** compilation and the poems composed but not formally compiled — the **To** appendices — form the basis of the new compilation of T, which is replicated with minimal changes of order in the first 200 items of E; by contrast, the second 200 poems of E do not correspond to the extant or reconstructable form of F, either in their order or in their contents. E duplicates seven *miragres*, all the duplicates occurring in the final 30 items, while F includes some pieces not incorporated in E or T.[30] It is generally assumed that E was commenced in parallel with T as an archive copy of the final compilation and an insurance policy against the possible (and latterly inevitable)

[28] The first fifty songs are marked out by the initial *loor* on the Seven Joys of the Virgin and then a closing *loor* on the Seven Sorrows (**To** 50, *cantiga* 408). **To** thus has the structure of a double *rosarium* (see fn 23), an organisation abandoned, along with *cantiga* 408, in the later compilations.

[29] It is not clear whether the appendix was intended to have a cognate structure to the main compilation: it begins with the seasonal poem *Ben vennas maio* [43], and includes a *cantiga de loor* numbered 10 but in fact eleventh in the cluster as the preceding *cantiga* is also numbered 10.

[30] In this Anthology, [31] appears twice, with minor variants, in E, as E267 and E373; [45] appears as E340 and E Festas 2, with variation in the order of the final strophes.

curtailment of the production of the luxurious T/F version: once the production of E caught up with the production of F the two teams were in competition for the master copies, and it became impossible for the two projects to maintain the same structure of compilation. The relatively humble production values of E are reflected in its many deficiencies of layout and the lower quality of its text and musical copy, resulting in the paradox of the only reasonably complete manuscript, and one on which any modern numbering scheme must be based, being the least reliable text on which to base an edition.

4. The *Cantigas de Santa Maria* as a Miracle Collection

As a collection of tales of miracles of the Virgin, the *CSM* belong to the late medieval tradition which begins with collections of Marian miracles in Britain and France, develops through the Latin compilations of the 11th century as the cult of the Blessed Virgin expanded, and developed into multiple vernacular traditions in the poetic collections of Gautier de Coinci, Gonçalo de Berceo, and the Norman poet Adgar.[31] Alfonso, as an exemplary devotee of the Virgin, was doing nothing that previous poets and collectors had not done, though he achieved it on a scale and with a lavishness befitting his station.

A typical miracle collection contains a selection of international and widely diffused miracles and clusters from smaller compilations of miracles associated shrines such as Canterbury, Laon, Rocamadour and Soissons, combined with more localised or generic miracles.[32] Where the *collection* is itself associated with a miraculous shrine, miracle stories exemplify the healing and protective power of the Virgin to the workmen constructing the shrine (as in [28]) or to the faithful attending it. In all these cases there is an established procedure for collecting, promoting and propagating miracle stories in which the devotional imperative outweighs modern concepts of evidentiality — in the 'miracle kitchen' stories are adapted, embroidered, relocated or cloned for the holy purpose of advancing the universal or local devotion to the Mother of God. The development of such collections was a combination of reproduction and proliferation. The relation between documented event and published narrative was at times tenuous, with miracle stories being constructed on standard models and attributed to specific locations and times for the purpose of developing local cults. [33]

The *Cantigas de Santa Maria* are a distinctive product of this tradition in various ways. They are developed as part of a very specific cultural and political agenda, to create a royal persona in which the poet-king Alfonso X was intermediary between the Virgin Mary and the kingdoms he placed under her protection.[34] They combine classic techniques of development of miracle narratives with a literary and poetic and iconographic framework in which aesthetic effect is as important as doctrinal consistency. They aim to promote not just one shrine but a whole series of Hispanic shrines of the Virgin, often in competition with other saints such as St James of Compostela. In this Anthology we include miracles associated with the Spanish shrines of Salas [8, 18], Montserrat [9], Castroxeriz [28], and Vilasirga [26], and with the Portuguese shrine of Terena [24, 35], as well as the French shrine of Rocamadour [8, 19, 21, 31]. Other tales have Spanish or Portuguese locations: [3] in Oña, [6] and [17] in Galicia, [25] in Ciudad Rodrigo, [22] in Faro and [38] in Estremoz.

What is most distinctive in the *CSM* is the systematic nature of the process of collection of miracle stories, and the close links between the processes of composition, which generated the stories, and compilation, which inscribed them in the four luxurious manuscripts together with their accompanying music and art. Whereas it had been relatively straightforward to locate the 89 miracle stories needed for the first compilation, using well-known collections of miracles, the challenge of the larger compilation obliged Alfonso to engage in active

---

[31] Bétérous 1984, Ward 1982. Collections of miracle stories formed part of the *mariale*, 'a collection of materials in praise of the Virgin, a sort of anthology or *summa* of Mary lore. Such volumes were useful in the monasteries and churches as sources of readings for Saturdays and the celebration of the great festivals of the Virgin Mary' (Wilson 1946: 30–31).

[32] International miracles include Hildefonsus (2), Theophilus (3), Chaste Empress (5), Incest (17), Julian the Apostate (15), Siege of Constantinople (28).

[33] Ward 1982, Signori 1996.

[34] Snow 1985, Scarborough 2009.

collection of miracle stories, from a wider range of hagiographical sources, and in particular to develop collections related to Hispanic shrines.[35] This is already evident in the small collection of poems appended to **To**, which draw heavily on the *Speculum historiale* of Vincent of Beauvais.[36] It also emerges in the large and compact nucleus of poems associated with the shrine of Santa Maria de Salas, and the even more independent *cancioneiro* of the new foundation of Santa Maria do Porto. Many schematic narratives crop up in more than one version, usually attributed to different places.[37]

The miracle tales used in the *CSM* cluster around four basic themes of rescue, revival, reward and reproof, with many tales illustrating more than one. Devotees are rescued from dismissal, pregnancy, adultery, loss and theft, possession and hallucination, illness, accident, drowning, fire, and imprisonment. The ultimate rescue, revival of the dead, is given to a murdered boy, a drowned priest, a suicidal pilgrim, and a crushed huntsman. Most of the cases of rescue are a reward for devotion, but reward does not always imply danger: rewards for devotion include a moving candle, free milk from goats, preferment, and entry into a church late at night. Many miracles are exemplary demonstrations of power, sometimes violent, sometimes comic, to reprove the doubting, wayward or blasphemous — monks and nuns, gamblers, lovers and spouses tempted to revenge or magic, disrespectful Jews and Moors.

The *CSM* portray women as no more nor less sinful than men, while being more natural recipients of the grace of the Queen of Heaven, particularly if they are also mothers. Female fragility in *cantigas* 7 [3], 59 [11], 64 [12] and 104 [17] is balanced by male immorality in 11 [5], 26 [6], 72 [14]; even incest and infanticide (17) are redeemable. The virtuous mistress of 68 [13] is no more to blame than the vengeful wife (and it is ultimately the errant husband who loses his *solaz*). In tales of spousals promoted or banned by the Virgin, gender equality is observed. Girls are enlightened by the Virgin (79, 251) to balance tales of boys feeding the Christ child (139, 353). Enterprising women are rescued (147 [19]) as are minstrels (8 [4]), merchants (267 [31]) and pilgrims (26 [6], 159 [21]). Nuns are more likely to be morally frail (7 [3], 59 [11]) while male clerics are larcenous (319, 322) as well as overtly blasphemous (283 [35]). Both male (72 [14]) and female (136, 294) *tafures* insult the Virgin, but male clerics are more likely to be given preferment (32 [7], 87 [16]) while female devotees are rewarded (246 [27]). Men are more likely to come to harm in the workplace (249 [28], 276 [32]).

Prominent in the *CSM* are miracles involving animals, of which the rich bestiary is well represented in this anthology: a goshawk is returned in 44 [8], goats give their milk in 52 [9] and a sheep its wool in 147 [19]; spiders threaten the faithful in 225 [25], and the King's pet ferret is protected from certain death in 354 [39]. Elsewhere, asses, bullocks, dogs, horses, and silkworms all play their part in the miraculous designs of the Blessed Virgin Mary, lovingly portrayed by the miniaturists.

This range of familiar situations is undoubtedly part of the overriding moral of the whole collection, which is that the devotees of the Virgin are protected by her in every part of life, from the humblest child and animal to the greatest in the land, King Alfonso himself, whose protection and healing by the Mother of God is intended to show exemplary reward and rescue, to reprove those who dare oppose him.

5. The *Cantigas de Santa Maria* as Hstory and Autobiography

While the earlier *CSM* are largely based on miracle stories drawn from international and local sources, as the compilations proceed we find greater numbers of references to contemporary events and to the life of Alfonso himself. In most cases the aim of the historical record is to establish a connection with familiar places and events,

---

[35] Updated lists of known sources of individual *cantigas* are provided by the *Cantigas de Santa Maria* Database. For studies of the sources, see Filgueira Valverde 1979 , Fidalgo 2002, Parkinson 2011a. The *CSM* include most of the tales recounted earlier by Gonçalo de Berceo in his *Milagros de Nuestra Señora*, but it is more probable that Alfonso's team used the same or a related source than that they directly consulted Berceo's text. Nascimento 1979 identifies a possible source manuscript from the library of the Portuguese monastery of Alcobaça.

[36] Alfonso owned a copy, which is explicitly mentioned in his will, as *los cuatro libros que llaman Espejo historial que mando facer el rey Luis de Francia*.

[37] See Parkinson 2011b for cases of duplication. *Cantiga* 225 [25] set in Spain is paralleled by a Portuguese version in *cantiga* 222; *cantiga* 249 [28] forms a pair with *cantiga* 252.

and to reinforce the immediacy of the narrative. At the same time the involvement of Alfonso as protagonist and beneficiary of miracles becomes part of the theme of the Virgin's role as protector of the king, in reward for his exemplary service, and this theme is taken up in the *loores* as well as the miracle narratives. In many cases the historical narrative is modified, in the context of its redesignation as a miraculous tale, so that the historicity of the *CSM* cannot be assumed. A typical example is cantiga 183 [22] referring to a miracle which took place in the Portuguese town of Faro when it was still in Arabic territory, as the explanation of the rubric makes clear: 'un miragre que mostrou Santa Maria en Faaron quando era de mouros'. The text refers more obliquely to a period in which the Algarve was ruled by a Moorish king 'Aben Mafon' alias Musa ibn Muhammad ibn Musiar ibn Mahfudh, King of Niebla until it was taken by Alfonso X. The narrative glosses over the fact that Faro was retaken by the Portuguese in 1249, and that the ownership of the Algarve was a matter of dispute between Alfonso X and Alfonso III of Portugal.[38]

The miracle stories linked to the foundation and construction of the church of Santa Maria do Porto, located at the very end of E, refer to very recent events, from the foundation of the settlement in 1262 to events close to the king's death.

With the exception of miracles linked to his family,[39] most of the personal miracles recounted by or for Alfonso refer to miraculous cures of his ever more frequent bouts of ill health, recorded from at least 1269 onwards. The king's poor health was part of the case made by his opponents for his incapacity to rule, and has been much debated.[40] The *CSM* rarely specify his symptoms but typically refer to him as being on the point of death. *Cantiga* 209 [33] is a typical narrative of this type, recounting a serious illness after the King's unsuccessful campaign for the title of Holy Roman Emperor, during the year he spent in Vitoria (1275–6) after meeting the Pope in Beaucaire in 1275.[41] The poem gives no more details than the reference to Vitoria (*jazendo en Bitoira enfermo assi*, 3.2) but attributes his healing to the miraculous powers of *o livro dela*, which the rubrics of E and F gloss as *o livro das cantigas de Santa Maria* and the caption of the miniature in F as *o libro das cantigas que el fez de Santa Maria*, leading to the conclusion that this must be a reference to **To** or its presumed lost original. (Whether this was a real event or another product of the 'miracle kitchen' cannot be determined, as there is no reference to this miraculous event in historical accounts of Alfonso's reign.) Other references to healing are even less precise. *Cantiga* 279 [34], half way between *miragre* and *loor*, could refer to any of the illnesses of this period (though as its first appearance is in the Appendix to **To**, it could not be linked to any event in which **To** itself appeared). Similarly *cantiga* 200, closing the first expansion of the compilations, but missing from T, refers to the king's *grandes enfermidades* (200, S3.2).

Alfonso also appears as indirect recipient of the benefices of miracles not included in this anthology. In *cantiga* 18 he is said to take possession of a veil miraculously woven by silkworms, while in *cantiga* 299 the Virgin orders a monk to give him a statue of her. In *cantiga* 169 he is the object of a corrective miracle, when the Virgin refuses to allow the Moors to take possession of a church which Alfonso has ceded to them.

The *CSM* are widely seen as a picture of social history of 13th-century Iberia, in particular in their portrayal of relations between Christians, Jews and Muslims. Surprise is often expressed at the apparent inconsistency between the generally antagonistic presentation of Muslims and particularly Jews in the *CSM* (consistent with the repressive provisions of the *Siete Partidas*), and the importance given to Arabic culture and science in Alfonso's cultural policy. In the case of the *CSM*, the presence of Arabic musicians in the miniatures of E, and the Arabic roots of the *zéjel* form (see section 7.2) are seen to add to the incongruity.

---

[38] Other historical sources (Ferreiro Alemparte 1972) give a different date.

[39] *Cantiga* 256 recounts the healing of his mother Beatriz, and *cantigas* 221 and 292 are tales of King Fernando II.

[40] For an extended discussion (at times compromised by the literal interpretation of the text and miniatures of the *CSM* as historical evidence), see Martínez 2003, chaps 6–7,

[41] Mettmann (1986–89, II, 259), wrongly assigns the event to 1276–77. The lengthy historical narrative of *cantiga* 235 locates this illness as the third of four healing events (following illnesses in Requena 1273 and Montpellier 1275 and preceding one in Valladolid 1278).

It is important to recognise that the *CSM* do not represent a unified picture of Iberia or a single personal viewpoint. Many of the tales whose anti-Semitic or anti-Muslim content are taken to be indicative of social attitudes are taken from the mainstream hagiographical literature in which the Jews are the enemies of Christ and Islam is the enemy of Christianity. A small number of Iberian miracles of the Reconquest (277, 374) present the Virgin as the defender of Christians, in the same way as she is invoked as protector of Spain and Alfonso in non-narrative *cantigas* such as the epilogal *Petiçon* [41] and the May song, 406 [43].

Running alongside this is the conversion topos in which individual Moors and Jews are virtuous people led astray by a false creed, and who require only the impulse of an exemplary miracle to bring them round. Here the special affinity of the Blessed Virgin Mary to mothers, infants and girls is manifest, in the more general context of a willingness to perform miracles for either group.[42]

Cantiga 6 [2] is a good example of a tale with a very long history. The story of the singer who is murdered by a Jew because he sings a religious song which itself refers to the Jews as in error goes back to English sources and is developed by Gautier and others in much more aggressively anti-Semitic terms. The miracle is used to exemplify the topoi of revenge and restoration, and the Jewish offender is ancillary rather than centre stage. In the other early miracle of a similar kind, *cantiga* 4, the rescue of the Jewish boy cast into the furnace by his father, the Jew's sin is to resist the conversion of his son, and his death is set against the conversion of the boy and his mother.[43]

Once we get past this corpus of inherited miracles, a different pattern emerges. Jewish girls and mothers are as deserving of the Virgin's favours as Christian ones: miraculous deliveries benefit a Christian woman in *cantiga* 86 and a Moorish one in 89; the rescue of the Jewish girl Marisaltos, cast from a cliff as punishment for adultery (107), is mirrored by the rescue of the lady of Puy in 344. The Muslim who reveres an image of the Virgin (46) counterbalances the one who defiles it (34). The Moors of Faro (183 [22]) are easily persuaded of their error, just as the Muslim captive in 192 [23] who is forced to choose between damnation and conversion, makes a sound choice.

6. The *Cantigas de Santa Maria* as Literature

The *Cantigas de Santa Maria* form part of the medieval Galician-Portuguese lyric, a Hispanic development of the European troubadour culture which developed from the late 12th century and flourished at the royal courts of Castile and Portugal in the mid to late 13th century.[44] The prestige of this literary movement resulted in a virtual monopoly for Galician and Portuguese as the language for courtly verse in 13th-century Iberia.

The secular lyric centres on three main genres. There are two separate genres of love poetry — the female voiced *cantiga de amigo* and the male voiced *cantiga de amor* — and a separate genre of satirical or humorous poetry (the *cantiga de escarnho e maldizer*) in which a number of different classes may be found. Each genre has one or more verse forms closely associated with it — the *cantiga de amor* cultivates the *cantiga de meestria*, refrainless but often ending in an *envoi* or *fiinda*, the *cantiga de amigo* (in its traditional form) develops parallelistic verse and refrains, and the *cantigas de escarnho e maldizer* use a wider range of polymetric forms as well as developing extended narratives using a wide range of refrain-based forms. The two genres of love poetry find their counterparts in the *Cantigas de Santa Maria*, not surprisingly in the context of the idea that Alfonso as troubadour

---

[42] This is encapsulated in the refrains for *cantiga* 167, *Quen quer que na Virgen fia / e a roga de femença / valer-ll'-á, pero que seja / doutra lee en creença* [If anyone trusts in the Virgin and earnestly implores her, she will help them even though they are of another creed] and *cantiga* 181, *Pero que seja a gente doutra lei e descreuda / os que a Virgen mais aman, a esses ela ajuda* [Even when people hold another faith and are unbelievers, the Virgin will aid those who most love her].

[43] Other early anti-Semitic items including *cantiga* 3 which presents as a Jew the intermediary in Theophilus' selling his soul; 12 recounting the tale of the Jews of Toledo crucifying an image of Christ; and 34 relating the defiling of an icon are all of international provenance. *Cantiga* 27, which tells of a dispute over a church, is one of a cycle of miracles located in the reign of Julian the Apostate, and portrays the Jews as vacillating, as they first sell their place of worship, then ask for it back, and accept the miraculous decision in favour of the Christians, before reverting to type *os judeus que sempr' acostumad' an / de querer mal aa do bon talan* ['the Jews who have always hated our Lady of goodness hated] and doing the bidding of the emperor.

[44] Tavani 1969, Cohen 2009.

of the Virgin is writing love poetry *a lo divino*: the *loores*, particularly the more discursive ones, have a larger proportion of refrainless poems while the more lyrical ones develop refined forms of parallelism. The *miragres*, on the other hand, are more closely aligned with the satirical poems. Both types are essentially narrative, using refrains to point to a common thread of meaning; both use a concrete vocabulary of everyday objects and events.[45] The overall tone of the *miragre* narratives, with their acerbic focus on the frailties and sinfulness of humankind, has a lot in common with the *cantiga de escarnho* (particularly where the sins and omissions of the clergy are concerned), and neither genre minces its words when it comes to accidents or misfortunes.[46]

The manuscript traditions of the two lyric corpora could hardly be more different. In contrast with the closely knit body of 13th-century manuscripts preserving the *Cantigas de Santa Maria* and their music for posterity, the secular lyric is primarily preserved in two 16th-century Italian copies of one or more now lost 15th-century collections bringing together a succession of smaller compilations of the poems of individuals or groups.[47] Only three medieval witnesses survive, of which only two small fragments have music, for 13 pieces out of a total corpus of over 1600 poems.

The main point of contact between the two bodies of lyric poetry is Alfonso himself. He was one of the great writers of satirical verse, and undoubtedly had a hand in the collective effort of collection and compilation of the secular lyric. (It has been suggested that the *Cantigas de Santa Maria* compilations were a model for the compilation of the secular lyric into structured *cancioneiros*, and that the generalised use of the term *cantiga*, in place of *cantar*, in the later compilations, was also influenced by the *Cantigas de Santa Maria*.)[48] The poets who composed, recomposed and extended the *Cantigas de Santa Maria* would undoubtedly have known, or even been part of the courtly lyric tradition, just as the musicians who composed the melodies would have known troubadour song.

The composition of the *Cantigas de Santa Maria* was essentially a team activity. Alfonso X, as prime mover, commissioner, director of the project and owner of the collections, is asserted as its author both textually (by the pervasive authorial 'I') and iconographically by the inclusion of the king in didactic poses both in the presentational miniatures at the beginning of T and E and in many of the miniatures accompanying the *loores*. The extent of his actual involvement in the composition phase of individual *cantigas* can only be a matter for conjecture. Only one poem appears attributed to Alfonso outside the *CSM* manuscripts — *cantiga* 40, a *loor*, is included in the secular poetry collections beside Alfonso's early *cantigas de escarnho*.[49] It appears beside another apparently Marian poem, which may well be a late interpolation, leaving open the possibility that the poem was included at a later date, and associated with Alfonso because of his reputation rather than through any direct connection. In the absence of any linguistic fingerprint identifying Alfonsine compositions or of documentary evidence associating the king with particular compositions, scholars have relied on judgements of probability, content and quality to identify a larger or smaller number of compositions which could be attributed to Alfonso.[50] The evidence of cases of emendation and of wholesale rewriting and of discontinuity between early and late sections suggest that many poems went through several redactions, or were composed in stages: it is thus not inconceivable that the royal poet may have begun a poem and left his clerks to complete it.[51] The poems most likely to be substantially by Alfonso are the Prologue, the opening *cantiga* (1 [1]) and Epilogue (*Petiçon*), a number of *loores* including 10 [10], 40, 60, 70 [20], 160 [30], and 300 [40]; the personal healing narratives of 209 [22] and 279 [23] and the May song, 406 [43]. For this reason they have a prominent place in this anthology.

---

45 Snow 1990.

46 Odber 1992, Parkinson 1992.

47 Tavani 1969, Oliveira 1994.

48 Miranda 2010.

49 CBN 409. The folio which should have contained *cantiga* 40 is missing from T, making it also possible that this loose sheet passed into the hands of the compilers of the secular collection, beside other loose sheets containing Alfonso's secular poetry.

50 On linguistic marks of authorship, see Schaffer 1997, Bertolucci 1985; for varying numerical assessments of Alfonso's input, see Mettmann 1987, Snow 1994.

51 Parkinson 1998, 2007, 2010b.

The miracle narratives follow a set pattern, with clear congruence between the textual narrative and the accompanying graphic narrative. The *zéjel* structure (section 7.2) dictates that the refrain, containing the *razon* of the story, opens the poem. The first strophe of the poem proper is usually a linking passage, previewing the narrative in terms of its location or the identity of its protagonist, attributing the story to a source, and associating it with the *razon*, after which the narrative proper typically begins in strophe 2, with a description of the context of the miracle, and the events leading up to the intervention of the Virgin. The completion of the miracle is usually followed by a closing paragraph of public or private recognition of the miracle, often associated with an act of praise.

Direct speech and dialogue are widely used to punctuate and advance the narrative. Postulants typically address the Virgin directly (147 [19]), and many believers and sinners are harangued by her (192 [23]) as are devils in 26 [6]. *Cantiga* 7 [3] has a dialogue between the abbess and her accusing bishop, while in *cantiga* 147 [19] a stolen sheep gives voice in the final strophe. Dialogue is often deployed in the verse structures involving short lines and insistent rhyme, emphasising the incisive quality of the direct speech.

7. Metrics and Poetics

The *Cantigas de Santa Maria* epitomise the values of the Galician-Portuguese lyric in their cultivation of precise and varied metrics. In three key areas — verse structure, strophic structure and rhyme — they show great virtuosity both in meeting the strict requirements of their formal models and in achieving great variety inside a tightly constrained framework.

7.1 Versification

The Galician-Portuguese lyric follows its Occitan role model in cultivating accentual-syllabic versification, in which line length is regulated by strict syllable count, adjusted to the final cadence of the line, so that equivalent lines require the same number of syllables up to the final stressed syllable. Studies of Galician-Portuguese metrics have followed the Franco-Italian model of notation, representing the length of a line by the number of syllables up to the final stress, with an apostrophe used to indicate the presence of a further unstressed syllable. The underlying assumption is that lines with masculine (oxtyonic, *agudo*) and feminine (paroxytonic, *grave*) endings are variants of the same type.[52] Traditional Spanish notation makes the same assumption but bases its labelling system on *grave* (paroxytonic) lines. Thus an *octosilabo* in Spanish has final stress on its seventh syllable, and corresponds to a *heptassílabo* in Galician-Portuguese; a Spanish *octosílabo agudo* thus has only seven phonetic syllables. An *octossílabo grave* in Galician-Portuguese has nine phonetic syllables including one post-stress, and is labelled *eneasílabo* in Spanish.

This notation with its underlying assumption nevertheless obscures three features of *CSM* metrics, shared to a greater or lesser extent by other parts of the Galician-Portuguese corpus.

a) In the *CSM* there is no freedom to mix corresponding *grave* and *agudo* rhyming lines.[53] In this respect the majority of *CSM* could be said to adopt a strict syllabic-accentual scheme in which both the absolute number of syllables and the final cadence have to match.

[52] By extension this equivalence would include proparoxytonic (*esdrúxula*) verses, but there are no examples in either the *CSM* or the secular lyric.

[53] This principle is enshrined in an injunction found in a fragmentary 14th-century poetic treatise appended to one of the Italian manuscripts of the Galician Portuguese lyric: *Poderá meter na cobra das ũas e das outras, se quiser, atanto que per qual guisa as meter en ũa cobra per tal guisa as meta nas outras* (Tavani 2007: 52) [(the poet) can put both types of rhyme in the strophe, if he wishes, so long as however he places the rhymes in one strophe, so must he place them in the others.] The *CSM* are more rigid in their observance of this principle than the secular lyric. Very few *CSM* infringe it, and those that do are suspect. *Cantiga* 173, which changes from *grave* to *agudo* rhyme midway through the poem, has been argued to be a hybrid (Parkinson 2013).

b) In a small number of *CSM*, line length seems to be regulated rhythmically or accentually, by the number of accents rather than the number of syllables, making it a precursor of the Spanish *arte mayor* genre, and linking it to the Galician-Portuguese *cantiga de amigo*. The refrain of *cantiga* 10 [10] is a case in point.[54]

c) In a very small number of cases, originally uncovered by the Italian scholar Adolfo Mussafia, the metre is based on purely syllabic counting, combining verse of the same number of phonetic syllables but different cadences. An example of this antirhythmic verse is *cantiga* 70 [20]. More examples are found in the Galician-Portuguese secular lyric.

Syllable counting in the *CSM* is sensitive to the metrical process of elision, by which two successive vowels may be deemed to count as a single metrical syllable. This is sometimes misrepresented either as a systematic avoidance of hiatus, or as the phonetic process of the same name in which vowel sequences run together or unstressed vowels are lost in continuous speech. In the accentual-syllabic verse of the *CSM* the poets deploy elision and hiatus to regulate line length, without elision being a mechanical or obligatory process. Elisions are generally represented in the manuscripts by the omission of one of the participating vowels, so that the written record contains the number of syllables matching the metrical count — especially important in matching text and music— but this should not be interpreted as implying the phonetic loss of the vowel concerned. Modern editions make elisions explicit by the use of the editorial apostrophe <’> in place of the omitted vowel, while leaving readers or singers to implement additional syllabic reductions required to make the verse conform to the syllabic pattern.[55] In this edition all such additional adjustments are made explicit in the accompanying metrical apparatus.

7.2 Strophic Structure

The overwhelming majority of the *CSM* base their strophic structure on a dominant refrain, which begins the poem as well as ends every strophe. The strophe itself has two sections, of which the second replicates all or some of the structure of the refrain, giving a highly structured pattern of repetition.

refrain
strophe a
strophe b (=refrain)
refrain

This structure is closely related to the 16th-century Spanish *villancico* and the 14th-century French *virelai*, but pre-dates both of them, being most probably related to the Arabic *zajal* (Spanish *zéjel*) form cultivated by Andalusian poets. The modern labels for the parts of the structure are anachronistically drawn from the *villancico*: the ‘free’ part of the strophe is labelled the *mudanzas* and the part prefiguring the return of the refrain is the *vuelta*.

In the most common *zajal* form, in which line length is uniform throughout the poem, the *vuelta* matches the refrain perfectly in line length and partially in rhyme, as in 44 [8]:

A	A	|	b	b	b	a	|	A	A
10	10	|	10	10	10	10	|	10	10

In many *cantigas*, however, either the refrain or the strophe is polymetric, giving many more opportunities for structural variety. See Table 1 for a full catalogue of forms in the anthology. Dorothy Clotelle Clarke noted

[54] Duffell 2007, Parkinson 2006b.

[55] Traditional metrical analysis (e.g. Cunha 1961) distinguishes *elision* from *synaloepha* (reduction in syllable count retaining all participating vowels) and *absorption* when vowels are discounted despite the formal conditions for elision or synaloepha not being met. In Parkinson 2006b I propose the cover term *conflation* for all these cases. Cunha 1961 concluded that the conjunctions *que*, *se*, *ca* and *e* were not subject to elision, a principle which seems too restrictive for the *CSM*.

TABLE 1. Catalogue of metrical forms

Cantiga de mestria		
7' 7' 7' 7' 3' 7' 7' 7' 7'	a a a b b b c c d	45
8 6' 8 6' 6' 8 6' 6' 8 6'	a b a b b a b b a b	1
10 10 10 10 10 10	a a a b a b	P
13 [6' 6] 13 [6' 6] 13 [6' 6] 13 [6' 6] 13 [6' 6] 13 [6' 6] 13 [6' 6] 13 [6' 6] 13 [6' 6] 13 [6' 6]	a a a a a a a a a a	41
Cantiga de refrão		
7 8 | 4'	a a | B	30
10' 10' 10' 10' | 4'	a a a a | B	43
Zajal		
7 7 | 7' 7 7' 7 7 7	A A | b c b c c a	11
8 8 | 8 8 8 8	A A | b b b a	13
8! 8! | 8! 8! 8! 8!	A A | b b b a	20
8' 8 | 8 8 8 8 8 8' 8	A B | c c c c c a b	35
10 10 | 10 10 10 10	A A | b b b a	8, 42
11' 11' | 11 11 11 11'	A A | b b b a	24
11' 11' | 11' 11' 11' 11'	A A | b b b a	31
11 11 | 11 11 11 11	A A | b b b a	33
11' [5' 5'] 11 [5' 5] | 11' [5' 5'] 11' [5' 5'] 11' [5' 5'] 5	A B | c c c b	15
13 [6' 6] 13 [6' 6] | 13 [6' 6] 13 [6' 6] 13 [6' 6] 13 [6' 6]	A A | b b b a	36
15 [7' 7] 15 [7' 7] | 15 [7' 7] 15 [7' 7] 15 [7' 7] 15 [7' 7]	A A | b b b a	17, 22, 27, 28, 37
15 [7' 7] 15 [7' 7] | 15' [7' 7'] 15' [7' 7'] 15' [7' 7'] 15 [7' 7]	A A | b b b a	26
15' [7' 7'] 15' [7' 7'] | 15 [7' 7] 15 [7' 7] 15 [7' 7] 15' [7' 7']	A A | b b b a	21
15' [7' 7'] 15' [7' 7'] | 15' [7' 7'] 15 [7' 7'] 15' [7' 7'] 15' [7' 7']	A A | b b b a	25, 38, 39
Polymetric zajal		
11 [3 8] 11 [3 8] | 7 7 12 [7 5]	A A | b b a	14
13 [7' 5] 14 [7' 6] | 10' 10' 13 [7' 5] 14 [7' 6]	A A | b b a a	6
8' 10' | 10 10 10 10'	A A | b b b a	10
10 10 | 9 9 10 10	A A | b b b a	18
11 13 | 13 13 13 13	A A | b b b a	12
12 12 | 10 10 12 10	A A | b b b a	9
12 [6 6] 12 [6 6] | 13 [6' 6] 13 [6' 6] 13 [6' 6] 13 [6' 6]	A A | b b b a	29
14' [7 7'] 14' [7 7'] | 14' [7' 6'] 14' [7' 6'] 15' [7' 7'/8 6'] 14' [7' 6'/7 7']	A A | b b b a [A B] [A B] | c c c b	2
9' [4' 4'] 11' [4' 6'] | 8' 8' 8' 8' 9' [4' 4'] 11' [4' 6']	A A | b b b b a a	44
15 [7' 7] 15 [7' 7] | 7' 7 7' 7 15 [7' 7] 15 [7' 7]	A A | b c b c c a	19
7 8 | 7 6' 7 8 [=6' 1]	A B | c d c b [d b]	32
Elaborated zajal		
8 6' | 8 8 8 6' | 8 6'	A B | c c c b | c B	16
10 10 4 | 10 10 10 10 10 4	A A B | a A a A a b	34
5' 5' 5 10 | 5' 5' 5' 5' 5' 5' 5 10 [4' 5]	A A B B | n c n c c c b b	7
10' 10 10' 10 | 5' 5 5' 5 5' 5' 5' 5 5' 5' 5' 5	A B A B | c d c d c c c b c c c b	23
5' 6 5' 6 | 7' 7' 7' 7' 3' 3' 7 3' 3' 7	A B A B | c d d c c c b c c b	40
7 7' 7 7' | 7' 7 7' 7 7' 7 7' 7'	A B A B | n c n c n c n b	4
7 7 6' 7 7 6' | 7 7 6' 7 7 6' 7 7 6' 7 7 6'	A A B A A B | c c d c c d a a b a a b	3
7' 5 4' 7' 5 4' | 7' 7' 7' 5 4' 7' 5 4'	A B C A B C | a a a b c a b c	5

without exaggeration that most of the line types and verse forms used in Castilian poetry are to be found in the *CSM*.[56]

Multiple variations on the *zajal* pattern are found. In 276 [32] the refrain is matched by a *vuelta* in which the final line is simultaneously two shorter lines with independent rhyme. In 87 [16] the refrain is variable and parallelistic. In 79 [14] the refrain is a four-line aaab structure replicated perfectly in the *vuelta*, while in 7 [3] the six-line refrain is as long as the *mudanzas*. In 279 [34] the first line of the refrain is repeated as an intercalated rhyme, in a structure related to the *rondel*, before being prefigured in the *vuelta* and then repeated. A number of non-narrative poems have a non-*zajal* structure, corresponding to the two main classes of strophic forms of the Galician-Portuguese lyric, the refrainless *cantiga de mestria* (Prologue, 1 [1], *Petiçon* [41], 340 [45]), or the *cantiga de refrão* with a metrically separate refrain repeated after the strophe (160 [30], 406 [43]), both examples showing the short refrains typical of the *cantiga de amigo*. *Cantiga* 160 [30] also appropriates the techniques of parallelism and *leixa pren* of the *cantigas de amigo*.

In many strophic structures there is a complex combination of long and short lines. The most common long line of the *CSM*, fifteen syllables, is usually broken down into two regular hemistichs without internal rhyme but with a constant cadence, while refrains and *vueltas* very often have rhymed short lines which combine to match long lines in the strophe or *mudanzas*.

7.3 Rhyme

Rhyming is a marker of virtuosity in the *CSM*. The *zajal* structure is typically based on a small number of rhymes, whose use is governed by two complementary principles:

(1) where a rhyme is repeated structurally throughout the poem (a refrain rhyme repeated in the *vuelta*) there can be no repetition of rhyme words.[57] *Cantiga* 246 [27] requires 23 *-er* words, and 225 [25] needs 13 in *-oso*; 183 [22] raids the rhyming dictionary for *-ado*.

(2) where different rhymes are used in successive strophes (as the *mudanzas*), there can be no repetition of rhymes. *Cantiga* 59 [12] requires 18 different *agudo* rhymes, and 246 [27] requires 22 of them.

This gives the longer narrative *cantigas*, where a story is spread over ten, fifteen or more strophes, a dimension of metrical difficulty not found in the shorter structures of the secular Galician-Portuguese lyric. In these longer poems, the poets must find increasing numbers of rhyme words for the *vuelta*, at the same time as exploring the lesser-used rhymes in the *mudanzas*.

The number of variant strophic forms incorporated in this scheme decreases as the project advances, so that there is much greater uniformity in the last 100 poems than in the first 100.[58]

8. Further Reading and Resources

The only complete textual editions of the *CSM* are Mettmann 1959–72 (still in print at the University of Coimbra, at the time of writing) and Mettmann 1986–89, which this editorial project seeks to supersede. Fidalgo 2003 is an edition of the *cantigas de loor*, with extensive textual commentary and paleographical apparatus. Colour facsimiles, often with extensive companion volumes, have been published of three of the four manuscripts: CCG 2004 for **To**, Edilan 1979, Testimonio 2011 for **T**, Edilan 1989 for **F**. The only facsimile of **E** is the black-and-white reproduction published in 1964 as Anglés 1943–64 vol. 1. Only Testimonio 2011 is still in print, though the Edilan publications are increasingly appearing on auction house lists. Copies may be found in major university libraries. Colour reproductions of **To** are freely available on the *Biblioteca Digital Hispánica* site of the Biblioteca

[56] Clarke 1955. Betti 2005 gives a full inventory, structured for easy comparison with the Occitan lyric.
[57] In a few poems the alternative constraint is applied, and the same rhyme words are used throughout, as in the case in 354 [39] which uses only the words *mercee* and *vee*.
[58] Parkinson 2000b.

Nacional de España <http://bdh-rd.bne.es>; none of the miniatures of T, F or E are available in this form (though unauthorised reproductions of images are widely available on the internet).

The *Cantigas de Santa Maria* Database <csm.mml.ox.ac.uk> is a searchable and browsable online resource containing full information on all 419 poems, with narrative summaries, descriptions of the miniatures, bibliography, discography, sources and analogues, metrical and layout analysis, as well as preliminary critical editions of many texts not included here. It is complemented by the *Cantigas de Santa Maria for Singers* site <www.cantigasdesantamaria.com> which provides syllabified texts for singers, using a regularised version of Mettmann's editions, with a glossary and concordance. BITAGAP <http://bancroft.berkeley.edu/philobiblon/bitagap_en.html> gives extensive information on the manuscripts, with bibliography for individual poems.

The only substantial monographic study of the *CSM* is Fidalgo 2002. Major collections of articles include Mondéjar and Montoya (eds) 1985, Katz & Keller (eds) 1987, Montoya 1999, Parkinson (ed) 2000, Fernández & Ruiz Sousa (coords) 2011. Snow 2012 is a recent bibliographical survey, to be complemented by Snow 2014. O'Callaghan 1998 tells Alfonso's life through the *CSM*, to complement biographies by Martínez 2003 and González 1993, and Procter's still influential 1951 survey of his activities as patron. Scarborough 2009 places the *CSM* in a political context. Domínguez and Treviño 2007 provide an illustrated introduction to the miniatures of the *códices de las histórias*, beside Guerrero Lovillo's 1949 account of their documentary value. The journal *Alcanate* is devoted to Alfonsine studies, following the now defunct *Cantigueiros*.

The online discography by Roberge and McComb is linked to the *CSM* database. The musical edition by Anglés remains the only full edition with critical credentials. Ferreira 2009b has samples of a new musical edition, based on a complete re-evaluation of the *CSM* notational system.

9. Editorial Principles

The edition has been designed for maximum readability and performability. Editorial, metrical, paleographical and codicological information is kept to the critical apparatus. The orthography is intended to be phonetically and syllabically transparent.

9.1 Apparatus

The following information is provided for each cantiga:

- Location in all manuscripts
- Linguistic and literary notes, with minimal bibliography (a full bibliography for every poem can be found in the *Cantigas de Santa Maria* Database)
- Metrical analysis
- Line-by-line metrical notes on elision and syllable-division
- Editorial variants from principal textual editions
  - The following abbreviations are used for major editions: **M** = Mettmann (**M1** = Mettmann 1959–72, **M2** = Mettman 1986–89); **V** = Valmar 1889; **Fid** = Fidalgo 2003; **C** = Cunningham 2000; **RL** = Lapa 1933; **A** = Anglés 1943–64. Purely orthographic variants are not listed
- Manuscript variants
- Rubrics and Index entries in all manuscripts
- Captions of miniatures in T and F

9.2 Metrics

Elisions explicit in manuscript readings are indicated in the edited text by the apostrophe, with full forms recorded in the metrical apparatus. Elided forms will always be transparently related to full forms, with the elimination of elision-related variants (e.g **logu'** and **branqu'** for **log(o)**, **branc(o)**, **un** for **ũ(a)**).

The metrical apparatus also indicates syllable division, inexplicit elisions (aka synaloepha) and possible resolutions of hypermetric or hypometric lines.

9.3 Abbreviations

Abbreviations have been tacitly expanded in the edited text. Logographic abbreviations are expanded using the normal full form (**sc̃a** and **sc̃o** are expanded to **santa/santo** and **Xpo** to **Cristo**; Tironian 'et' to **e**). Original manuscript readings, including explicit resolution of abbreviations, and retention of Tironian &, are preserved only in the critical apparatus for major manuscript variants.

9.4 Orthography

The orthography of the edition has been regularised in general conformity with current practice for editions of the Galician-Portuguese lyric (Ferreiro et al 2008).

- Double consonants are retained only where phonetically distinct from single consonants:
cc, ff, pp, etc. are eliminated
nn, ll are retained to represent palatal sounds
-**ss**- and -**rr**- are retained in intervocalic position, where they are distinguished from
-**s**- and -**r**-, but are eliminated elsewhere.
- **h** is used in cases of consistency (**hora** *vs* **ora**), but eliminated when orthographic bulk (**un** not **hun, niũa** not **nihũa**, etc.).
- **g, c** indicate hard [g], [k] before **a, o, u** (pronounced or elided), and soft [ʒ] [ts] before **i, e** (pronounced and elided).
- **gu, qu** indicate hard [g], [k] before **i, e** (pronounced or elided), and velar-labial sequences [gw], [kw] before **a, o, u** (pronounced or elided).
- double vowels are retained
when phonetically significant: -**ii**- *vs* -**i**-, -**uu**- *vs* -**u**-
when grammatically significant and subject to metrical process of elision: **a** *vs* **aa**.
- **i, j, y**:
i represents vocalic [i] including the second part of falling diphthongs (**ei, oi, ai**)
and the first part of rising diphthongs (**ia, io**, etc.)
j represents consonantal j [ʒ]
y is not used.
- **u, v**:
u represents vocalic [u] including the second part of diphthongs (**eu, ou, au**)
v represents consonantal [v].
- vowel nasality is indicated by the tilde [˜] over **a, i, e, o, u**, when followed by a second vowel symbol, by -**m**- when followed by **p** or **b** and by -**n**- in other contexts (e.g. **ampar** for manuscript readings of *anpar, ampar*, and *ãpar*).
- a distinction is maintained between the endings -**inno**/-**inna** and their historical antecedent -**ĩo**/-**ĩa**
- reduced forms of 3rd person preterite endings combined with the object pronoun **o** have been expanded: **matou o** replacing **matoo** (**matou-o** in **M**).
- the acute accent [ˊ] is used sparingly in the text to indicate unpredictable stress. In the manuscript variants it is used to indicate the fine angled lines (*plicas*) used in the manuscripts as reading aids to specify letter and word separation (e.g. *uíu, fillé*), when these are of particular relevance (e.g. *cantiga* 225 [25], S3.4: quisó).
- the grave accent is not used. Mettmann employs it to indicate vowel contraction (**à agua** for **a‿a agua**): in this edition such instances (e.g. *cantiga* 11 [5], S9.6) are given as double vowels in the text (**aa agua**), with the metrical (rather than grammatical) contraction recorded in the apparatus ('*necessary elision* a‿a').

- capital letters are used for beginnings of sentences and proper names. No use is made of devotional capitals or line- or strophe-initial capitalisation.
- 'Jeso Cristo' and 'Jesu Cristo' are always given as 'Jesucristo' (one word, unless divided over two lines).

9.5 Word Profiles

In addition to orthographic regularisation, the edition reduces internal variation by selecting a preferred form for words of known variability, including place names and personal names. This selection is based on *word profiles* for each relevant lexical item, establishing the majority form, defining patterns of variation across manuscripts and scribal hands, and distinguishing metrical doublets (different forms corresponding to different syllable counts or patterns of elision) from orthographic or lexical variants. For examples of word profiles in action, see nos [6], [27], and [44] in this Anthology. In many cases of poems transmitted by a single manuscript (usually **E**) word profiling justifies the replacement of peripheral forms such as **Gloriosa** and **cibdade** by the majority forms **Groriosa, cidade**. See Parkinson and Barnett (2013) for extended examples.

9.6 Word Division and Hyphenation

- word separation is observed in **por en(de)**; **se non** (except in **senon se/que** 'except that'); **tan tost**.
- word separation is maintained in **quen o, quen a**; **non o, non a, con o, con a, nen no**; **sobre lo(s)**; contraction is observed in **eno, ena** (beside **no, na**) and **ao, aa**.
- hyphenation has been kept to a minimum and is not used for post-verbal pronouns. It is only used for embedded pronouns (e.g. **contar-lo-emos**) in compound futures, and in fused word sequences where a final -**s** or -**r** has been elided (**poi-lo, vo-la, leva-lo**).

Cantigas de Santa Maria

Commissioned by ALFONSO X, The Learned

Don Afonso de Castela,
de Toledo, de Leon
rei, e ben des Compostela
ta o reino d'Aragon [...]
este livro, com' achei
fez a onra e a loor
da Virgen Santa Maria
que éste madre de Deus
en que ele muito fia.
Por en dos miragre seus
fezo cantares con sões
saborosos de cantar
todos de sennas razões
com' i podedes achar.

Intitulatio, ll. 1–4, 18–28

Alfonso, King of Castile, Toledo and León, ruler from Compostela as far as the kingdom of Aragon, [...], made this book, as I heard tell, in honour and praise of the Blessed Virgin Mary, Mother of God, in whom he puts great trust. Thus he made songs about her miracles, with music which is most pleasurable to sing. Each song has its own theme, as you will find within.

To f. 1v, **T** f. 5r, **E** f. 28v. See Parkinson 2010a for the status of this text.

25] **To** fez cen cantares e sões, *amended by a later hand to* fezo cantares con sões.

Prologue

1 Porque trobar é cousa en que jaz
entendimento, por en quen o faz
á o d' aver e de razon assaz,
per que entenda e sábia dizer
o que entend' e de dizer lle praz
ca ben trobar assi s' á de fazer.

Making verse is a business which demands wisdom, so he who would be a trovador must have it and intelligence in good measure, so that he can understand, and be able to express what he understands and what he would say — that is how the good trovador must work.

2 E macar eu estas duas non ei
com' eu querria, pero provarei
a mostrar ende un pouco que sei
confiand' en Deus, ond' o saber ven
ca per ele tenno que poderei
mostrar do que quero algũa ren.

And though I have neither of these gifts as much I would wish to have, nevertheless I will try to display a little of what I know of them putting my trust in God, the source of all knowledge, for I hold that by his power I will be able to show some small amount of what I wish to show.

3 E o que quero é dizer loor
da Virgen, madre de Nostro Sennor,
Santa Maria, que ést' a mellor
cousa que el fez, e por aquest' eu
quero seer oimais seu trobador,
e rogo lle que me queira por seu

And what I mean to do is praise the Blessed Virgin, mother of Our Lord, Holy Mary, who is the best of all he created; and for that reason I would be her trovador from this day forth and I pray to her that she may accept me

4 trobador e que queira meu trobar
receber, ca per el quer' eu mostrar
dos miragres que ela fez, e ar
querrei me leixar de trobar des i
por outra dona, e cuid' a cobrar
per esta quant' enas outras perdi.

as her trovador, and hear my verses, for in them I mean to reveal some of the miracles she performed; what is more I will cease from composing poetry for any other lady; for I expect to regain through her all that I lost in wooing the others.

5 Ca o amor desta sennor é tal
que quen o á sempre per i mais val
e poi-lo gaannad' á, non lle fal
senon se é per sa grand' ocajon
querendo leixar ben e fazer mal
ca per esto o perd' e per al non.

For the love of this lady is so wondrous that whosoever owns it is more worthy thereby, and when a man has won her love, it does not fail him, save by his own grievous fault, if he turns away from good and does wrong — thus and only thus is her love lost.

To Prologue, T Prologue, E Prologue

Metrics

10 10 10 10 10 10
a a a b a b

1.3] =de‿aver 1.4] sa·bia 1.5] =entende‿e 1.6] =se‿á 2.2] =como‿eu 2.4] =confiando‿en; onde‿o 3.3] =éste‿a 3.4] =aquesto‿eu 3.5] se·er 4.2] =quero‿eu 4.5] =cuido‿a 4.6] =quanto‿en 5.3] =ga·a·nna·do‿a 5.4] =grande‿ocajon 5.6] =perde‿e 6.1] =quero‿eu 6.6] =sempre‿ela; o·iu 7.3] =lle‿aprouguer 7.4] =como‿ela 7.5] a·os

Editorial variants

1.3] **Fid** áo d' aver, e de gran razon assaz 1.4] **V** perque 2.2] **C** peró 3.2] **M1**, **V** nostro 3.6] **Fid** e rogolle 4.4] **Fid** querreime 4.6] **V** en as 5.3] **Fid** poi' lo **V** poil-o 5.4] **Fid** se non; ocaijon 5.6] **M1** perde **C** perde; per 6.1] **Fid** Por én 6.3] **V** én 6.5] **M** merçee

6 Por en dela non me quer' eu partir
ca sei de pran que se a ben servir
que non poderei en seu ben falir
de o aver, ca nunca i faliu
quen llo soube con mercee pedir
ca tal rogo sempr' ela ben oiu.

And so I will not forsake her, for I know surely that if I serve her truly with her good will I will not fail to have her love, for none has failed to have it who has beseeched her to give it — such a request she has always granted.

7 Onde lle rogo, se ela quiser,
que lle praza do que dela disser
en meus cantares, e se ll' aprouguer
que me dé gualardon com' ela dá
aos que ama, e quen o souber,
por ela mais de grado trobará.

And so I implore her, if she will, to be pleased with what I say about her in my songs, and, if it is acceptable to her, to give me the reward that she gives to those she loves. Whoever knows he has her favour will then the more willingly be her trovador.

Manuscript variants
5.1] E senor 5.4] To ocaijo*n*

Rubric (E Ind)
Prologo das Cantigas de Santa Maria ementando as cousas que á mester eno trobar.

Postscript (T)
Aqui se acaba o prologo das Cantigas de Santa Maria.

Cantigas de Santa Maria

1. *Cantiga de loor* (*The Seven Joys*)

1 Des oge mais quer' eu trobar
pola Sennor onrada,
en que Deus quis carne fillar
bẽeita e sagrada,
por nos dar gran soldada
no seu reino e nos erdar
por seus de sa masnada
de vida perlongada,
sen avermos pois a passar
per mort' outra vegada.

2 E por en quero começar
como foi saudada
de Gabriel u lle chamar
foi: "Benaventurada
Virgen, de Deus amada,
do que o mund' á de salvar
ficas ora prennada
e demais ta cunnada
Elisabet que foi dultar
é end' envergonnada".

3 E demais quero ll' enmentar
como chegou cansada
a Beleem e foi pousar
no portal da entrada
u pariu sen tardada
Jesucrist' e foi o deitar
como moller menguada
u deitan a cevada
no presev' e apousentar
ontre bestias d'arada.

4 E non ar quero obridar
com' angeos cantada
loor a Deus foron cantar
e paz en terra dada
nen como a contrada
aos tres reis en ultramar
ouv' a estrela mostrada,
por que sen demorada
vẽeron sa oferta dar
estranna e preçada.

5 Outra razon quero contar
que ll' ouve pois contada
a Madalena com' estar
viu a pedr' entornada
do sepulcr' e guardada
do angeo que lle falar
foi e disse: "Coitada
moller, sei confortada
ca Jesu que vẽes buscar
ressurgiu madurgada."

6 E ar quero vos demostrar
gran lediç' aficada
que ouv' ela u viu alçar
a nuv' enlumẽada
seu fill' e pois alçada
foi, viron angeos andar
entr' a gent' assũada,
mui desaconsellada,
dizend': "Assi verrá julgar
est' é cousa provada."

[1] From this day forth my song will be of our worthy Lady, the blessed and holy one in whom God was pleased to take human flesh, to give us a great reward in his kingdom, and to win us as members of his household, in life everlasting, without our having to pass through death again.

[2] And so I will begin my song with how she was greeted by the angel Gabriel, who hailed her "Happy maid, beloved of God, you now carry a child who will save the world; look at your sister-in-law Elizabeth, who did not believe, and is now put to shame."

[3] And next I will relate how she travelled wearily to Bethlehem, and found shelter in the gateway where she soon bore Christ Jesus, and, like a pauper, laid him in the manger where fodder is put, and sheltered him among beasts of the plough.

[4] And I will not forget to tell how the angels' song was "Praise to God and peace on Earth", nor how the star showed the Three Kings from over the sea the way to that country, so that straight away they came to give their rare and precious gifts.

[5] The next thing I will relate, which Mary Magdalen told her, was how she saw the stone rolled away from the tomb, and an angel guarding it, saying to her: "Sorrowing woman, take comfort, for Jesus whom you came here to seek rose from the dead this morning."

[6] And then I will show you the great heartfelt joy she felt when she saw her son ascend in the fiery cloud, and when it had ascended, angels were seen to pass among the assembled throng who were full of wonder and they said: "Thus will he come in judgement, so it is written."

7
Nen quero de dizer leixar
de como foi chegada
a graça que Deus enviar
lle quis atan grãada
que por el' esforçada
foi a companna que juntar
fez Deus e ensinada
d' espirit' avondada
por que souberon preegar
logo sen alongada.

8
E par Deus non é de calar
como foi corõada,
quando seu fillo a levar
quis des que foi passada
deste mund' e juntada
con el no ceo, par a par
e reĩa chamada,
filla, madr' e criada,
e por en nos dev' ajudar
ca x' é noss' avogada.

Cantiga 1 (To 1, T 1, E 1)

Metrics

8 6' 8 6' 6' 8 6' 6' 8 6'
a b a b b a b b a b

1.1] =quero‿eu 1.4] bẽ·ei·ta 1.10] =morte‿outra 2.2] sa·u·da·da 2.6] =mundo‿á 2.10] =ende‿envergonnada 3.1] =lle‿enmentar 3.3] Be·le·em 3.6] =Jesucristo‿e 3.9] =preseve‿e 3.10] =de‿arada 4.2] =como‿an·ge·os 4.6] a·os 4.7] =ouve‿a‿estrela, *necessary elision* 4.9] vẽ·e·ron 5.2] =lle‿ouve 5.3] =como‿estar 5.4] =pedra‿entornada 5.5] =sepulcro‿e 5.6] an·ge·o 5.9] vẽ·es 6.2] =lediça‿aficada 6.3] =ouve‿ela 6.4] =nuve‿enlumẽada 6.5] =fillo‿e 6.6] an·ge·os 6.7] =entre‿a gente‿assũada 6.9] =dizendo‿Assi 6.10] =esto‿é 7.4] grã·a·da 7.5] =ela‿esforçada 7.8] =de‿espirito‿avondada 7.9] pre·e·gar 8.5] =mund‿e 8.7] re·ĩ·a 8.8] =madre‿e 8.9] =deve‿ajudar 8.10] =xe‿é nossa‿avogada

Editorial variants

2.1] **Fid** E por én 2.3] **Fid** le 2.4] **M1, RL** Ben aventurada 2.9] **M** Elisabeth 3.1] **Fid** queroll 3.3] **V, RL** a Belleem **Fid** a Beleen 3.6] **Fid** foio 3.10] **Fid** entre 4.5] **V** acontrada 4.7] **M** ouv' a strela 5.6] **Fid** le 5.10] **M** resurgiu 6.1] **Fid** querovos 6.4] **C** a nuven lumeada 6.7] **M** ontr' 6.9] **M** juygar **Fid** julgar 7.4] **Fid** le **V** granada 7.6] **M1** compan[n]a **RL** compan[h]a 7.7] **V** enssinnada **C** ensinnada 7.8] **M** de Spirit **Fid** d' espirit' **C** d' Esperit' 8.4] **V** desque 8.7] **V** et Reynna **Fid** é Reinna **C** e Reinna

Manuscript variants

3.10] **To** entre 4.7] **To, T, E** ouua strela 5.1] **To** Autra 6.7] **E** ontr 6.9] **T** juigar **E** iuygar 7.6] **E** compana 7.7] **To** enssi*nn*ada 8.7] **To** reÿna

Rubric

De loor de Santa Maria ementando os VII goios que ouve de seu fillo.

To, To Ind los **To Ind, E Ind** sete **T Ind** *missing* **E Ind** de fillo

Captions (T)

1. Como o angeo saudou a Santa Maria. 2. Como Santa Maria pariu Jesucristo e o pos no preseve. 3. Como o angeo pareceu aos pastores. 4. Como os tres reis deron sa oferta a Jesucristo. 5. Como Madalena disse a Santa Maria que ressurgira seu fillo. 6. Como Jesucristo subiu aos ceos na nuve. 7. Como o Spirito Santo vẽo sobelos Apostolos. 8. Como Jesucristo corõou Santa Maria nos ceos.

4] ouferta 5] resurgira 8] *text badly rubbed*

[7] And I will not fail to tell of the coming of the grace which God sent in such abundance, by which the company of apostles which God brought together was encouraged and taught so that they could instantly preach the word.

[8] And by Our Lord I cannot keep silent on how she was crowned, once she had passed on from this world, when it pleased her son to take her to be reunited with him in heaven, at his side. There she was hailed as queen, daughter, mother and handmaiden; and so she must help us for she is our advocate.

2. *The Murdered Chorister*

R 1 *A que do bon rei Davi de seu linnage decende*
2 *nembra lle, creed' a mi, de quen por ela mal prende.*

1 1 Por end' a sant' escritura que non mente nen erra
2 nos conta un gran miragre que fez en Engraterra
3 a Virgen Santa Maria con que judeus an gran guerra
4 porque naceu Jesucristo dela, que os reprende.
R *A que do bon rei Davi de seu linnage decende ...*

2 1 Avia en Engraterra ũa moller menguada
2 a que morreu o marido con que era casada
3 mas ficou lle del un fillo con que foi mui confortada
4 e log' a Santa Maria o ofereu por ende.
R *A que do bon rei Davi de seu linnage decende ...*

3 1 O menĩ' a maravilla er' apost' e fremoso
2 e d' aprender quant' oia era muit' engẽoso
3 e de mais tan ben cantava tan mans' e tan saboroso
4 que vencia quantos eran en sa terr' e alende.
R *A que do bon rei Davi de seu linnage decende ...*

4 1 E o cantar que o moço mais aposto dizia
2 e de que se mais pagava quen quer que o oia
3 era un cantar en que diz: "Gaude Virgo Maria"
4 e pois diz mal do judeu que sobr' aquesto contende.
R *A que do bon rei Davi de seu linnage decende ...*

5 1 Este cantar o menĩo atan ben o cantava
2 que qualquer que o oia tan toste o fillava
3 e por leva-lo consigo con os outros barallava
4 dizend': "Eu dar-ll-ei que jante e de mais que merende."
R *A que do bon rei Davi de seu linnage decende ...*

6 1 Sobr' esto diss' o menĩo: "Madre, fe que devedes,
2 des oge mais vos consello que o pedir leixedes
3 pois vos dá Santa Maria por mi quanto vos queredes
4 e leixad' ela despenda pois que tan ben despende."
R *A que do bon rei Davi de seu linnage decende ...*

7 1 Depois, un dia de festa en que foron juntados
2 muitos judeus e crischãos e que jogavan dados
3 enton cantou o menĩo. E foron en mui pagados
4 todos, se non un judeu que lle quis gran mal des ende.
R *A que do bon rei Davi de seu linnage decende ...*

Believe you me, that Lady, who is of the line of good King David, will always be mindful of those who suffer for her sake.

[1] Holy Scripture, which has no lies or falsehoods, tells us a great miracle which was performed in England by Our Lady with whom the Jews are ever at war, for she bore Jesus Christ who rebukes them.

[2] In England there lived a poor woman who lost the man to whom she was married, but he left her a son who was a great comfort to her, and so she pledged him to Our Lady.

[3] The boy was wondrously fine and fair, and had great skill at learning anything he heard, and he sang so sweetly and softly that he charmed all the people of his region and beyond.

[4] The song which the boy sang most sweetly, and which gave most pleasure to whoever heard it, was a song which runs "Gaude Virgo Maria" and condemns the Jews who dispute her divinity.

[5] The boy sang this song so well that whoever heard it would promptly look after him and would vie with the others to take him home, saying: "I will give him his supper, and more besides."

[6] Knowing this, the boy said to his mother: "Believe me, Mother, from this day forth I tell you that you do not need to beg for money, because Our Lady gives you all you need through me. Let her provide for us, as she provides so well."

[7] Later, on a festival day, when many Christians and Jews were together playing dice, the boy sang his song, and everyone took pleasure in it, except a Jew, who bore him ill will thereby.

8 1 No que o moço cantava o judeu meteu mentes
2 e levou o a sa casa pois se foron as gentes
3 e deu lle tal dũa acha que ben atro enos dentes
4 o fendeu bẽes assi ben como quen lenna fende.
R *A que do bon rei Davi de seu linnage decende ...*

9 1 Poi-lo menĩo foi morto o judeu muit' agĩa
2 soterrou o na adega u sas cubas tĩia.
3 Mas deu mui maa noite a sa madre, a mesquĩa,
4 que o andava buscando e dalend' e daquende.
R *A que do bon rei Davi de seu linnage decende ...*

10 1 A coitada por seu fillo ia muito chorando
2 e a quantos ela via a todos preguntando
3 se o viran. E un ome lle diss': "Eu o vi ben quando
4 o judeu o levou sigo que os panos revende."
R *A que do bon rei Davi de seu linnage decende ...*

11 1 As gentes, quand' est' oiron, foron alá correndo
2 e a madre do menĩo braadand' e dizendo:
3 "Di me que fazes, meu fillo, ou que estás atendendo
4 que non vẽes a ta madre que ja sa mort' entende."
R *A que do bon rei Davi de seu linnage decende ...*

12 1 Pois diss': "Ai, Santa Maria, Sennor, tu que es porto
2 u arriban os coitados, dá me meu fillo morto
3 ou viv' ou qual quer que seja, se non, farás me gran torto
4 e direi que mui mal erra quen o teu ben atende."
R *A que do bon rei Davi de seu linnage decende ...*

13 1 O menĩ' enton da fossa, en que o soterrara
2 o judeu, começou logo en voz alta e clara
3 a cantar "Gaude Maria" que nunca tan ben cantara
4 por prazer da Groriosa que seus servos defende.
R *A que do bon rei Davi de seu linnage decende....*

14 1 Enton tod' aquela gente que i juntada era
2 foron corrend' aa casa ond' essa voz vẽera
3 e sacaron o menĩo du o judeu o posera
4 viv' e são, e dizian todos: "Que ben recende!"
R *A que do bon rei Davi de seu linnage decende ...*

15 1 A madr' enton a seu fillo preguntou que sentira
2 e ele lle contou como o judeu o ferira
3 e que ouvera tal sono que sempre depois dormira
4 ata que Santa Maria lle disse: "Leva t' ende,
R *A que do bon rei Davi de seu linnage decende ...*

[8] The Jew thought on the boy's song, and took him back to his house once the people had dispersed, and struck him such a blow with an axe that he cleft his head to the jaw, just like you split firewood.

[9] After he had killed the boy, the Jew quickly buried him in his cellar, where he kept his wine butts. But the boy's wretched mother had no rest, and went looking for him hither and thither.

[10] The poor woman wept all the while for her son, asking everyone she met if they had seen him. A man said: "I saw him just when he was being taken away by the Jewish cloth merchant."

[11] When the people heard this, they went running to the place with the boy's mother crying aloud and saying: "Tell me what you are doing, my son, or what you are waiting for, since you do not come to your mother who feels her death is nigh."

[12] Then she said "Mary, Our Lady, you who are the port where the afflicted take refuge, give me back my son, dead, alive, or however it my be; if you do not, you will do me great wrong, and I will proclaim that anyone who hopes for favours from you is sorely mistaken."

[13] Then the boy, in a loud, clear voice, from the pit in which the Jew had buried him, began to sing his "Gaude Maria" better than he had ever sung it before, at the bidding of our Glorious Lady, who aids her servants.

[14] And then all the people who were gathered there went running to the house from where that singing had come, and brought out the boy safe and sound from where the Jew had hidden him, and everyone said "How sweet he smells!"

[15] The mother asked her son what he had been through, and he told of how the Jew had struck him and how he had felt so sleepy that he had slept until he heard Our Lady tell him "Awake,

16 1 ca muito per ás dormido dormidor te feziste
2 e o cantar que dizias meu ja escaeciste.
3 Mas leva t' e di o logo mellor que nunca dissiste
4 assi que achar non possa null' om' i que emende."
R *A que do bon rei Davi de seu linnage decende ...*

17 1 Quand' esto diss' o menĩo quantos s' i acertaron
2 aos judeus foron logo e todolos mataron.
3 E aquel que o ferira eno fogo o queimaron
4 dizendo: "Quen faz tal feito desta guisa o rende."
R *A que do bon rei Davi de seu linnage decende ...*

Cantiga 6 (To 5, T 6, E 6)

Metrics

14' [7 7']	14' [7 7'] | 14' [7' 6']	14' [7' 6']	15' [7' 7'/8 6']	14' [7' 6'/7 7']
A	A | b	b	b	a
[A B]	[A B] | c	c	c	b

Strophe 4 line 3 is an anomalous line, apparently hypometric and with exceptional caesura [8 6']. Musical analysis suggests that the hypometry is deliberate, to allow the initial syllable of 'Gaude' to be aligned with the second figure of the music, which quotes a Marian responsory 'Quae est ista quae processit'. Music associated with 'Gaude Maria Virgo' underlies *cantiga* 100 (anthology 44; Ferreira 1999–2000: 38–39).

In most strophes the division of line 4 is congruent with the remainder of the strophe, with the caesura following the 7th syllable, and a *grave* cadence. Strophes 4, 7, and 8 match the division of the refrain, with the caesura in line 4 following the 7th syllable and an *agudo* cadence. In strophes 4 and 7 the stressed word is the keyword 'judeu'.

R.2] =cre·ede‿a 1.1] =ende‿a santa‿escritura 2.4] =logo‿a 3.1] =era‿aposto‿e 3.2] =de‿aprender quanto‿o·i·a; muito‿engẽoso 3.3] =manso‿e 3.4] =terra‿e 4.2] o·i·a 4.3] era un cantar en que diz: ( ) "Gaude Virgo Maria"; *see above* 4.4] =sobre‿aquesto; *see above on caesura* 5.2] o·i·a 5.4] =dizendo‿Eu dar-lle‿-ei 6.1] =Sobre‿esto disse‿o 6.4] =leixade‿ela 7.4] *see above on caesura* 8.4] *see above on caesura* 9.1] =muito‿agĩa 9.3] *hypometric first hemistich resolved by dieresis of* de·u *or* mu·i; ma·a 9.4] =dalende‿e 10.1] i·a 10.2] vi·a = vi‿i·a 10.3] =disse‿Eu 11.1] =quando‿esto‿o·i·ron 11.2] =bra·a·dan·do‿e 11.4] vẽ·es 12.1] =disse‿Ai 12.3] =vivo‿ou 13.1] =menĩo‿enton 14.1] =toda‿aquela 14.2] =correndo‿a·a; onde‿essa; 14.4] =vivo‿e 15.1] =madre‿enton 15.4] =Leva te‿ende 16.2] es·ca·e·cis·te 16.3] =leva te‿e 16.4] =nullo‿ome‿i 17.1] =Quando‿esto disse‿o; se‿i 17.2] a·os

Editorial variants

R] M *laid out in short lines* 2.3] M1 [mui confortada] 3.1] V menynn' 3.2] V engennoso 4.3, 4.4] M *no caesura* 4.4] M1 a[que]sto [c]ontende 5.1] V menynno 6.2] V conssello 7.3] V menynno 7.4] M *no caesura* 8.2] M levó-o 8.3] V atró en os 8.4] M *no caesura* 9.1] M2 fo V Poil-o menynno; agynna 9.2] M soterró-o V tiynna 9.3] M2 mesqỹa M1 mesq[u]ỹa V mesquynna 11.2] V menynno 11.4] M2 vees 13.1] V menynn' 14.2] M1, V correndo 14.3] V menynno 15.4] V Leuat' ende 16.3] V leuat' e 17.1] V menynno quantos ý acertaron 17.3] V en o

Manuscript variants

2.1] E meguada 2.3] E foi, *remainder of line missing* 3.1] To minỹ 4.4] E asto 5.1] To minỹo 5.4] E iãte de 6.1] To minỹo 7.3] To minỹo 8.2] To, T, E leuoo 9.1] To minỹo 9.2] To, T soterroo E soterro o 9.3] T mdre E mesqỹa 9.4] T dalende & E buscado 10.2] To viia, T, E vija; T tods 11.2] To minỹo 12.1] To dis 12.2] E ariban 13.1] To minỹ 14.2] T, E correndo 14.3] To minỹo 15.2] To firira 17.1] To minỹo 17.3] To firira

Rubric

Como Santa Maria ressucitou ao menĩo que o judeu matara porque cantava "Gaude Virgo Maria".

To resucitou o minỹo To Ind resocitou ao minỹo T Ind *missing* E Ind resuscitou ao menino

Captions (T)

1. Como lle morreu o marido e oferiu o fillo a Santa Maria. 2. Como o menĩo cantava "Gaude Maria" e pesou ao judeu por en. 3. Como o judeu levou ao menĩo a sa casa e o matou. 4. Como o soterrou na adega ontr' as cubas. 5. Como Santa Maria ressucitou o menĩo por rogo de sa madre. 6. Como queimaron aquel judeu que matara o menĩo.

5] mdre

[16] you have slept too long, and become a sluggard, and you have already forgotten the song you used to sing for me. Get up and sing it now, better than you have ever sung before, so that no man can find fault with it."

[17] When the boy had said all this, all the people gathered there went to the Jewry and killed them all. And they burnt at the stake the Jew who had wounded him, saying "For what he has done, thus shall he be paid."

3. *The Pregnant Abbess*

R *Santa Maria amar*
devemos muit' e rogar
que a sa graça ponna
sobre nos por que errar
non nos faça nen pecar
o demo sen vergonna.

1 Por ende vos contarei
un miragre que achei
que por ũ' abadessa
fez a madre do gran Rei
ca per com' eu apres' ei
era xe sua essa.
Mas o demo enartar
a foi por que emprennar
s' ouve dun de Bolonna
ome que de recadar
avia e de guardar
seu feit' e sa besonna.
R *Santa Maria amar …*

2 As monjas pois entender
foron esto e saber
ouveron gran lediça
ca porque lles non sofrer
queria de mal fazer
avian lle maiça.
E foron a acusar
ao bispo do logar
e el ben de Colonna
chegou i, e pois chamar
a fez, vẽo sen vagar
leda e mui risonna.
R *Santa Maria amar …*

3 O bispo lle diss' assi:
"Dona, per quant' aprendi
mui mal vossa fazenda
fezestes, e vin aqui
por esto que ante mi
façades end' emenda."
Mas a dona sen tardar
a Madre de Deus rogar
foi, e come quen sonna
Santa Maria tirar
lle fez o fill' e criar
lo mandou en Sansonna.
R *Santa Maria amar …*

4 Pois s' a dona espertou
e se guarida achou
log' ant' o bispo vẽo
e el muito a catou
e desnua-la mandou
e pois lle viu o sẽo
começou Deus a loar
e as donas a brasmar
que eran d' ordin d' Onna
dizendo: "Se Deus m' ampar
por salva poss' esta dar
que non sei que ll' aponna."
R *Santa Maria amar …*

Cantiga 7 (To 6, T 7, E 7)

Note

1.9, 2.9, 3.12, 4.9] On the comic effect of the fantastic and ambiguous geography of the 'Bolonna', 'Colonna', 'Sansonna', and 'Onna' rhymes, see Parkinson 1992: 53–54. 'Bolonna' is intended to refer to the Burgundian dynasty of Portuguese monarchs so that 'un de Bolonna' is a satirical reference to Alfonso III, viewed by Alfonso X as a usurper (Ramos & Rossi 2004). 'Colonna' could be either Colonna (Italy) or Cologne (Germany), neither of which has any relation to Iberian monasticism. 'Onna' is mentioned in *cantiga* 221. See Maia 1984 for the folk etymology of this name.

Metrics

7	7	6'	7	7	6'	|	7	7	6'	7	7	6'	7	7	6'	7	7	6'
A	A	B	A	A	B	|	c	c	d	c	c	d	a	a	b	a	a	b

R.2] =muito‿e 1.3] =ũa‿abadessa 1.5] =como‿eu apreso‿ei 1.9] =se‿ouve 1.12] =feito‿e 2.6] ma·i·ça 2.8] a·o 3.1] =disse‿assi 3.6] =ende‿emenda 3.11] =fillo‿e 4.1] =se‿a 4.3] =logo‿ante‿o 4.5] des·nu·a-la 4.9] =de‿ordin de‿Onna 4.10] =me‿ampar 4.11] =posso‿esta 4.12] =lle‿aponna

We should truly love
Our Lady, and pray
her to send us her grace,
so that the shameless
Devil lead us not into
sin and error.

[1] On this theme I will tell you
of a miracle of which I heard,
which the mother of the great King
performed for an abbess
because, so I was told,
she was devoted to Her.
But the Devil ensnared her
so that she fell pregnant
by a man from Bologna
who was charged with
her accounts and business.

[2] When the nuns learned
of this, there was
great rejoicing
for since the abbess was loath
to pardon their misdeeds
they bore her much ill-will.
And they denounced her to
their bishop
who came straight away from Cologne
and when he had her summoned,
she came unhurried,
happy and smiling.

[3] The bishop spoke to her thus:
"Madam, as I have heard,
your conduct has been very
bad; and this is why I have come
so that in my presence
you can make amends."
But the abbess straight away
went to entreat the Mother of God
and, as she slept,
Our Lady had the child
taken from her body
and sent it to be raised in Soissons.

[4] Then the abbess awoke
and found herself restored
and she at once went to the bishop.
And he examined her closely
and had her disrobed.
And when he saw her naked body
he began to praise God
and to berate the nuns
(who were of the order of Oña)
saying: "As God is my witness
this lady can be declared faultless
for I can find nothing against her."

Editorial variants

R.4] V porque 1.2] M1 dun V d' un 1.8] V porque 1.10] A racadar 2.7] V fóron-a 2.9] V Collonna 3.1] V lles

Manuscript variants

R.2] To muit rogar (2R & 4R) 1.2] E dun 1.7] To mais 1.10] E racadar 2.1] To enteder 2.4] To les 2.9] E Collonna 3.1] To le E lles 3.11] To le 4.6] To le

Rubric

Como Santa Maria livrou a abadessa prenne que adormecera ant' o seu altar chorando.

T Ind *missing*

Captions (T)

1. Como as monjas acusaron ant' o bispo a abadessa que era prenne. 2. Como o bispo foi veer a abadessa ao moẽsteiro. 3. Como vẽeron ant' o bispo a abadessa e as monjas que a acusaron. 4. Como Santa Maria fez sacar o fillo a abadessa pelo costado. 5. Como o angeo deu a criar o fillo da abadessa a un ermitan. 6. Como a abadessa se despojou ant' o bispo e foi livre da acusaçon.

4. *The Minstrel of Rocamadour*

R *A Virgen Santa Maria*
todos a loar devemos
cantand' e con alegria
quantos seu ben atendemos.

1 E por aquest' un miragre
vos direi, de que sabor
averedes poi-l' oirdes,
que fez en Rocamador
a Virgen Santa Maria
madre de Nostro Sennor.
Ora oid' o miragre
e nos contar-vo-lo-emos.
R *A Virgen Santa Maria ...*

2 Un jograr de que seu nome
era Pedro de Sigrar
que mui ben cantar sabia
e mui mellor violar
e en todalas eigrejas
da Virgen que non á par
un seu lais sempre dizia
per quant' en nos aprendemos.
R *A Virgen Santa Maria ...*

3 O lais que ele cantava
era da Madre de Deus
estand' ant' a sa omagen
chorando dos ollos seus
e pois diss': "Ai, Groriosa,
se vos prazen estes meus
cantares, ũa candea
nos dade a que cẽemos."
R *A Virgen Santa Maria ...*

4 De com' o jograr cantava
Santa Maria prazer
ouv', e fez lle na viola
ũa candea decer.
Mas o monge tesoureiro
foi lla da mão toller
dizend': "Encantador sodes
e non vo-la leixaremos."
R *A Virgen Santa Maria ...*

5 Mas o jograr que na Virgen
tĩia seu coraçon
non quis leixar seus cantares
e a candea enton
ar pousou lle na viola.
Mais o frade mui felon
tolleu lla outra vegada
mais toste ca vos dizemos.
R *A Virgen Santa Maria ...*

6 Pois a candea fillada
ouv' aquel monge des i
ao jograr da viola,
foi a põer ben ali
u x' ant' estav' e atou a
mui de rij' e diss' assi:
"Don jograr, se a levardes
por sabedor vos terremos."
R *A Virgen Santa Maria ...*

All we who wait for the favour of Our Lady
should sing her praises with joy.

[1] So I will tell you a miracle which you will enjoy when you hear it, which Our Lady, mother of God, performed in Rocamadour. Now hear the miracle as we tell it.

[2] There was a jogral called Pedro de Sigrar, who was a good singer and a better fiddler, and who knew a *lai* of the matchless Virgin which he sang in every church of hers, as I learned.

[3] The *lai* was to the Mother of God, and he sang it before a statue of her, tears in his eyes, and said: "O Glorious Virgin, if these songs of mine please you, send me a candle so that we may dine."

[4] Our Lady was pleased with the jogral's singing, and so she made a candle come down and land on his fiddle. But the friar-almoner took it from his hand, saying: "You are a sorcerer, and we will not allow it."

[5] But the jogral, whose heart belonged to Our Lady, would not stop his singing, and the candle once more settled on his fiddle. And the wrathful friar took it away again as fast as it takes to say it.

[6] When that friar had seized the candle from the jogral's fiddle, he put it back up where it had been, and tied it very firmly there, saying "Sir jogral, if you take it now we will know you are a magician."

7 O jograr por tod' aquesto
non deu ren mas violou
como x' ante violava
e a candea pousou
outra vez ena viola.
Mas o monge lla cuidou
fillar, mas disse ll' a gente:
"Esto vos non sofreremos."
R *A Virgen Santa Maria ...*

8 Poi-lo monge perfiado
aqueste miragre viu
entendeu que muit' errara
e logo s' arrepentiu
e ant' o jograr en terra
se deitou e lle pediu
perdon por Santa Maria
en que vos e nos creemos.
R *A Virgen Santa Maria ...*

9 Poi-la Virgen groriosa
fez este miragr' atal
que deu ao jograr dõa
e converteu o negral
monge, dali adeante
cad' an' un grand' estadal
lle trouxe a sa eigreja
o jograr que dit' avemos.
R *A Virgen Santa Maria ...*

Cantiga 8 (To 8, T 8, E 8)

Linguistic note

R.2] 'a' could be the feminine singular pronoun (direct object of 'loar') or a preposition in the construction 'dever a loar', which alternates freely with the simpler construction 'dever loar'.

Metrics

7	7'	7	7'	|	7'	7	7'	7	7'	7	7'	7'
A	B	A	B	|	n	c	n	c	n	c	n	b

or

7	7'	7	7'	|	15 [7' 7]	15 [7' 7]	15 [7' 7]	15' [7' 7']
A	B	A	B	|	c	c	c	b

R.3] =cantando‿e 1.1] =aquesto‿un 1.3] =poi-lo‿o·ir·des 1.7] =o·i·de‿o 2.8] =quanto‿en 3.3] =estando‿ante‿a 3.5] =disse‿Ai 3.8] cẽ·e·mos 4.1] =como‿o 4.3] =ouve‿e 4.7] =dizendo‿encantador 5.2] tĩ·i·a 6.2] =ouve‿aquel 6.3] a·o 6.5] =xe‿ante‿estava‿e 6.6] =rijo‿e disse‿assi 7.1] =todo‿aquesto 7.3] =xe‿ante 7.7] =lle‿a 8.3] =muito‿errara 8.4] =se‿arrepentiu 8.5] =ante‿o 8.8] cre·e·mos 9.2] =miragre‿atal 9.3] a·o 9.6] =cada‿ano‿un grande‿estadal 9.8] =dito‿avemos

Editorial variants

1.3] V poy-l'-oirdes **RL** poyl' oirdes 1.8] V contar-uol-o-emos **A** contar vo-lo emos 3.1] **M1**, **RL** Aquel lais que el cantava **V** Aquel lais que él cantaua 4.5] **M** may-lo **V** mayl-o **RL** maylo 4.8] **V** uol-a 5.2] **V** tijnna 6.6] **M** rrig' 7.5] **V** en a 8.1] **V** Poil-o **RL** Poilo 8.8] **M1** nos e vos **V** nós et uós **RL** nós et vós 9.1] **V** Poyl-a **RL** Poyla

Manuscript variants

1.3] **T** poiloyirdes 2.3] **To** catar 3.1] **T**, **E** Aquel lais *que* el cantaua 4.5] **E** maylo 4.8] **T** lla 6.6] **To** rrig e **T**, **E** rrige 7.6] **T** mai lo 8.8] **E** nos & uos

Rubric

Como Santa Maria fez en Rocamador decender ũa candea na viola do jograr que cantava ant' ela.

To ent ela **To Ind** ent ela e a loaua **T Ind** *missing*

Captions (T)

1. Como o jograr violava ant' o altar de Santa Maria e lle pediu ũa candea. 2. Como a candea lle deceu na viola e a fillou o monge. 3. Como o monge tornou a candea en seu lugar e a atou. 4. Como a candea lle deceu outra vez e o monge lla quis fillar. 5. Como o monge rogou ao jograr que o perdõasse. 6. Como o jograr tragia cad' ano ũa candea a Santa Maria.

[7] The jogral took no notice of all this, but played as he did before, and the candle once more came down onto his fiddle. And the friar made to take it, but the onlookers said: "We will not allow you to do this."

[8] When the stubborn monk saw this miracle he understood that he had done a great wrong, and he straight away saw his error and knelt before the jogral to ask his forgiveness in the name of Our Lady in whom we all believe.

[9] After the Glorious Virgin had performed this miracle which rewarded the jogral and converted the black-hearted monk, from that day forward every year the jogral of whom we speak brought a large altar candle for her shrine.

5. The Drowned Sacristan

R *Macar ome per folia*
agĩa caer
pod' en pecado
do ben de Santa Maria
non dev' a seer
desasperado.

1 Por en direi todavia
com' en ũa abadia
un tesoureiro avia,
monge que trager
con mal recado
a sa fazenda sabia
por a Deus perder,
o malfadado.
R *Macar ome per folia ...*

2 Sen muito mal que fazia,
cada noit' en drudaria
a ũa sa druda ia
con ela tẽer
seu gasallado,
pero ant' "Ave Maria"
sempr' ia dizer
de mui bon grado.
R *Macar ome per folia ...*

3 Quand' esto fazer queria
nunca os sinos tangia,
e log' as portas abria
por ir a fazer
o desguisado,
mas no rio que soia
passar foi morrer
dentr' afogado.
R *Macar ome per folia ...*

4 E u ll' a alma saia,
log' o demo a prendia
e con mui grand' alegria
foi pola põer
no fog' irado,
mas d' angeos compannia
pola socorrer
vẽo privado.
R *Macar ome per folia ...*

5 Gran referta i crecia,
ca o demo lles dizia:
"Ide daqui vossa via,
que dest' alm' aver
é juigado,
ca fez obras noit' e dia
sempr' a meu prazer
e meu mandado."
R *Macar ome per folia ...*

6 Quand' est' a compann' oia
dos angeos, se partia
dali triste, pois viia
o demo seer
ben razõado,
mas a Virgen que nos guia
non quis falecer
a seu chamado.
R *Macar ome per folia ...*

7 E pois chegou, lles movia
sa razon con preitesia
que per ali lles faria
a alma toller
do frad' errado,
dizendo lles: "Ousadia
foi d' irdes tanger
meu comendado."
R *Macar ome per folia ...*

8 O demo, quand' entendia
esto, con pavor fogia,
mas un angeo corria
a alma prender
led' aficado,
e no corpo a metia
e fez lo erger
ressucitado.
R *Macar ome per folia ...*

Even if a man fall lightly into sin, he should not despair of Our Lady's mercy.

[1] And so I will tell how there was an almoner in an abbey, a monk who was well versed in doing wrong and lost God's favour, sinner that he was.

[2] His great folly was to go out each night to tryst with his mistress and have his pleasure of her. But beforehand he would always say "Ave Maria" with all his heart.

[3] And when he was at this business, he would never ring the church bell but would quickly open the abbey door to go on his foolishness. But one day he drowned in the river he crossed each night.

[4] And as his soul departed the Devil quickly seized it and with great glee went to cast it in the angry fire, but a troop of angels hastened to help him.

[5] A furious skirmish broke out there, for the Devil said to them: "Go on your way, for it is decreed that this soul is mine, for he did evil day and night, at my command and as it pleased me."

[6] When the company of angels heard this they departed in sorrow, for they saw that the Devil's case was good, but the Virgin who is our guide would not abandon her follower.

[7] And as she came she set out the case by which she would make them yield the soul of the errant monk, saying: "You were rash to lay hands on my devotee."

[8] When the Devil heard these words he fled in terror; but an angel ran to rescue the soul in great joy, and returned it to the body so that he came back to life.

9 1 O convento atendia
2 o sino a que s' ergia,
3 ca des peça non durmia,
4 por en sen lezer
5 ao sagrado
6 foron, e aa agua fria,
7 u viron jazer
8 o mui culpado.
R *Macar ome per folia ...*

10 1 Tod' aquela crerezia
2 dos monges logo liia
3 sobr' ele a ledania,
4 polo defender
5 do denodado
6 demo, mas a Deus prazia,
7 e logo viver
8 fez o passado.
R *Macar ome per folia ...*

Cantiga 11 (To 11, T 11, E 11)

Linguistic note
9.6] 'aa agua': the edition restores the sequence of preposition 'a' and article 'a' which is eliminated through elision in the manuscript witnesses. Mettmann's reading ('à') assumes an anachronistic morphological contraction of the two vowels.

Metrics

7'	5	4'	7'	5	4'	|	7'	7'	7'	5	4'	7'	5	4'
A	B	C	A	B	C	|	a	a	a	b	c	a	b	c

R.2] a·gĩ·a ca·er R.3] =pode‿en R.5] =deve‿a se·er 1.2] =como‿en 1.6] sa·bi·a 2.2] =noite‿en 2.3] i·a 2.6] =ante‿Ave 2.7] =sempre‿i·a 3.1] =Quando‿esto 3.3] =logo‿as 3.6] so·i·a 3.8] =dentro‿afogado 4.1] =lle‿a; sa·i·a 4.2] =logo‿o 4.3] =grande‿alegria 4.5] =fogo‿irado 4.6] =de‿an·ge·os 5.4] =desta‿alma‿aver 5.5] ju·i·ga·do 5.6] =noite‿e 5.7] =sempre‿a 6.1] =Quando‿esto‿a companna‿o·i·a 6.2] an·ge·os 6.3] vi·i·a 6.4] se·er 7.5] =frade‿errado 7.7] =de‿irdes 8.1] =quando‿entendia 8.3] an·ge·o 8.5] =ledo‿aficado 9.2] =se‿ergia 9.5] a·o 9.6] *necessary elision* a‿a, *see Linguistic note above* 10.1] =Toda‿aquela 10.2] li·i·a 10.3] =sobre‿ele

Editorial variants
R.2] **M** aginna 1.1] **A** toda via 2.3] **M2** hua **M1**, **V** hũa 4.6] **M1** conpan[n]ia 6.1] **M** Quando 8.2] **M** fugia 9.6] **M** e à agua 10.1] **V** Tot' aquela

Manuscript variants
R.2] **E** aginna R.6] **To** desesperado 4.6] **To** co*mpa*n*n*ia **T** compania **E** conpania 6.1] **E** Qvando 6.5] **T** rezõado *corrected to* razõado **E** rezõado 8.2] **E** fugia 9.6] **To**, **T**, **E** a agua 10.1] **E** Tot 10.3] **E** Lodania *corrected to* Ledania

Rubric
Como Santa Maria tolleu a alma do monge que s' afogara no rio ao demo e feze o ressucitar.

To, **To Ind** resocitar **T** ressocitar **T Ind** *missing* **E** ressocitar **E Ind** resusçitar

Captions (T)
1. Como o monge dizia "Ave Maria" ant' o altar. 2. Como o monge abriu as portas por ir a sa barragãa. 3. Como o monge morreu no rio e os diaboos lle levaron a alma. 4. Como Santa Maria tolleu a alma do monge aos diaboos. 5. Como Santa Maria ressucitou o monge. 6. Como os monges loaron todos a Santa Maria.

[9] Meanwhile the abbey was waiting for the bell calling them to rise, for they had been awake for some time, and so with haste they went to the churchyard and there saw the sinner lying in the cold water.

[10] Straight away the whole community of monks recited the litany over him, to protect him from the foul fiend, but God was merciful and at once brought the dead man back to life.

6. The Pilgrim to Santiago

R 1 *Non é gran cousa se sabe | bon joizo dar*
2 *a madre do que o mundo | tod' á de joigar.*

1 1 Mui gran razon é que sábia dereito
2 quen Deus troux' en seu corp' e de seu peito
3 mamentou, e del despeito | nunca foi fillar.
4 Por en de sen me sospeito | que a quis avondar.
R *Non é gran cousa se sabe | bon joizo dar …*

2 1 Sobr' esto, se m' oissedes, diria
2 dun joizo que deu Santa Maria
3 por un que cad' ano ia | com' oí contar
4 a San Jam' en romaria | porque se foi matar.
R *Non é gran cousa se sabe | bon joizo dar …*

3 1 Este romeu con bõa voontade
2 ia a Santiago de verdade
3 pero desto fez maldade | que ant' albergar
4 foi con moller sen bondade | sen con ela casar.
R *Non é gran cousa se sabe | bon joizo dar …*

4 1 Pois esto fez, meteu s' ao camĩo
2 e non se mãefestou o mesquĩo
3 e o demo mui festĩo | se lle foi mostrar
4 mais branco que un armĩo | polo tost' enganar.
R *Non é gran cousa se sabe | bon joizo dar …*

5 1 Semellança fillou de Santiago
2 e disse: "Macar m' eu de ti despago,
3 a salvaçon eu cha trago | do que fust' errar
4 por que non cáias no lago | d' iferno, sen dultar.
R *Non é gran cousa se sabe | bon joizo dar …*

6 1 Mas ante farás esto que te digo
2 se sabor ás de seer meu amigo
3 talla o que trages tigo | que te foi deitar
4 en poder do ẽemigo | e vai te degolar."
R *Non é gran cousa se sabe | bon joizo dar …*

7 1 O romeu que sen dovida cuidava
2 que Santiag' aquelo lle mandava
3 quanto lle mandou tallava. | Poi-lo foi tallar
4 log' enton se degolava | cuidando ben obrar.
R *Non é gran cousa se sabe | bon joizo dar …*

8 1 Seus companneiros poi-lo mort' acharon
2 por non lles apõer que o mataron
3 foron s' e logo chegaron | a alma tomar
4 demões que a levaron | mui toste sen tardar.
R *Non é gran cousa se sabe | bon joizo dar …*

9 1 E u passavan ant' ũa capela
2 de San Pedro muit' aposta e bela
3 San James de Compostela | dela foi travar
4 dizend': "Ai, fals' alcavela, | non podedes levar
R *Non é gran cousa se sabe | bon joizo dar …*

10 1 a alma do meu romeu que fillastes
2 ca por razon de mi o enganastes.
3 Gran traiçon i pensastes | e se Deus m' ampar
4 pois falsament' a gãastes | non vos pode durar."
R *Non é gran cousa se sabe | bon joizo dar …*

11 1 Responderon os demões louçãos:
2 "Cuja est' alma foi fez feitos vãos
3 por que somos ben certãos | que non dev' entrar
4 ante Deus pois con sas mãos | se foi desperentar."
R *Non é gran cousa se sabe | bon joizo dar …*

12 1 Santiago diss': "Atanto façamos:
2 pois nos e vos est' assi rezõamos,
3 ao joizo vaamos | da que non á par
4 e o que julgar façamos | logo sen alongar."
R *Non é gran cousa se sabe | bon joizo dar …*

We should not wonder that Our Lady gives true judgements,
as she is the mother of he who will judge the world.

[1] It is not strange that she judges well, she who bore God in her body and nursed him at her breast, and never was wronged by him. And so I am sure that he filled her with wisdom.

[2] On this theme, if you pay heed to me, I will tell you of the judgement of Our Lady on a man who, as I heard tell, would go to Compostela on pilgrimage every year, and who killed himself.

[3] This pilgrim indeed would go to Santiago with good intentions, but on this occasion he did wrong, for first he spent the night with a woman of ill repute, to whom he was not married.

[4] After this, he set off on his pilgrimage without making confession, and the Devil with great speed appeared to him, whiter than ermine, to deceive him at once.

[5] He took the form of Santiago, and said "Though I am displeased with you, I bring you salvation for the sin you committed, to keep you from being surely cast into the fiery lake of hell.

[6] Instead, you must do precisely what I tell you, if you wish to gain my favour: cut off that part of you by which you fell into the power of the ancient foe, and then cut your own throat."

[7] The pilgrim, who was sure that it was Santiago who gave him this command, cut off the part he was bidden. And when he had done this he promptly cut his own throat, thinking that he was acting wisely.

[8] When his companions found him lying dead, they ran off, for fear of being accused of killing him; and then devils immediately came to carry off his soul, with no delay.

[9] And as they passed a fine rich chapel dedicated to St Peter, Santiago himself stood in their way, saying: "False band of villains, you will not take away

[10] the soul of this pilgrim of mine that you have stolen, for you deceived him by taking my place. You have devised a great treachery, so help me God, and as you took this soul by deceit, you may not keep it."

[11] The proud devils replied: "The man whose soul it was did evil deeds and so we are sure that he will not be admitted to stand before God, as he ended his own life with his own hand."

[12] Santiago replied "This is what we will do, as you and I have both made our cases, let us go to judgement before she who has no equal, and whatever she decrees, we will do without delay."

13 1 Log' ante Santa Maria vẽeron
2 e rezõaron quanto mais poderon.
3 Dela tal joiz' ouveron: | que fosse tornar
4 a alma onde a trouxeron, | por se depois salvar.
R *Non é gran cousa se sabe | bon joizo dar …*

14 1 Este joizo logo foi comprido
2 e o romeu morto foi ressurgido
3 de que foi pois Deus servido | mas nunca cobrar
4 pod' o de que foi falido | con que fora pecar.
R *Non é gran cousa se sabe | bon joizo dar …*

Cantiga 26 (To 24, T 26, E 26)

Linguistic note

R.2, 12.4] The alternation between *joigar* (3 syllables) and *julgar* (2 syllables) is a metrical doublet, confrmed by the word profile for this set of forms.

14.4] 'pod'' (='pode') is preterite, not present.

Metrics

13 [7' 5]	14 [7' 6]	|	10'	10'	13 [7' 5]	14 [7' 6]
A	A	|	b	b	a	a

R.1] jo·i·zo R.2] =todo‿a; jo·i·gar 1.1] sa·bia 1.2] =trouxe‿en; corpo‿e 2.1] =sobre‿esto; me‿o·i·sse·des 2.2] jo·i·zo 2.3] =cada‿ano; como‿o·i 2.4] =Jame‿en (*compare* 'James', 9.3) 3.1] vo·on·ta·de 3.2] i·a a San·ti·a·go 3.3] =ante‿albergar 4.1] =se‿a·o 4.4] =toste‿enganar 5.1] San·ti·a·go 5.2] =me‿eu 5.3] =fuste‿errar 5.4] =de‿iferno; cai·as 6.2] se·er 7.2] =San·ti·a·go‿aquelo 7.4] =logo‿enton 8.1] =morto‿acharon 8.2] a·põ·er 8.3] =se‿e 9.1] =ante‿ũa 9.2] =muito‿aposta 9.4] =dizendo‿Ai falsa‿alcavela 10.3] =me‿ampar; tra·i·çon 10.4] =falsamente‿a gã·as·tes 11.2] =Cuja esta‿alma foi, *alt.* Cuja‿esta alma foi 11.3] =deve‿entrar 12.1] =San·ti·a·go disse‿Atanto 12.2] =esto‿assi 12.3] a·o jo·i·zo va·a·mos 13.1] =logo‿ante 13.3] =jo·i·zo‿ouveron 13.4] *necessary elision* a‿alma onde a trouxeron (*compare* 11.2), *alt.* a alma‿onde a trouxeron *or* a alma onde‿a trouxeron 14.1] jo·i·zo 14.4]=pode‿o

Editorial variants

R.1] **M2** joyzo 4.1] **V** camynno 4.2] **M2** mesqỹo **M1** mesq[u]ỹo **V** maenfestou; mesquynno 4.3] **M2** le **V** festynno 4.4] **V** armynno 5.4] **M1** [no] 6.4] **V** enemigo 7.3] **V** poil-o 8.1] **V** poil-o 10.4] **V** gannastes 12.4] **V** iulgar' 14.2] **M** resorgido

Manuscript variants

4.1] **To** camĩo, **T** caminno, **E** camỹo 4.2] **To** mesquĩo **T** mesquinno **E** mesqỹo 4.3] **To** festĩo **T** festinno **E** festỹo; le 4.4] **To** armĩo **T** arminno **E** armỹo 5.4] **E** caies lago **T** inferno 9.3] **T** jaymes 14.2] **To** resurgido **T, E** resorgido

Rubric

Como Santa Maria juigou a alma do romeu que ia a Santiago que se matou na carreira por engano do diaboo que tornass' ao corpo e fezesse pẽedença.

To que que ia; fizesse **To Ind** ioigou; tornas **T, E** diabo **T Ind** *missing*

Captions (T)

1. Como Santa Maria mamentou Jesucristo, seu fillo, do seu peito. 2. Como o demo pareceu ao romeu en forma de Santiago no camĩo. 3. Como o romeu cortou sa natura e se degolou por consello do demo. 4. Como Santiago quis fillar ao demo a alma do seu romeu. 5. Como Santiago e o demo vẽeron a joizo ante Santa Maria pola alma do romeu. 6. Como o romeu ressurgiu per mandado de Santa Maria.

6] resurgiu

[13] And so they went before Our Lady, and argued their case as best they could. And her judgement was that they should return the soul whence they had taken it, so that he could find salvation.

[14] The Virgin's judgement was carried out, and the dead pilgrim was returned to life, and served God faithfully, but he never could recover the part he had lost which had led him into sin.

7. *The Priest who Only Knew One Mass*

R *Quen loar podia*
com' ela querria
a madre de quen
o mundo fez seria de bon sen.

1 Dest' un gran miragre
vos contarei ora
que Santa Maria
fez, que por nos ora
dũu que al, fora
a sa missa, ora-
çon nunca per ren
outra sabia | dizer mal nen ben.
R *Quen loar podia …*

2 Onde ao bispo
daquele bispado
en que el morava
foi end' acusado
e ant' el chamado
e empreguntado
foi, se era ren
o que oia | del. Respos: "O ben."
R *Quen loar podia …*

3 Poi-lo bispo soube
per el a verdade
mandou lle tan toste
mui sen piedade
que a vezindade
leixass' da cidade
tost' e sen desden
e que sa via | logo se foss' en.
R *Quen loar podia …*

4 Aquela noit' ouve
o bispo veuda
a Santa Maria
con cara sannuda
dizendo lle: "Muda
a muit' atrevuda
sentença, ca ten
que gran folia | fezist'. E por en
R *Quen loar podia …*

5 te dig' e ti mando
que destas perfias
te quites, e se non,
d' oj' a trinta dias
morte prenderias
e alá irias
u o dem' os seus ten
na sa bailia | ond' ome non ven."
R *Quen loar podia …*

6 O bispo levou se
mui de madurgada
e deu ao preste
sa raçon dobrada
e: "Missa cantada
com' acostumada
ás," disse, "manten
da que nos guia | ca assi conven."
R *Quen loar podia …*

Cantiga 32 (To 34, T 32, E 32)

Metrics

5'	5'	5	10	|	5'	5'	5'	5'	5'	5'	5	10 [4' 5]
A	A	B	B	|	n	c	n	c	c	c	b	b

The '–ia' endings in ll. 1.3 and 4.3 create incidental rhymes with the refrain, but are not part of the metrical structure.

R.2] =como‿ela 1.1] =Desto‿un 1.5] dũ·u 2.1] a·o 2.4] =ende‿acusado 2.5] =ante‿el 2.8] o·i·a 3.6] leixass' *apocopated form of* leixasse *(for another example see cantiga 227 [anthology 26], 3.4)* 3.7] =toste‿e 3.8] =fosse‿en 4.1] =noite‿ouve 4.6] =muito‿atrevudo 4.8] =feziste‿E 5.1] =digo‿e 5.3] *the metrical accent falls on* se 5.4] =de‿oje‿a 5.7] =u‿o demo‿os 5.8] =onde‿ome 6.3] a·o 6.6] =como‿acostumada

Editorial variants

1.5] V d'uun 2.1] V Unde 2.8] V d'él 3.1] V Poil-o 3.6] **M2** leixas' **M1** leixas[s]' 3.7] V toste sen 4.8] V fecist' 5.4] V d'oi 5.7] M u dem', *footnote u = u o* 6.1] V se leuou 6.3] V at ao capelan 6.4] V deu raçon

The man who can do her will
and sing the praise of the mother of Him
who made the world, he is a man of wisdom.

[1] Now I will tell you a great miracle on this theme, which Our Lady, who prays for us, performed for a priest who for good or ill knew no other prayers, other than her mass.

[2] For this he was denounced to the bishop of the diocese where he lived, and was summoned to appear before him to say if what was reported was true. And he replied: "It is."

[3] When the bishop heard the truth from his mouth, he showed no pity and immediately ordered him to leave the city precincts, at once and without complaint, and to depart and go on his way.

[4] That night the bishop had a vision of Our Lady, with wrathful countenance, who said: "Change your bold decree, and know that you have done a very foolish thing.

[5] I tell you and order you to be done with such quarrels. If you do not, within thirty days you will breathe your last and go where the Devil keeps his own in his domain, whence no man returns."

[6] The bishop arose early that morning and doubled the priest's stipend, saying: "Hold to the singing of the mass of Our Lady who guides us, as you have been wont to do, for so it should be."

Manuscript variants

1.3] T q*ue* | que 1.5] E dun 2.1] T, E Unde 3.6] To, T, E leixas 5.7] To, T, E u dem 6.1] To leuousse, *over erasure* T, E se leuou 6.3] To deu ao preste, *over erasure* T, E e ao capelan 6.4] To ssa raço*n*, *over erasure* T, E deu raçon

Rubric

Como Santa Maria amẽaçou o bispo que descomungou o crerigo que non sabia dizer outra missa se non a sua.

T Ind *missing*

Captions (T)

1. Como o crerigo dize missa de Santa Maria ca non sabia outra. 2. Como o acusaron ant' o bispo porque non sabia dizer outra missa se non de Santa Maria. 3. Como o bispo mandou ao crerigo que non cantasse missa en toda a cidade. 4. Como Santa Maria diss' ao bispo mui sannudamente que se partisse do seu clerigo. 5. Como o bispo mandou ao crerigo que cantasse e deu lle razon dobrada. 6. Como o crerigo cantou sempre d' ali adeante missa de Santa Maria como soía.

5] mando

8. *The Knight whose Goshawk was Returned by Santa Maria de Salas*

R 1 *Quen fiar na madre do Salvador*
2 *non perderá ren de quanto seu for*

Whosoever trusts in the mother of Our Lord will never be parted from what he owns.

1 1 Quen fiar en ela de coraçon,
2 averrá lle com' a un ifançon
3 avẽo eno reino d' Aragon,
4 que perdeu a caça un seu açor,
R *Quen fiar na madre do Salvador …*

Whoever trusts in her with all their heart will be served as was a nobleman in the kingdom of Aragon who during the hunt lost one of his goshawks

2 1 que grand' e mui fremos' era, e ren
2 non achava que non fillasse ben
3 de qual prijon açor fillar conven,
4 d' ave pequen' atro ena maior.
R *Quen fiar na madre do Salvador …*

which was a big and handsome bird, and easily caught everything it came upon of the kinds of prey a goshawk is wont to take, from the smallest to the largest of birds.

3 1 E daquest' o ifançon gran pesar
2 avia de que o non pod' achar,
3 e por ende o fez apregõar
4 pela terra toda en derredor.
R *Quen fiar na madre do Salvador …*

And the nobleman was very sad that he could not find it, and so had the news proclaimed throughout the land around.

4 1 E pois que por esto non o achou,
2 pera Salas seu camĩo fillou
3 e de cera semellança levou
4 de sa av', e diss' assi: "Ai, Sennor
R *Quen fiar na madre do Salvador …*

And when even then he could not find it he set off to Salas and took with him a wax image of his bird, and said: "O my Lady

Cantiga 44 (To 58, T 44, E 44)

Metrics

10 10 | 10 10 10 10
A A | b b b a

1.2] =como‿a 1.3] =de‿Aragon 2.1] =grande‿e; fremoso‿era 2.4] =de‿ave pequena‿atro 3.1] =daquesto‿o 3.2] =pode‿achar; a·vi·a 4.4] =ave‿e disse‿assi 5.3] mio (*single syllable*) 5.4] =aver-me‿-ás 6.2] =sempre‿andarei 7.1] o·ir 7.3] =se‿en; lle‿o; vĩ·ir 7.4] =onde‿ouve‿el 8.1] =ouvesse‿ende‿el 8.2] =lle‿o 8.3] =logo‿a 9.1] =muito‿a 9.2] lo·ou 9.3] =dizendo‿Ai

Editorial variants

1.3] V en o 2.4] M pequena tro V en a 4.1] M nono 4.2] V camynno 5.3] V mi-o 7.2] M1, V partir- 8.2] V en a 9.4] M amor!

Manuscript variants

2.3] E quall 6.3] To pregõado 9.3] To tatos

Rubric

Como o cavaleiro que perdera seu açor e foi o pedir a Santa Maria de Salas e estando na eigreja posou lle na mão.

To pidir; igreja T Ind *missing*

Captions (T)

1. Como o ifançon foi a caça e lançou o açor aas perdizes. 2. Como o infançon andava buscando o açor e non o podia achar. 3. Como o ifançon fez pregõar o açor per toda a vila e as aldeas. 4. Como o ifançon levou o açor de cera a Santa Maria de Salas que lli desse o seu que perdera. 5. Como estando o ifançon ant' o altar de Santa Maria vẽo o açor e posou lli na mão. 6. Como o ifançon loou muito Santa Maria e contou end' aa gente todo o feito.

5 1 Santa Maria, eu venno a ti
2 con coita de meu açor que perdi,
3 que mio cobre, e tu fas lo assi,
4 e aver-m'-ás sempre por servidor.
R *Quen fiar na madre do Salvador …*

Mary, I come to you in distress at the loss of my goshawk so that you may recover it for me: do as I ask and you will always have me as your servant.

6 1 E demais esta cera ti darei
2 en sa figura, e sempr' andarei
3 pregõando teu nome e direi
4 como dos santos tu es la mellor."
R *Quen fiar na madre do Salvador …*

Moreover I will give you this wax in the likeness of the bird, and I will continually proclaim your name and will tell how you are the greatest of all the saints."

7 1 Pois esto disse, missa foi oir
2 mui cantada, mas ante que partir
3 s' en quisesse, fez ll' o açor vĩir
4 Santa Maria, ond' ouv' el sabor.
R *Quen fiar na madre do Salvador …*

When he had said this, he went to hear a full sung mass, but before he could prepare to depart, Holy Mary made his goshawk come back to him, which gave him great joy.

8 1 E que ouvess' end' el maior prazer
2 fez ll' o açor ena mão decer,
3 come se ouvesse log' a prender
4 caça con el como faz caçador.
R *Quen fiar na madre do Salvador …*

And to give him the greater pleasure, she had the goshawk come to rest on his hand, as if it had just taken some game as a hunting bird does.

9 1 E el enton muit' a Madre de Deus
2 loou, e chorando dos ollos seus,
3 dizend': "Ai Sennor, tantos son os teus
4 bẽes que fazes a quen ás amor."
R *Quen fiar na madre do Salvador …*

And then he gave hearty praise to the Mother of God, his eyes full of tears, saying: "O my Lady, many are the favours that you do for those you love."

9. The Mountain Goats that Gave Milk to the Monks of Montserrat

R *Mui gran dereit' é d' as bestias obedecer*
a Santa Maria, de que Deus quis nacer.

1 E dest' un miragre, se Deus m' ampar,
mui fremoso vos quer' ora contar
que quiso mui grand' a Groriosa mostrar,
oide-mio, se ouçades prazer.
R *Mui gran dereit' é d' as bestias obedecer …*

2 En Monsarrat, de que vos ja contei,
á ũ' eigreja, per quant' apres' ei,
feita no nome da madre do alto rei
que quis por nos morte na cruz prender.
R *Mui gran dereit' é d' as bestias obedecer …*

3 Aquel logar a pé dun mont' está
en que muitas cabras montesas á
ond' estrãia maravilla avẽo ja,
ca foron todas ben juso decer
R *Mui gran dereit' é d' as bestias obedecer …*

4 ant' a eigreja qu' en un vale jaz,
e ant' a porta paravan s' en az
e estavan i todas mui quedas en paz,
ta que os monges las ian monger.
R *Mui gran dereit' é d' as bestias obedecer …*

5 E quatr' anos durou, segund' oí,
que os monges ouveron pera si
assaz de leite, que cada noite ali
vĩian as cabras esto fazer,
R *Mui gran dereit' é d' as bestias obedecer …*

6 atẽes que un crerizon sandeu
furtou un cabrit' en e o comeu,
e das cabras depois assi lles conteceu
que nunca mais las poderon aver.
R *Mui gran dereit' é d' as bestias obedecer …*

7 E desta guisa a Madre de Deus
quis governar aqueles monges seus,
por que depois gran romaria de romeus
vẽeron polo miragre saber.
R *Mui gran dereit' é d' as bestias obedecer …*

Cantiga 52 (**To** 66, **T** 52, **E** 52)

Textual Note
2.1] 'de que vos ja contei': this refers to a preceding poem set in Montserrat (*cantiga* 48, **To** 62).

Metrics

12	12	|	10	10	12	10
A	A	|	b	b	b	a

R.1] =dereito‿é de‿as bes·tias 1.1] =desto‿un; me‿ampar 1.2] =quero‿ora 1.3] =grande‿a Gro·ri·o·sa 1.4] oi·de-mi·o; *musical notation confirms 10-syllable line* 2.2] =ũa‿eigreja; quanto‿apreso‿ei 3.1] =monte‿está 3.3] =onde‿es·trã·ia 4.1] =ante‿a; que‿en; *alt.* ante‿a eigreja que nun vale jaz *or* ante‿a eigreja que en un val jaz *or* ante‿a‿eigreja que en un vale jaz 4.2] =ante‿a; se‿en 4.3] *alt.* quedas e‿en paz 4.4] i·an 5.1] =quatro‿anos; segundo‿o·í 5.4] vĩ·i·an 6.1] a·tẽ·es 6.2] =cabrito‿en 7.3] ro·ma·ri·a 7.4] vẽ·e·ron

Editorial variants
R.1] **A** beschas (1R) 1.4] **V** Oýde-mi-o **A** o-y-de-mio 2.1] **M1**, **V** Monsarraz 2.2] **V** apres 3.3] **V** estranya 5.1] **V** segund' óy 5.4] **V** uijnnan

Manuscript variants
1.4] **E** se de*us* u*os* amostre prazer 1.R] **T** beschas 2.1] **T** Monssarraz **E** mon sarraz 2.2] **To**, **T**, **E** un **E** igreia 3.3] **To**, **E** estrãya **T** estraỹa 4.4] **E** moger 6.4] **E** nuca

Most right it is that animals should be obedient
to holy Mary, in whom God was pleased to be born.

[1] On this theme, with God's help, I will tell you a very fine and mighty miracle, which the Glorious Virgin performed — listen to me, if you wish to hear a pleasant tale.

[2] In Montserrat, of which I have already told you, there is a church, as I heard tell, built in honour of the mother of the great King who died for us on the cross.

[3] That place is at the foot of a mountain where there are many wild goats, whereby a strange miracle was wrought, for they would all come down the mountain

[4] to the church, which sits in a valley, and they would line up in a row before the church door, and stand there calmly and peacefully until the monks came to milk them.

[5] For four years, as I heard, the monks had all the milk they needed, as the goats came every night to give them it,

[6] until a foolish priest stole a kid from them and ate it, and from then on it befell that the goats came no more to them.

[7] And in this way the Mother of God provided for her monks; and thereafter many came there in pilgrimage to hear tell of that miracle.

Rubric

Como Santa Maria fez vĩir as cabras montesas a Monsarrat e leixavan se ordennar aos monges cada dia.

To monssarrat **To Ind** las cabras; monssarad; ordinnar **T** Monssarrad **T Ind** *missing* **E** las cabras; monssarraz; se leixaven **E Ind** monssarraz; se leixaron ordenar; *final two words*, cada dia, *missing*

Captions (T)

1. Como as cabras montesas decendian da montanna que as mongessen os monges. 2. Como as cabras se paravan todas en az e as mongian os monges. 3. Como os monges comian leite daquelas cabras quanta lles era mester. 4. Como os monges loavan Santa Maria por aquela mercee que llis fazia. 5. Como un crerizon furtou un cabrito daquelas cabras e o comeu. 6. Como as cabras fugiron e nunca mais i vẽeron por aquel cabrito que tomaron.

10. *Cantiga de loor*

R *Rosa das rosas, flor das flores,*
dona das donas, sennor das sennores.

1 Rosa de beldad' e de parecer
e flor d' alegria e de prazer,
dona en mui piadosa seer,
sennor en toller coitas e doores.
R *Rosa das rosas, flor das flores ...*

2 Atal sennor dev' ome muit' amar
que de todo mal o pode guardar
e pode ll' os pecados perdõar,
que faz no mundo per maos sabores.
R *Rosa das rosas, flor das flores ...*

3 Devemo-la muit' amar e servir
ca punna de nos guardar de falir,
des i dos erros nos faz repentir
que nos fazemos come pecadores.
R *Rosa das rosas, flor das flores ...*

4 Esta dona que tenno por sennor
e de que quero seer trobador,
se eu per ren poss' aver seu amor,
dou ao demo os outros amores.
R *Rosa das rosas, flor das flores ...*

Cantiga 10 (**To** 10, T 10, E 10)

Linguistic note
In 2.1 and 3.1 alternative readings are possible with the construction 'dever a':
2.1 Atal sennor dev' ome muit' amar =muito‿a‿amar
3.1 Devemo-la muit' amar e servir =muito‿a‿amar.

Metrics
The refrain is best treated as a couplet of accentual lines, with four metrical accents to each line:

Rosa das rosas, *flor* das flores,
dona das donas, sennor das sennores

The syllabic irregularity produced by this structure is attenuated but not eliminated by the insertion of 'e' in the version copied by all manuscripts. The music of the refrain aligns its accents with the verbal accents (with the exception of the intrusive 'e' which receives the musical accent intended for 'flor'), while no such alignment is found in the strophe.

8'	10'	|	10	10	10	10'
A	A	|	b	b	b	a

1.1] =beldade‿e 1.3] se·er 2.1] =deve‿ome muito‿amar, *see Linguistic note above* 2.2] =de‿alegria 2.3] =lle‿os 2.4] ma·os 3.1] =muito‿amar, *see Linguistic note above* 4.2] =se·er 4.3] =posso‿aver 4.4] a·o

Editorial variants
R.1] **M** Fror das frores **Fid** flor das flores **C** Rosa das rosas | e Fror das frores 1.2] **M** Fror **Fid** flor 2.3] **Fid** e podell' os **M** peccados **C** pecados 3.1] **Fid** Devemosla **V** Deuemol-a 4.1] **V**, **RL**, **C** Dona

Manuscript variants
R.1] T, E fror 1.2] T, E fror 2.3] E peccados

Rubric
De loor de Santa Maria, como é fremosa e bõa e á gran poder.

T Ind *missing*

Captions (T)
1. Como Santa Maria é rosa das rosas. 2. Como Santa Maria é fror das frores. 3. Como Santa Maria é dona das donas. 4. Como Santa Maria é sennor das sennores. 5. Como Santa Maria tolle coitas e doores. 6. *missing*

Rose of roses, Flower of flowers,
Lady of ladies, Queen of queens.

[1] Rose of beauty, rose of grace
flower of joy, flower of pleasure
lady who is most merciful
queen who takes away grief and pain.
Rose of roses, Flower of flowers ...

[2] Such a lady deserves great love
for she can guard us from all ill
and forgive us the sins
that we commit in this world for vain pleasure.
Rose of roses, Flower of flowers ...

[3] We must love and serve her truly
for she strives to keep us from falling
and makes us repent of the errors
that we sinners commit.
Rose of roses, Flower of flowers ...

[4] This gracious lady who is my Lady
and whose trovador I would be
if by any means I may win her love
I will send all other loves to the Devil.
Rose of roses, Flower of flowers ...

11. *The Nun who was Slapped by a Crucifix*

R *Quen a Virgen ben servir*
nunca poderá falir.

Whosoever serves the Virgin
will never come to ill.

1 E daquesto un gran feito
dun miragre vos direi
que fez mui fremos' afeito
a madre do alto Rei
per com eu escrit' achei
se me quiserdes oir.
R *Quen a Virgen ben servir ...*

On this theme, if you will hear me, I will tell you of a great deed, a fine splendid miracle which the mother of the high King performed, as I found in writing.

2 Esto foi dũa donzela
que era en Fontebrar
monja fremosa e bela
que a Virgen muit' amar
sabia, se Deus m' ampar,
mais da orden quis sair
R *Quen a Virgen ben servir ...*

The tale is of a maiden who was a nun, a fair and beauteous one, in the convent of Fontevrault. She loved the Virgin dearly, as God is my help, but she decided to leave her order

3 con un cavaleir' aposto
e fremos' e de bon prez,
e non catou seu dẽosto
mais como moller rafez
quisera s' ir dessa vez.
Mais non a quis leixar ir
R *Quen a Virgen ben servir ...*

to go off with a handsome, fair and valiant knight. And she did not think of her dishonour, but like a common woman wanted to go at this time. But the Blessed Virgin Mary would not let her go.

4 a Virgen Santa Maria
a que mui de coraçon
saudava noit' e dia
cada que sa oraçon
fazia, e log' enton
ia beijar sen mentir
R *Quen a Virgen ben servir ...*

The nun would greet the Virgin lovingly whenever she went to pray, and every day, in truth she would kiss

5 os pees da magestade
e dun crucifiss' assi
que i de gran santidade
avia, com' aprendi,
e pois s' ergia dali
ia as portas abrir
R *Quen a Virgen ben servir ...*

zthe feet of the crucifix which hangs there, which as I heard tell was an object of great devotion. And then she would arise and open the doors

6 da igrej', e sacristãa
era, com' oí dizer,
do logar, e a campãa
se fillava a tanger
por s' o convento erger
e a sas oras vĩir.
R *Quen a Virgen ben servir ...*

of the church, as she was the sacristan of the convent, as it is told, and she would ring the bell for the convent to awake and come to say their Hours.

7 Fazend' assi seu ofiço
mui gran temp' aquest' usou
atẽes que o proviço
a fez que se namorou
do cavaleir' e punnou
de seu talante comprir.
R *Quen a Virgen ben servir ...*

Performing her duties in this way, she passed many years, until the Devil made her fall in love with that knight, and she did all she could to do his will.

8 E por end' ũa vegada
a meia noite s' ergeu
e com' era costumada
na igreja se meteu
e aa omagen correu
por se dela espedir.
R *Quen a Virgen ben servir ...*

And so one night she arose at midnight, as was her wont, and went into the church and ran to the statue of the Virgin to say her farewell.

9 E ficando os gẽollos
disse: "Con graça, Sennor"
mas chorou logo dos ollos
a madre do Salvador
en tal que a pecador
se quisesse repentir.
R *Quen a Virgen ben servir ...*

And she knelt before it and said "Forgive me, my Lady", but the mother of our Saviour wept so sorrowfully that the sinful woman was near to repentance.

10 1 Enton s' ergeu a mesquĩa
2 por s' ir log' ante da luz
3 mas o crucifiss' agĩa
4 tirou a mão da cruz
5 e com' ome que aduz
6 de rijo a foi ferir
R *Quen a Virgen ben servir ...*

Then the wretched nun arose to make her escape before dawn, but the crucified Christ freed its hand from the cross, and like a man waving his arm dealt her a mighty blow

11 1 e ben cabo da orella
2 lle deu orellada tal
3 que do cravo a semella
4 teve sempre por sinal
5 por que non fezesse mal
6 nen s' assi foss' escarnir.
R *Quen a Virgen ben servir ...*

and struck her so fiercely by the ear that she bore a welt in the shape of a nail for the rest of her life, as a sign for her to sin no more and not put herself to shame.

12 1 Desta guisa come morta
2 jouve tolleita sen sen
3 trões u o convent' a porta
4 britou e espantou s' en
5 quand' ela lles contou quen
6 a firiu pola partir
R *Quen a Virgen ben servir ...*

With the blow the nun fell senseless to the ground and lay there as if dead, until the nuns broke open the door, and they were amazed when she told them who had struck her to stop her

Cantiga 59 (**To** 75, T 59, E 59)

Linguistic notes

12.3] The construction in use here, 'trões u', was obscured by the invisible elision of 'u'. The **To** scribe attempted to restore the alternative construction, 'trões que', by the insertion of 'que', creating a non-standard elision: 'trões que‿o'.

6.1, 8.4] The variant 'igreja', usually found in alternation with our preferred form 'eigreja', appears in all witnesses of this *cantiga*. See Parkinson & Barnett 2013: 469–70 and 475–77 on the distribution of variants of 'eigreja' throughout the *CSM*.

Note

2.2] The location in 'Fontebrar' (the convent of Fontevrault) seems to be an innovation of the *CSM* version of this tale. The T and **To** readings 'Fontenbrar' might suggest Fontainebleau, probably known to Alfonso X as a favourite residence of Louis IX, and with a chapel dedicated to the Virgin but no convent.

Metrics

7	7	|	7'	7	7'	7	7	7
A	A	|	b	c	b	c	c	a

1.3] =fremoso‿afeito 1.5] =escrito‿achei 1.6] o·ir 2.4] =muito‿amar 2.5] =me‿ampar; sa·bi·a 3.1] =cavaleiro‿aposto 3.2] =fremoso‿e 3.5] =se‿ir 4.3] =noite‿e; sa·u·da·va 4.5] =logo‿enton 4.6] i·a 5.1] pe·es 5.2] =crucifisso‿assi 5.4] =como‿aprendi 5.5] =se‿ergia 5.6] i·a 6.1] =igreja‿e 6.2] =como‿o·í 6.5] =se‿o 6.6] vĩ·ir 7.1] =Fazendo‿assi 7.2] =tempo‿aquesto‿usou 7.3] a·tẽ·es 7.5] =cavaleiro‿e 8.1] =ende‿ũa 8.2] =se‿ergeu; mei·a 8.3] =como‿era 8.5] *necessary elision* e a‿a *or* aa‿omagen 10.1] =se‿ergeu 10.2] =se‿ir logo‿ante 10.3] =crucifisso‿a·gĩ·a 10.5] =come‿ome 11.6] =se‿assi fosse‿escarnir 12.3] *necessary elision* u‿o, *see Linguistic note above*; =convento‿a 12.4] =se‿en 12.5] =quando‿ela 12.6] fi·riu 13.1] =grande‿erro 14.1] =ende‿o 14.2] =logo‿en 14.6] =esto‿a

13 do grand' erro que quisera
fazer, mas que non quis Deus
nen a sa madre que fera-
mente quer guarda los seus
segund Lucas e Mateus
e os outros escrivir
R *Quen a Virgen ben servir …*

committing the great sin she had wished to do, for this was not God's will, nor that of his mother who fiercely protects her own, as Luke, Matthew and the others

14 foron. Por end' o convento
se pararon log' en az
u avia mil e cento
donas, todas faz a faz,
e cantado ben assaz
est' a Deus foron gracir.
R *Quen a Virgen ben servir …*

wrote in their gospels. And so the whole convent, one thousand one hundred nuns in all, assembled in their ranks, one opposite another, and with singing gave thanks to God for this miracle.

Editorial variants

R] M Quena V Quén á; seruir' A Quen â 1.2] M1, V dum 2.4] V á 2.5] V m' anpar' 2.6] M1 Mais da orden quis sayr V Mais da órden quis sayr 3.3] V denosto 3.5] V quiséra-ss' ir 3.6] M2 nona 5.1] M2 majestade V Maiestade 6.1] M2 ygreg'; sancristãa 6.4] V filaua 8.1] M1 porende 8.5] M2 à omagen 10.1] M2 mesquinna 10.2] V logo ánte 10.3] M2 aginna 10.6] M2 ferir 12.3] M2 trões o convent' *footnote*: trões o = trões u o 12.6] M2 feriu 13.3] M2 nena 13.5] M2 segun; Matheus

Manuscript variants

1.2] E dum 2.2] To, T font enbrar E font ebrar 2.6] To mais quis da orde*n* sair T mais quis da orden sair 3.3] T deõsto 3.4] E mas 4.6] To beyar 5.1] T, E maiestade 6.1] To, T igreg e E ygreg e sancristãa 6.3] To canpãa 6.4] E filaua 7.1] T ossiço E offiçio 8.1] E porende hũa 8.5] E & a omagen 10.3] T, E agi*n*na 10.5] To, T a aduz 10.6] To firir 11.1] E orela 12.3] To trões *que* o, *superscript* q̃ *added by later hand* T, E trões o 12.6] T, E feriu 13.1] E Con 14.5] E asaz

Rubric

Como o crucifisso deu a palmada a onra de sa madre aa monja que posera de s' ir con seu entendedor.

To sa sa T Ind *missing* E aa onrra; monja de font ebrar E Ind como cruçifixo; palmadas; font ebar

Captions (T)

1. Como ũa monja pos de s' ir con un cavaleiro. 2. Como a monja se foi espedir da omage de Santa Maria e a omage fillou s' a chorar. 3. Como o crucifisso deu gran palmada aa monja que se queria ir. 4. Como a monja caeu en terra amortida da ferida que lle deu o crucifisso. 5. Como acordou a monja e contou ao convento o que ll' avẽera. 6. Como todo o convento das monjas loaron muito Santa Maria e seu fillo Jesucristo.

1] dess con

12. *The Woman who could not Remove her Slipper*

R 1 *Quen mui ben quiser o que ama guardar*
2 *a Santa Maria o dev' a encomendar.*

1 1 E dest' un miragre, de que fiz cobras e son,
2 vos direi mui grande, que mostrou en Aragon
3 Santa Maria, que a moller dun ifançon
4 guardou de tal guisa, por que non podess' errar.
R *Quen mui ben quiser o que ama guardar …*

2 1 Esta dona, per quant' eu dela oí dizer,
2 aposta e ninna foi e de bon parecer
3 e por aquesto a foi o ifançon prender
4 por moller, e foi a pera sa casa levar.
R *Quen mui ben quiser o que ama guardar …*

3 1 Aquel ifançon un mui gran temp' assi morou
2 con aquela dona, mais pois s' ir dali cuidou
3 por ũa carta de seu sennor que lle chegou
4 que avia guerra e que o foss' ajudar.
R *Quen mui ben quiser o que ama guardar …*

4 1 Ante que movesse, disse ll' assi sa moller:
2 "Sennor, pois vos ides, fazede, se vos prouguer,
3 que m' encomendedes a alguen, ca m' é mester
4 que me guarde e que me sábia ben consellar."
R *Quen mui ben quiser o que ama guardar …*

5 1 E o ifançon lle respondeu enton assi:
2 "Muito me praz ora daquesto que vos oí
3 mais ena eigreja mannãa seremos i
4 e enton vos direi a quen vos cuid' a leixar."
R *Quen mui ben quiser o que ama guardar …*

6 1 Outro dia foron ambos a missa oir
2 e pois foi dita, u se lle quis el espedir,
3 chorand' enton ela lle começou a pedir
4 que lle désse guarda por que ouvess' a catar.
R *Quen mui ben quiser o que ama guardar …*

7 1 E ar ele, chorando muito dos ollos seus,
2 mostrou ll' a omagen da Virgen, madre de Deus,
3 e disse ll': "Amiga, nunca os pecados meus
4 sejan perdõados, se vos a outri vou dar
R *Quen mui ben quiser o que ama guardar …*

Whoever wishes to keep what is dear to him, should entrust it to Holy Mary.

[1] Of this I will tell you — and both the verse and the music are mine — a very fine miracle, which the Virgin Mary performed in Aragon, where she protected the wife of a nobleman and kept her from going astray.

[2] This lady, according to the tale, was fair and young and of pleasant appearance, and so the nobleman took her as his wife and carried her off to his house,

[3] And that nobleman lived with the lady for many years, but then he was minded to go away, as he had received a letter from his liege lord telling of a war and asking for his aid.

[4] Before he left, his wife spoke to him thus: "My lord, as you are going away, if it so please you, dispose that you entrust me to someone, who will protect me and give me good counsel, for I have need of it."

[5] And the nobleman replied in this wise: "I am greatly pleased by what you have said. Tomorrow we will go to the church, and then I will tell you in whose care I will leave you."

[6] The next day they both went to hear mass, and when it was over, as he made ready to take his leave of her, she wept and asked him to give her a guardian to watch over her.

[7] And then, with eyes full of tears, he pointed to the statue of the Blessed Virgin, mother of God, and said: "My dearest, may my sins never be forgiven if I commend you to anyone

8 1 se non a esta, que é sennor espirital,
2 que vos pode ben guardar de posfaz e de mal
3 e por ende a ela rog' eu que pod' e val,
4 que mi vos guarde e leix' a mi cedo tornar."
R *Quen mui ben quiser o que ama guardar …*

9 1 Foi s' o cavaleiro logo dali. Mais que fez
2 o diabr' arteiro por lle toller seu bon prez
3 a aquela dona? Tant' andou daquela vez
4 que un cavaleiro fezo dela namorar.
R *Quen mui ben quiser o que ama guardar …*

10 1 E con seus amores a poucas tornou sandeu
2 e por end' ũa sa covilleira cometeu
3 que lle fosse bõa, e tanto lle prometeu
4 que por força fez que fosse con ela falar.
R *Quen mui ben quiser o que ama guardar …*

11 1 E disse ll' assi: "Ide falar con mia sennor
2 e dizede lle como moiro por seu amor,
3 e macar vejades que lle desto grave for,
4 non a leixedes vos por en muito d' aficar."
R *Quen mui ben quiser o que ama guardar …*

12 1 A moller respos: "Aquesto de grado farei
2 e que a ajades quant' eu poder punnarei
3 mais de vossas dõas me dad', e eu llas darei,
4 e quiçai per esto a poderei enganar."
R *Quen mui ben quiser o que ama guardar …*

13 1 Diss' o cavaleir': "Esto farei de bon talan."
2 Log' ũas çapatas lle deu de bon cordovan
3 mais a dona a trouxe peior ca a un can
4 e disse que per ren non llas queria fillar.
R *Quen mui ben quiser o que ama guardar …*

14 1 Mais aquela vella, com' era moller mui vil
2 e d' alcaiotaria sabedor e sotil,
3 por que a dona as çapatas fillasse, mil
4 razões lle disse, trões que llas fez tomar.
R *Quen mui ben quiser o que ama guardar …*

15 1 Mais a mesquĩa, que cuidava que era ben,
2 fillou logo as çapatas, e fez i mal sen,
3 ca u quis calça-la ũa delas, ja per ren
4 fazer non o pode, nen a do pee sacar.
R *Quen mui ben quiser o que ama guardar …*

[8] except this lady, who is our spiritual liege, and who will truly protect you from disgrace and evil and so I ask her, as she is powerful, to look after you on my behalf and bring me quickly home."

[9] And the knight departed thence. But what did the cunning Devil devise to steal that lady's good name? He tried so hard that he made another knight fall in love with her.

[10] And quickly his love drove him out of his mind, and so he found a go-between, and persuaded her to help him, and made her so many promises that he forced her to go and talk to the lady.

[11] And he said to the bawd: "Go and talk to my lady, and tell her that I am dying of love for her, and even if you can see that she is not willing, do not give her any way to resist you."

[12] The woman replied: "I will gladly do this, and will do all I can for you to have her, but first give me gifts, and I will give them to her, for perhaps in this way we can ensnare her."

[13] Said the knight: "This will I gladly do." And so he gave her some slippers of fine leather. But the lady treated the bawd like a cur, and said that nothing would make her take them.

[14] But that old woman, who was a wicked creature, and sly and wise in matters of harlotry, tried a thousand arguments to persuade the lady to accept the slippers, and finally made her take them.

[15] And the poor young woman, who thought she was not doing wrong, took the slippers, which was a great mistake, for as soon as she tried to put one on, she found she could not get it on or off her foot.

16 1 E assi estede un ano e ben un mes,
2 que a çapata ao pee assi se ll' apres
3 que, macar de toller lla provaron dous nen tres,
4 nunca lla poderon daquel pee descalçar.
R *Quen mui ben quiser o que ama guardar ...*

17 1 E depos aquest' a poucos dias recodiu
2 seu marid' a ela, e tan fremosa a viu
3 que a logo quis, mas ela non llo consentiu
4 ata que todo seu feito ll' ouve a contar.
R *Quen mui ben quiser o que ama guardar ...*

18 1 O cavaleiro disse: "Dona, desto me praz,
2 e sobr' esto nunca averemos se non paz
3 ca sei que Santa Mari', en que todo ben jaz,
4 vos guardou." E a çapata lle foi en tirar.
R *Quen mui ben quiser o que ama guardar ...*

Cantiga 64 (To 52, T 64, E 64)

Metrics

The unusual alternation of 11 and 13 lines in the refrain is probably an error from the first examplars, but is present in all witnesses and has been incorporated into the musical structure. R.2 could be scanned as 11 syllables: 'a Santa Maria‿o dev' a‿encomendar'.

11	13	|	13	13	13	13
A	A	|	b	b	b	a

R.2] =deve‿a 1.1] =desto‿un 1.4] =podesse‿errar 2.1] =quant‿eu; o·í 3.1] =tempo‿assi 3.2] =se‿ir 3.4] =fosse‿ajudar 4.1] =lle‿assi 4.2] prou·guer 4.3] =me‿encomendedes; me‿é 4.4] sá·bia 5.2] o·í 5.4] =cuida‿a 6.1] o·ir 6.3] =chorando‿enton 6.4] =ouvesse‿a 7.2] =lle‿a 7.3] =lle‿Amiga 8.3] =rogo‿eu; pode‿e 8.4] =leixe‿a 9.1] =se‿o 9.2] =di·ab·re‿ar·tei·ro 9.3] =tanto‿andou 10.2] =end‿ũa 11.1] =lle‿assi; mia (*single syllable*) 11.4] =de‿aficar 12.2] =quanto‿eu 12.3] =dade‿e 13.1] =Disse‿o cavaleiro‿Esto 13.2] =Logo‿ũas 14.1] =como‿era 14.2] =de‿al·cai·o·ta·ri·a 15.4] pe·e 16.2] =lle‿apres; *necessary elision* çapata‿ao pe·e 16.4] pe·e 17.1] =aquesto‿a 17.2] =marido‿a 17.4] =lle‿ouve 18.2] =sobre‿esto 18.3] =Maria‿en

Editorial variants

R.1] M1, V Quem (1–13R) 1.4] V porque 3.1] V así 4.1] M2 diss-ll' 6.2] V e depois 8.1] V Sennora espirital 8.2] V pos faz 8.3] V porend' 8.4] V guard' 9.2] V seu mui bon 11.1] M1 disse-l' assi V disse-l' así 12.1] V respos' 12.2] V poder' 12.3] V uosas 13.1] M1, V Disse o 13.3] M1 [a] troxe V dona troxe peor ca un can 14.3] M1 a[s] çapatas fillas[e] 14.4] M1 fez fillar V troes que ll' as fez fillar 15.3] V calçal-a 16.1] M esteve 16.2] V ll' a apres 17.1] V de pos 17.2] M1 marido dela, e tan fremosa [a] viu V marido d' ela e tan fremos' a uiú 17.3] M1 ll[o] V ll' consentiú 17.4] M1 ll' o[u]ve V ll'oue 18.3] M1 Santa Maria, en V Santa María, en

Manuscript variants

R.1] E Quem (1–6R & 8–13R); Quem a s*anta* mui: *the underlining of* a santa *indicates erasure* (3R) 1.3] T jfanco*n* 1.4] To, T per 2.2] To nina 2.3] T un jfançon 3.1] E asi 3.2] E srr 3.3] T lli 5.3] E yg*re*ia T mannaa 6.2] E e depois 7.2] E omge*n* 8.1] E sennora 8.2] To posfaç T posfac 8.3] E porend a ela 8.4] T, E guard e E mi*n* 9.2] E seu mui 10.4] To, T per 11.1] E dissel 12.3] E uosas 13.1] E Disse o 13.3] To q*ue* a T la dona; que a E troxe peor ca un can 14.3] E dona açapatas fillass 14.4] E fez fillar 15.1] To mesquỹa T mesqỹna E mesq*uiñ*a 15.4] T non pode 16.1] E esteue 16.2] To pe assi si E lla apres 17.2] E marido dela; fremosa uiu 17.3] E no*n* ll 17.4] E oue 18.3] E Maria en

[16] And so she remained for a year and a month, with the slipper stuck to her foot, and though two or three people tried to take it off, none could ever remove it from her foot.

[17] And a few days later her husband returned to her, and was so struck by her beauty that he desired her that very hour, but she would not yield until she had told him the whole story.

[18] And the knight declared "My lady, this pleases me greatly, and there will never be anything but peace between us, for I know that Holy Mary, the seat of all goodness, has protected you." And with that he took the slipper from her foot.

Rubrics

To Como a moller que o marido leixara en comenda a Santa Maria non podo calçar a çapata que lle dera seu entendedor mais de ate ena meadade do pe, nen a ar pode descalçar ta que o marido lla descalçou.

To Ind, **T**, **E** Como a moller que o marido leixara en comenda a Santa Maria non podo a çapata que lle dera seu entendedor meter no pee nen descalçar.

T podo calçar **T**, **E** nen descalçala **T Ind** *missing* **E Ind** encomendada; *the last four words*, no pee nen descalçar, *are missing*

Captions (T)

1. Como un cavaleiro casou con ũa donzela mui fremosa. 2. Como seu sennor lle enviou dizer per sa carta que o fosse servir. 3. Como o cavaleiro comendou sa moller a Santa Maria que lla guardasse de desonra. 4. Como un cavaleiro rogou a ũa alcaiota que lli fezess' aver aquela dona. 5. Como a dona non pude calçar nen descalçar a çapata que lli deu a alcaiota. 6. Como vẽo da oste seu marido, da dona, e lli descalçou a çapata.

13. *The Wife and the Mistress*

R 1 *A Groriosa grandes faz*
2 *miragres por dar a nos paz.*

The Glorious Virgin performs fine miracles to restore peace.

1 1 E dest' un miragre direi
2 fremoso, que escrit' achei,
3 que fez a madre do gran Rei
4 en que toda mesura jaz
R *A Groriosa grandes faz …*

Now I will tell you a fine miracle, which I found in writing, performed by the mother of the high King, full of wisdom

2 1 pola moller dun mercador
2 que porque seu marid' amor
3 avia con outra, sabor
4 dele perdia e solaz.
R *A Groriosa grandes faz …*

for the wife of a merchant, who had lost the pleasure and comfort she used to have of him, because he loved another woman.

3 1 E por esto queria mal
2 a sa combooça mortal,
3 e Santa Maria sen al
4 rogava que lle déss' assaz
R *A Groriosa grandes faz …*

And so she bore mortal hatred for her husband's other woman, and openly begged the Virgin Mary to give her all possible

4 1 coita e mal por que perder
2 lle fazia o gran prazer
3 que seu marido lle fazer
4 soía na vila d' Arraz.
R *A Groriosa grandes faz …*

sorrow and pain, because it was she who made her lose the great pleasure she once had of her husband, there in the town of Arras.

5 1 E pois fez esta oraçon
2 adormeceu se log' enton
3 e dormindo viu en vijon
4 Santa Maria con grand' az
R *A Groriosa grandes faz …*

And when she had spoken this prayer she fell asleep and saw a vision of the Blessed Virgin with a great host

Cantiga 68 (**To** 68, **T** 68, **E** 68)

Metrics

8	8	|	8	8	8	8
A	A	|	b	b	b	a

R.1] Gro·ri·o·sa 1.1] =desto‿un 1.2] =escrito‿achei 2.2] =marido‿amor 3.2] com·bo·o·ça 3.4] =désse‿asaz 4.4] =de‿Arraz; so·í·a 6.1] =de‿an·ge·os; disse‿assi 6.2] o·í 6.4] cru·e·za 7.2] =ante‿o; gẽ·o·llos 7.3] sa·u·dar 7.4] =põ·ende‿en 8.1] =Tantoste‿aquela se‿espertou 8.2] =foi se‿e 8.4] =ante‿ela disse‿o 9.2] =me‿este 10.1] a·vĩ·ir 10.3] =xe‿ante‿avian

Editorial variants

2.1] **M1** dum **V** Por la moller d'um mercador 4.4] **M1, V** Araz 6.1] **M1** ll[e] **V** que-ll' diss' assí 7.3] **M1** saudar- **V** saudar- 7.4] **M1** me, poend' **V** me poend' 8.1] **M1, V** se espertou 8.2] **M2** foi-ss'; e 9.4] **V** non o

Manuscript variants

2.1] **E** dum 7.4] **To, T** mi **E** poend 8.1] **E** se espertou 8.4] **To, T** disse malvaz

6 1 d' angeos que lle diss' assi:
2 "A ta oraçon ben oí
3 mais pero non conven a mi
4 fazer crueza nen me praz.
R *A Groriosa grandes faz ...*

of angels, and the Virgin said to her: "I have heard your prayer but it is not my way nor does it please me to be cruel.

7 1 Demais aquela vai ficar
2 os gẽollos ant' o altar
3 meu e cen vezes saudar
4 me, põend' en terra sa faz."
R *A Groriosa grandes faz ...*

What is more, that woman goes to kneel at my altar and gives thanks to me a hundred times a day, bowing her head to the ground."

8 1 Tan tost' aquela s' espertou
2 e foi s' e na rua topou
3 con a outra que se deitou
4 ant' ela e diss': "O malvaz
R *A Groriosa grandes faz ...*

No sooner had the wife awoken than she went out to the street and met the other woman, who knelt before her and said: "It was the wicked

9 1 demo foi, chus negro ca pez,
2 que m' este torto fazer fez
3 contra vos, mais ja outra vez
4 non o farei, pois vos despraz."
R *A Groriosa grandes faz ...*

Devil, black as pitch, who led me to wrong you in this way, but I will do it no more, as it grieves you."

10 1 Assi a Virgen avĩir
2 fez estas duas, sen falir,
3 que x' ant' avian, sen mentir,
4 denteira come con agraz.
R *A Groriosa grandes faz ...*

And so the Blessed Virgin truly reconciled these two, who previously, without exaggeration, were at each other's throats.

Rubric
Como Santa Maria avẽo as duas combooças que se querian mal.

T Ind *missing* E Como santa avẽo E **Ind** queriam

Captions (T)
1. Como ũa bõa moller siia en sa casa e seu marido fazia mal sa fazenda con otra. 2. Como o mercador marido da bõa dona trebellava con sa barragaa. 3. Como a moller do mercador orava por mal de sa combooça e dormeceu ant' o altar e Santa Maria lli pareceu. 4. Como a combooça da moller do mercador beijava a terra ant' o altar de Santa Maria rogando lli que a perdõasse. 5. Como a moller do mercador topou con sa combooça na rua e a combooça lli pediu perdon. 6. Como a moller do mercador e sa combooça fezeron paz e se quitou a combooça daquel pecado.

3] li

14. *The Blasphemer who was Struck Dead*

R 1 *Quen diz mal da reĩa espirital,*
2 *log' é tal que merec' o fog' infernal.*

1 1 Ca non pod' dela dizer
2 mal, en que a Deus tanger
3 non aja, que quis nacer dela por Natal.
R *Quen diz mal da reĩa espirital …*

2 1 E desto quero contar
2 miragre que quis mostrar
3 Deus por sa madre vingar dun mui mentiral,
R *Quen diz mal da reĩa espirital …*

3 1 que na taverna beveu
2 e aos dados perdeu
3 alg' e por en descreeu mui descomunal-
R *Quen diz mal da reĩa espirital …*

4 1 mente, ca a Deus dẽostou
2 e sa madre non leixou,
3 e en seus nembros travou come desleal.
R *Quen diz mal da reĩa espirital …*

5 1 E u quis do ventre seu
2 dizer mal, morte lle deu
3 Deus come a fals' encreu que de razon sal.
R *Quen diz mal da reĩa espirital …*

6 1 Seu padre, quand' est' oiu,
2 de sa cas' enton saiu,
3 na via un morto viu ben di natural,
R *Quen diz mal da reĩa espirital …*

7 1 que lle diss' atal razon:
2 "Teu fillo, mui mal garçon,
3 é mort' e en perdiçon, que nunca mais fal,
R *Quen diz mal da reĩa espirital …*

8 1 non porque de Nostro Sennor
2 disse mal, mais que da flor,
3 sa madre, disse peior, e por en sinal
R *Quen diz mal da reĩa espirital …*

9 1 ti dou, que o acharás
2 pelas costas tod' atras
3 partid', e ll' o cor verás assi per igual
R *Quen diz mal da reĩa espirital …*

10 1 a testa e a serviz,
2 porque da Emperadriz
3 disse mal, Deus foi joiz que pod' e que val."
R *Quen diz mal da reĩa espirital …*

11 1 O padre foi log' ali
2 e achou seu fill' assi
3 como vos ja retraí, ben oistes qual.
R *Quen diz mal da reĩa espirital …*

Cantiga 72 (To App 13, T 72, E 72)

Metrics

The composite 11- or 12-syllable lines in the refrain and at the end of the *vuelta* are set to the same musical motif. All manuscript versions have an unsystematic alternation between 7- and 8-syllable lines in strophe 1, which can be assumed to have been in the exemplar(s) from which the manuscript versions were copied. The uncertainty probably derives from continuators' failure to notice the haplology in 1.1: 'Ca non pod' dela dizer'. The unresolvable hypermetry of 8.1 has been retained.

11 [3 8]	11 [3 8]	|	7	7	12 [7 5]
A	A	|	b	b	a

R.1] re·ĩ·a R.2] =logo‿e; merece‿o fogo‿infernal 1.1] =pode‿dela (*haplology*) 3.2] a·os 3.3] =algo‿e; des·cre·eu 4.1] *necessary elision* ca‿a 5.3] =falso‿encreu 6.1] =quando‿esto‿o·iu 6.2] =casa‿enton sa·iu 6.3] *alt.* e na via‿un 7.1] =disse‿atal 7.3] =morto‿e 8.1] *hypermetric line* 9.2] =todo‿atras 9.3] =partido‿e lle‿o 10.3] jo·iz 10.4] =pode‿e 11.1] =logo‿ali 11.2] =fillo‿assi 1.3] re·tra·í; o·is·tes

Editorial variants

R.1] M1, V Quem (*and* 7–11R) M2 Reynna M1 Reyn[n]a 1.1] M pode 2.1] M desto vos 3.1] M Que ena V Que en a 3.3] M algu', e 4.1] M1 [a] 6.2] V cassa 7.1] M disse 7.3] M1, V morto en 8.2] V de flor 9.1] M Te 10.1] M Da testa 11.1] M E o padre

He who maligns the heavenly queen,
has truly earned his place in hell.

[1] For no-one can speak ill of her without insulting God, who was born of her at Christmas.

[2] And so I will tell a miracle which God saw fit to vouchsafe to avenge his mother of a scoundrel

[3] who got drunk in a tavern and lost money at dice, and so blasphemed most wild-

[4] ly for he insulted Our Lord and did not spare his mother, and faithlessly spoke of her body.

[5] And when he scorned her womb, God brought him death as a foul unbeliever, who has lost his reason.

[6] When the man's father heard the news, he went out from his house, and in the street met a dead neighbour,

[7] who said: "Your son, a bad lot, has died and gone to hell, without reprieve

[8] not because he spoke ill of Our Lord but because he said worse things of his mother, the rose, and I give you a sign,

[9] you will find him with his back torn open and his heart revealed, and so

[10] also his head and his neck, for because he spoke ill of the Empress, God all powerful judged him."

[11] And his father went to the place and found his son as I have described, and you have heard.

Manuscript variants

R.1] E Qvem; Quem (7–11R) **To** reỹa espirital; reỹa esperital (1–11R) **T** reỹa esperital; reỹa (1–4R & 8–11R); reynna (5R); reyna (6R); reỹna (7R); esperital (3–11R) **E** reỹna espirital; reỹna (1R, 3–4R, 6–7R, 10–11R); reyna (2R, 5R, 8–9R); sp*er*ital (1–4R); espirital (5–6R & 8–11R); esperital (7R) 1.1] **To**, **T**, **E** pode dela 1.3] **T** naer **E** naçer 2.1] **To**, **T**, **E** desto uos 3.1] **To**, **T**, **E** Que ena 3.3] **E** descreu 4.1] **E** ca deus deostou 5.3] **To** falss cre 6.2] **E** cassa 7.1] **To**, **T**, **E** disse 7.3] **E** morto en 8.2] **E** de flor 8.3] **E** peor 9.1] **E** Te 10.1] **To**, **E** Da testa **T** **E** a testa

Rubric

Como o demo matou a un tafur que dẽostou a Santa Maria por que perdera.

T Ind *missing* **E**, **E Ind** deostou

Captions (T)

1. Como ũus tafures jogavan os dados en ũa taverna. 2. Como un tafur perdeu aos dados et dẽostou Santa Maria e seu fillo Jesucristo. 3. Como o demo abriu aquel tafur pelas espaldas e lli partiu o coraçon per meogo. 4. Como un ome morto pareceu ao padre do tafur e lli disse que seu fillo era morto. 5. Como o ome boo achou seu fillo morto daquela guisa que ja oistes. 6. Como o ome boo e seus parentes levaron o tafur a soterrar.

1] huus; hua 2] deostou 6] et

15. *Musa, the Girl Taken to Paradise*

R *Ai Santa Maria, | quen se per vos guia*
quit' é de folia | e sempre faz ben.

O Holy Mary, whoever is guided by you
is cured of folly and always prospers.

1 Por end' un miragre | vos direi fremoso
que fezo a madre | do Rei grorioso
e de o oir ser-vos-á saboroso,
e prazer-mi-á en.
R *Ai Santa Maria, | quen se per vos guia ...*

And so I will tell you a fine miracle wrought by the mother of the glorious King — you will enjoy hearing it and that will please me.

2 Aquesto foi feito | por ũa minĩa
que chamavan Musa, | que mui fremosĩa
era e aposta, | mas garridelĩa
e de pouco sen.
R *Ai Santa Maria, | quen se per vos guia ...*

The miracle was performed for a girl called Musa, who was very pretty and elegant, but a chatterbox and a flibbertigibbet.

3 E esto fazendo, | a mui Groriosa
pareceu ll' en sonnos, | sobejo fremosa
con muitas minĩas | de maravillosa
beldad', e por en
R *Ai Santa Maria, | quen se per vos guia ...*

And the Glorious Virgin appeared to her in a dream, beautiful beyond measure, accompanied by many maidens of wondrous beauty, and so

4 quisera se Musa | ir con elas logo
mas Santa Maria | lle diss': "Eu te rogo
que se mig' ir queres | leixes ris' e jogo
orgull' e desden.
R *Ai Santa Maria, | quen se per vos guia ...*

Musa wanted to follow them, but Our Lady said: "What I ask of you, is that if you wish to come with me, leave behind mirth and play, pride and mockery.

5 E se esto fazes, | d' oj' a trinta dias
seerás comig' entr' estas compannias
de moças que vees, | que non son sandias,
ca lles non conven."
R *Ai Santa Maria, | quen se per vos guia ...*

If you can do this, in thirty days from now you will join me in these companies of damsels that you see, who are not foolish, for it does not become them."

Cantiga 79 (**To** 42, **T** 79, **E** 79)

Metrics

11' [5' 5']	11 [5' 5]	|	11' [5' 5']	11' [5' 5']	11' [5' 5']	5
A	B	|	c	c	c	b

The long lines of the strophe mainly divide 5'+5', with a small number (1.3, 5.2, 10.1) divided 5+6'. The false correction in 10.1 in **To** reflects an attempt to impose a 5'+5' division on such lines, as part of short-line layout.

R.2] =quito‿e 1.1] =ende‿un 1.3] o·ir ser=se‿er: *musical copy in all manuscripts subdivides a long note into two breves with a melodic dip to accommodate an extra syllable* 1.4] =prazer-mi‿-á 3.2] =lle‿en 3.4] =beldade‿e 4.2] =disse‿Eu 4.3] =migo‿ir; riso‿e 4.4] =orgullo‿e 5.1] =de‿oje‿a 5.2] =se·e·rás comigo‿entre‿estas 5.3] ve·es 6.1] =Atanto‿ouve 6.3] =logo‿outras 7.1] =padre‿e; quando‿esto 7.2] =lle‿o·i·ron 7.3] mer·ce·e 7.4] aa (*single syllable*) 8.1] =A·os 8.2] =logo‿a 8.3] =lle‿ouve‿apareçuda 10.2] jo·i·zo 10.3] =de‿erro‿e 10.4] =dizede‿Amen

Editorial variants

R.1] **M1**, **V** quem 1.3] **V** seer-uos á 1.4] **A** prazer m' á en 2.1] **M** mennynna 2.2] **M** fremosinna 2.3] **M** garridelinna 3.3] **M** meninnas 4.2] **V** dis' 5.1] **V** d' oi 5.2] **M1**, **V** serás comigo 6.2] **M** vision 7.1] **M1**, **V** padre e 7.4] **M** à que 8.1] **M A** vint' e seis dias 10.2] **V** que en o 10.3] **M1**, **V** ache sen erro e sen pecado

6 Atant' ouve Musa | sabor das compannas
que en vison vira, | que leixou sas mannas
e fillou log' outras, | daquelas estrannas,
e non quis al ren.
R *Ai Santa Maria, | quen se per vos guia ...*

Musa was so eager to join the companions that she had seen in her dream, that she put aside her old ways and took up new ones, unlike the others, and would not be moved.

7 O padr' e a madre, | quand' aquesto viron,
preguntaron Musa, | e pois que ll' oiron
contar o que vira, | mercee pediron
aa que nos manten.
R *Ai Santa Maria, | quen se per vos guia ...*

When her father and mother saw this, they asked Musa about it, and when she recounted what she had seen, they begged forgiveness of the Lady who protects us.

8 Aos quinze dias | tal fever aguda
fillou log' a Musa, | que jouve tenduda
e Santa Maria | ll' ouv' apareçuda,
que lle disse: "Ven,
R *Ai Santa Maria, | quen se per vos guia ...*

Fifteen days later, a terrible fever took hold of Musa, who took to her bed and Our Lady appeared to her, and said: "Come,

9 ven pora mi toste." | Respos lle: "De grado."
E quando o prazo | dos dias chegado
foi, seu espirito | ouve Deus levado
u dos outros ten
R *Ai Santa Maria, | quen se per vos guia ...*

come quickly." And Musa replied: "Gladly."And when the thirtieth day came, her soul was taken up by God to where all the saints

10 santos. E por en seja de nos rogado
que eno joizo, | u verrá irado,
que nos ache quitos | d' err' e de pecado,
e dized': "Amen."
R *Ai Santa Maria, | quen se per vos guia ...*

abide. And so let us beseech him that on the Day of Judgement, when he comes in wrath, he will find us free of sin and error — and all say "Amen!"

Manuscript variants

R.1] E *Maria* lei (2R); quem R.2] E fola (6R); be (7R) 1.3] **To**, T, E seer 1.4] T prazer ma 2.1] T meninna E menỹna 2.2] T fremosiinna 2.3] T garridelinna E garridelina E 3.1] T fazeno 3.2] T pareceo 3.3] **To** minỹas T menỹas E meninas 4.2] E dis 5.2] E seras T companias 6.2] E visio*n* 6.3] E est*r*anas 7.1] E padre 7.4] **To**, T, E a que 8.1] E A uinte seis dias 9.1] T pera 9.3] E se*n* 9.4] T deus 10.1] **To** denos *marked for replacement by* nos **To** iuizo E iuyzo 10.3] T ache sen erro e sen peccado E ache se*n* erro e se*n* pecado

Rubric

Como Santa Maria tornou a minĩa que era garrida corda e levou a sigo a paraiso.

T menỹa T **Ind** *missing* E menĩa; garida; levo E **Ind** menina; garida; levo a sig a

Captions (T)

1. Como a menĩa Musa estava fazendo garridenças con pouco siso. 2. Como Santa Maria pareceu con gran companna de menĩas a Musa u jazia dormindo. 3. Como Musa mudou seus costumes e o padr' e a madre se maravillavan. 4. Como a menĩa Musa contou a seu padr' e a sa madre o que ll' avẽera con Santa Maria. 5. Como a menĩa adoeceu e Santa Maria ll' apareceu e disse lli que se fosse con ela. 6. Como a menĩa Musa morreu e Santa Maria con sas virgẽes lli levaron a alma.

2] pareceu gran 4] quel

16. *Hieronymus is Made Bishop of Pavia*

R0 1 *Muito punna d' os seus onrar*
2 *sempre Santa Maria.*

S1 1 E desto vos quero contar
2 un gran miragre que mostrar
3 quis a Virgen que non á par
4 na cidad' de Pavia.
R1 1 *Muito punna d' os seus onrar*
2 *sempre Santa Maria.*

S2 1 Un crerig' ouv' i sabedor
2 de todo ben e servidor
3 desta groriosa Sennor
4 quant' ele mais podia.
R2 1 *D' onrar os seus á gran sabor*
2 *sempre Santa Maria.*

S3 1 Ond' avẽo que conteceu,
2 poi-lo bispo dali morreu,
3 a un sant' om' apareceu
4 a Virgen que nos guia.
R3 1 *Aos seus onrou e ergeu*
2 *sempre Santa Maria.*

S4 1 E pois lle foi aparecer,
2 começou ll' assi a dizer:
3 "Vai, di que façan esleer
4 cras en aquele dia
R4 1 *Os seus faz onrados seer*
2 *sempre Santa Maria.*

S5 1 por bisp' un que Geronim' á
2 nome, ca tanto sei del ja
3 que me serve e servid' á
4 ben, com' a mi prazia."
R5 1 *Os seus onrou e onrará*
2 *sempre Santa Maria.*

S6 1 Poi-lo sant' ome s' espertou,
2 ao cabidoo contou
3 o que ll' a Virgen nomeou
4 que por bispo queria.
R6 1 *D' os seus onrar muito punnou*
2 *sempre Santa Maria.*

S7 1 Acordados dun coraçon
2 fezeron del sa esleiçon,
3 e foi bisp' a pouca sazon,
4 ca ben o merecia.
R7 1 *Os seus onrou con gran razon*
2 *sempre Santa Maria.*

Cantiga 87 (To 21, T 87, E 87)

Metrics

This poem has an individual *zajal* structure, with a variable parallelistic refrain occupying the position of the normal invariable refrain.

8 6' | 8 8 8 6' | 8 6'
A B | c c c b | c B (NB in S.1 c=A)

All the manuscript witnesses of this poem misrepresent its structure and expand the text with repetitions of the initial form of the refrain, inserted in error as a consequence of their failure to recognise its variable refrain:

To, T AB |^{1} c c c b | AB |$^{2-7}$ c c c b c B | A B
E AB |^{1} c c c b | AB |$^{2-7}$ c c c b | AB | c B | A B

An alternative structure, closer to the manuscript witnesses and favoured by musical editors, would have the variable refrain followed by the invariable refrain, in a kind of of double *vuelta*:

A B | c c c b c B | A B

This solution would imply that the first strophe, already unusual in that the A-rhyme of the refrain is reused as the rhyme of the *vuelta*, would also have an unrepresentative structure, with the invariable refrain repeated, once as variable refrain and once as invariable refrain:

AB | a a a b A B | A B

Holy Mary always strives to bring honour to her own.

[1] On this I will tell a great miracle which the matchless Virgin wrought in the city of Pavia.
Holy Mary always strives to bring honour to her own.

[2] In that town there was a priest of great virtue who served that glorious Lady with all his strength.
Holy Mary always takes great pleasure in bringing honour to her own.

[3] And it came to pass that the bishop of the place died, and the Virgin who is our guide appeared to a holy man.
Holy Mary has always honoured and raised up her own.

[4] And when she had appeared to him, she said: "Go and make sure that tomorrow they elect
Holy Mary always has honour bestowed on her own.

[5] the man called Hieronymus as bishop, for I know him well and he serves and has served me well, as it pleased me."
Holy Mary has always honoured and will always honour her own.

[6] When the holy man awoke, he told the chapter who the Virgin had named as the man she wanted as her bishop.
Holy Mary has always striven to bring honour to her own.

[7] United in one mind, they made him their choice, and he was made bishop in a very short time, and well he deserved it.
Holy Mary has always brought due honour to her own.

R0.1] =de‿os S1.4] =cidade‿de (*haplology*) S2.1] =crerigo‿ouve‿i S2.3] gro·ri·o·sa S2.4] =quanto‿ele R2.1] =De‿onrar S3.1] =Onde‿avẽo S3.3] =santo‿ome‿apareceu R3.1] A·os seus S4.2] =lle‿assi S4.3] es·le·er R4.1] se·er S5.1] =bispo‿un; Geronimo‿á S5.3] =servido‿á S5.4] =come‿a S6.1] =santo‿ome se‿espertou S6.2] a·o ca·bi·do·o S6.3] =lle‿a; no·me·ou R6.1] De‿os S7.2] es·lei·çon S7.3] =bispo‿a

Editorial variants
R0.1] **V** dos S1.4] **M** çidad' **V** na cidad' S3.2] **V** poi-lo S4.3] **M1**, **V** façam S4.4] **M1** aquel[e] S5.1] **M2** Jeronim' R5.1] **M** onrrou; onrrará S6.1] **M1** se espertou **V** Poil-o sant' ome se espertou R6.1] **M1** [D]'os, pun[n]ou **V** Os seus R6.2] **M1** Sempre S7.1] **M1**, **V** dum S7.3] **M1**, **V** bispo

Manuscript variants
S4.3] E façam S4.4] E aquel S5.1] E ieronim S5.3] E seru e S6.1] E se espertou R6.1] E Os seus; punou S7.1] E dum S7.3] E bispo a

Rubric
Como Santa Maria mandou que fizessen bispo ao crerigo que dizia sempre sas oras.

T dizia sas T, E, E **Ind** fezessen T **Ind** *missing*

Captions (T)
1. Como un crerigo servia sempre mui ben a Santa Maria en todas sas oras. 2. Como morreu o bispo ond' era este crerigo servo de Santa Maria. 3. Como Santa Maria disse a un sant' ome que dissess' ao cabidoo que fezessen bispo a Geronimo. 4. Como o sant' ome diss' ao cabidoo o que lli mandou Santa Maria que llis dissesse. 5. Como todo o cabidoo alçaron por bispo Geronimo, crerigo de Santa Maria, con "Te Deum Laudamus". 6. Como Geronimo o bispo loava Santa Maria e ela o bẽezeu por en.

3] disses 4] dis

17. *The Bleeding Host*

R 1 *Nunca ja pod' aa Virgen | ome tal pesar fazer*
2 *como quen ao seu fillo | Deus coida escarnecer.*

1 1 E o que o fazer coida | creed' aquesto por mi
2 que aquel escarnno todo | á de tornar sobre si.
3 E daquest' un gran miragre | vos direi, que eu oí
4 que fezo Santa Maria | oide-mio a lezer.
R *Nunca ja pod' aa Virgen | ome tal pesar fazer ...*

2 1 Aquesto foi en Galiza, | non á i mui gran sazon
2 que ũa sa barragãa | ouve un escudeiron
3 e por quanto s' el casara | tan gran pesar ouv' enton
4 que con gran coita ouvera | o siso end' a perder.
R *Nunca ja pod' aa Virgen | ome tal pesar fazer ...*

3 1 E con gran pesar que ouve | foi seu consello buscar
2 enas outras sas vezĩas | e atal llo foron dar
3 que sol que ela podesse | ũa ostia furtar
4 das da eigreja que logo | o poderia aver
R *Nunca ja pod' aa Virgen | ome tal pesar fazer ...*

4 1 pois que lle tal ben queria. | E ela toste, sen al,
2 foi se a ũa eigreja | da Virgen espirital
3 que nas nossas grandes coitas | nos guarda sempre de mal
4 e diss' enton que queria | logo comoion prender.
R *Nunca ja pod' aa Virgen | ome tal pesar fazer ...*

5 1 E o crerigo sen arte | de a comungar coidou,
2 mai-la ostia na boca | aquesta moller guardou,
3 que per niũa maneira | non a trociu nen passou,
4 e punnou quanto mais pode | de se dali log' erger.
R *Nunca ja pod' aa Virgen | ome tal pesar fazer ...*

6 1 Pois que saiu da eigreja, | os dedos enton meteu
2 ena boca e tan toste | tirou a end' e odeu
3 a ostia ena touca, | e nada non atendeu,
4 ante se foi muit' agĩa | por provar est' e veer
R *Nunca ja pod' aa Virgen | ome tal pesar fazer ...*

7 1 se lle disseran verdade | ou se lle foran mentir
2 aquelas que lle disseran | que lle farian vĩir
3 log' a ela seu amigo | e ja mais nunca partir
4 dela se ja poderia, | e de con ela viver.
R *Nunca ja pod' aa Virgen | ome tal pesar fazer ...*

No one can cause as much pain to the Virgin as they who would insult God her Son.

[1] Whoever would insult him, believe you me that all that insult will come back to him. Whereon I will tell you of a great miracle of which I heard, which Holy Mary wrought — sit back and listen to me.

[2] This took place in Galicia, not long ago, where a squire had a mistress, and because he had taken a wife she felt such sadness that with the pain of it she had nearly gone out of her mind.

[3] And in her great sorrow she went to seek counsel with her neighbours, and this is what they advised her: that if she could only steal a host, as they use in church, she would at once be able to get him back

[4] as she loved him so dearly. And she immediately went to a church of the Holy Virgin, who always protects us from ill in our deep sorrows, and she said that she wanted to take communion that instant.

[5] And the unsuspecting priest thought he was giving her communion but that woman kept the host in her mouth, and made sure she did not eat or swallow it, but she made haste to depart from there as fast as she could.

[6] And as soon as she left the church, she put her fingers in her mouth and took out the host and wrapped it in her headscarf, and did not wait for anything but hastened away to test and see

[7] whether they had told her true, or whether they had lied to her when they had said that they would make her lover come to her at once, and he would never be able to leave her, and would come to live with her.

8 1 E entrant' a ũa vila | que dizen Caldas de Rei
2 ond' aquesta moller era, | per com' end' eu apres' ei,
3 avẽo en mui gran cousa | que vos ora contarei,
4 ca lle viron pelas toucas | sangue vermello correr.
R *Nunca ja pod' aa Virgen | ome tal pesar fazer ...*

9 1 E a gent' enton dizia | quando aquel sangue viu:
2 "Di, moller, que foi aquesto | ou quen te tan mal feriu?"
3 E ela maravillada | foi tanto que est' oiu
4 assi que nunca lles soube | niũa ren responder.
R *Nunca ja pod' aa Virgen | ome tal pesar fazer ...*

10 1 E pos a mão nas toucas | e sentiu e viu mui ben
2 que era sangue caente | e disso assi por en:
3 "A mi non me feriu outre | senon quen o mundo ten
4 en seu poder, por grand' erro | que me ll' eu fui merecer."
R *Nunca ja pod' aa Virgen | ome tal pesar fazer ...*

11 1 Enton contou lles o feito, | tremendo con gran pavor,
2 todo como ll' avẽera, | e deron por en loor
3 todos a Santa Maria | madre de Nostro Sennor
4 e a seu fillo bẽeito, | chorando con gran prazer.
R *Nunca ja pod' aa Virgen | ome tal pesar fazer ...*

12 1 A moller se tornou log' aa eigreja outra vez,
2 e deitou s' ant' a omagen | e disse: "Sennor de prez
3 non cates a meu pecado | que mi o demo fazer fez."
4 E log' a un mõesteiro | se tornou monja meter.
R *Nunca ja pod' aa Virgen | ome tal pesar fazer ...*

Cantiga 104 (To 96, T 104, E 104)

Linguistic note

1.2] The manuscript form 'escarno' represents the Galician-Portuguese word more normally written 'escarnio' or 'escarnho'. We use the form 'escarnno' which appears consistently in all manuscript witnesses in *cantigas* 316 and 318.

Note

This story is probably a transposition to Galicia of the 13th-century Portuguese Eucharistic miracle of Santarém. 'Caldas de Rei' (8.1), which Mettmann speculatively associates with Caldas de Reyes (Pontevedra), may well come from the Portuguese town of Caldas da Rainha.

Metrics

15 [7' 7]	15 [7' 7]	|	15 [7' 7]	15 [7' 7]	15 [7' 7]	15 [7' 7]
A	A	|	b	b	b	a

R.1] =pode‿a·a *and subsequent refrains* 1.1] =coi·da | cre·e·de‿aquesto 1.3] =daquesto‿un; o·í 1.4] o·i·de-mio 2.2] ba·rra·gã·a 2.3] =se‿el; ouve‿enton 2.4] =ende‿a 3.3] os·ti·a 4.4] =disse‿enton; co·moi·on 5.2] os·ti·a 5.3] ni·ũ·a 5.4] =logo‿erger 6.1] sa·iu 6.2] =ende‿e 6.3] os·ti·a 6.4] =muito‿agĩa; esto‿e ve·er 7.2] vĩ·ir 7.3] =logo‿a 8.1] =entrante‿a 8.2] =onde‿aquesta; como‿ende‿eu apreso‿ei 9.1] =gente‿enton 9.3] =esto‿o·iu 9.4] ni·ũ·a 10.2] ca·en·te 10.4] =grande‿erro; lle‿eu 11.2] =lle‿a·vẽ·e·ra 11.4] bẽ·ei·to 12.1] =logo‿a·a (*elision across caesura*) 12.2] =se‿ante‿a 12.3] *necessary elision* mi‿o 12.4] =logo‿a

[8] And as she arrived at a town called Caldas de Rei, where that woman came from, as I discovered, a great wonder took place, which I will now narrate, for people saw red blood running down her headscarf.

[9] And when people saw that blood, they said: "Tell us, woman, what has happened here, or who has wounded you so badly?" And when she heard this she was so amazed that she was not able to give them any answer.

[10] And she put her hand on the headscarf and both felt and saw that it was indeed warm blood, and so she said: "The only wound I have comes from he who holds the world in his power, on account of a great misdeed by which I have deserved it of him."

[11] And then trembling and in great fear she told them what she had done, and what had befallen her, and they all wept with great gladness and gave hearty thanks to Holy Mary, mother of Our Lord, and to her blessed son.

[12] And the woman went again to the church, and prostrated herself before the statue of the Virgin, saying: "Worthy lady, turn your face from the sin which the Devil made me commit." And she at once went to a convent and became a nun.

Editorial variants

R.1] **M1** [ja] (8–10R & 12R) 1.2] **M** escarno 2.2] **V** barragana 3.2] **V** uezinnas 5.3] **M, V** nehũa 6.4] **M, V** agynna 8.1] **M1** entrand', *corrected in errata* 8.2] **M** apres **V** apres' 10.3] **M** queno 11.4] **M2** o seu 12.1] **M** log[o] à

Manuscript variants

R.1] **E** Nunca pod (8–10R & 12R) R.2] **T** cuida 1.1] **T** cuida 1.2] **To, T, E** escarno, *see Linguistic note above* 2.4] **T** con coita 3.2] **To** uizĩas 4.4] **To** comuyon 5.1] **T** cuidou 5.2] **To, T** mais la 5.3] **T, E** ne hũa 6.4] **To** agĩa **T** agynna **E** agỹna 10.1] **To** poso a 10.4] **T** gran 12.1] **T, E** A moller; a eigreia **To** logo 12.4] **To** moesteiro

Rubric

Como Santa Maria fez aa moller que queria fazer amadoiras a seu amigo con el corpo de Jesucristo e que o tragia na touca que lle corresse sangue da cabeça ata que o tirou ende.

To,To Ind que lli **T, E** sangui **T Ind** *missing* **E** omo, *missing decorated initial*

Captions (T)

1. Como un escudeiro se casou e sa barragãa ouve gran pesar por en. 2. Como demandou a sas vezĩas como fezess' amadoiras a seu amigo. 3. Como foi comungar e furtou o Corpus Christi na boca e atou o no cabo da touca. 4. Como ela indo pela rua viron lli correr sangui vivo pelas toucas. 5. Como mostrou o Corpus Christi aa gente e llis contou todo o feito. 6. Como se repentiu e se meteu monja en un mõesteiro.

3] atoo

18. *The Possessed Man who was Exorcised at Salas*

R 1 *Razon an os diabos de fogir*
2 *ant' a Virgen que a Deus foi parir.*

1 1 Dereito fazen de s' ir perder
2 ant' a de que Deus quiso nacer
3 ca per ela perderon seu poder
4 de guisa que nos non poden nozir.
R *Razon an os diabos de fogir …*

2 1 Dest' un miragre quero contar
2 que fez a Virgen que non á par
3 nen averá mentr' o mundo durar
4 esto vos posso jurar sen mentir.
R *Razon an os diabos de fogir …*

3 1 O miragre foi en tal razon
2 cinco diabos ũa sazon
3 s' assũaron e fillaron enton
4 todos un ome polo mal bailir.
R *Razon an os diabos de fogir …*

4 1 Pera Salas en camĩ' entrou.
2 Quand' a vista do logar chegou,
3 essa companna assi s' espantou
4 que o non leixaron adeant' ir
R *Razon an os diabos de fogir …*

5 1 aquel ome, segund' aprendi,
2 ta que dous frades vẽeron i
3 mẽores, que o levaron dali
4 aa eigreja logo sen falir,
R *Razon an os diabos de fogir …*

6 1 querelando se, com' apres' ei,
2 os demões da madre do Rei
3 dos ceos en como vos eu direi:
4 "Esta nos fará dest' ome partir."
R *Razon an os diabos de fogir …*

7 1 Un judeu os conjurou por Deus
2 que dissessen porque os judeus
3 non fillavan. Diss' un demo: "Ca meus
4 sodes e punnades de me servir
R *Razon an os diabos de fogir …*

8 1 por esto non vos fazemos mal
2 ca sodes todos nossos sen al
3 mai-los que do batismo o sinal
4 tragen, aqueles imos percodir."
R *Razon an os diabos de fogir …*

9 1 Esto dito, fogiu o judeu
2 mai-los diabos, com' aprix eu,
3 cada un deles logo sinal deu
4 quando ouveron do om' a sair.
R *Razon an os diabos de fogir …*

10 1 Desto deron todos gran loor
2 a Santa Maria, que sabor
3 á de valer sempr' ao pecador
4 e d' os diabos sempre destroir.
R *Razon an os diabos de fogir …*

Cantiga 109 (T 109, E 109)

Metrics

10	10	|	9	9	10	10
A	A	|	b	b	b	a

T follows an exemplar which corrects all strophes to a symmetrical 10 10 10 10 pattern. The music copied above strophe 1 is inconsistent with this emendation, and neither text nor music has been adjusted.

R.2] =ante‿a 1.1] =se‿ir 1.2] =ante‿a 2.1] =Desto‿un 2.3] =mentre‿o 3.3] =se‿assũaron 4.1] =camĩo‿entrou 4.2] =Quando‿a 4.3] =se‿espantou 4.4] =ad·e·an·te‿ir 5.1] =segundo‿aprendi 5.2] dous (*single syllable*); vẽ·er·on 5.4] a·a 6.1] =como‿apreso‿ei 6.3] ce·os 6.4] =deste‿ome 7.3] =Disse‿un 9.1] fo·giu 9.2] =como‿aprix 9.4] =ome‿a sa·ir 10.3] sempre‿a·o 10.4] =de‿os

Editorial variants

R.1] M1 [os] (7R) 3.3] V s' asũaron 4.1] V camynn' 5.3] V menores 7.2] V por qué 8.3] V mail-os 9.2] V mail-os; aprix' eu

With good reason do devils flee
from the presence of the Blessed Virgin who gave birth to God.

[1] With good reason do they take flight from the Lady in whom God was pleased to be born, for it is through her that they have lost their power, so that they can harm us no more.

[2] On this theme I will tell a miracle, wrought by the Blessed Virgin Mary, who has no equal nor ever will have so long as the world endures, this I can truly swear to you.

[3] This is how the miracle took place. Five devils once came together and all took possession of a man, to treat him ill.

[4] The man set off to Salas. When he came within sight of the town, the company of devils was so alarmed that they would let the man go no further,

[5] as I heard tell, until two Franciscan monks came by, who took him thence and bore him at once to the church,

[6] while the devils, as I was told, complained of the mother of the King of Heaven in these words: "She will surely make us leave this man."

[7] Then a Jew required them, in the name of God, to tell him why they did not possess Jews. A devil replied: "Because you are already mine, and work to do my will

[8] and so we do not do you any harm, because you are without question of our number, while those who bear the sign of baptism, those are the ones we pursue."

[9] At this the Jew made off, but the devils, as I heard, all left the man, each one crying out as they did.

[10] And all gave hearty thanks to Holy Mary, who always takes pleasure in helping sinners and in destroying devils.

Manuscript variants

R.1] T an diabos (5R); fugir (1–10R); E a*n* diabos (7R) 1.1] T Gran dereito 1.2] T ant aquela de q*ue* de*us* quis 2.1] T miragre u*os* quero 2.2] T non ouve par 3.1] T E o miragre 3.2] T diabos aquela fazon 3.4] T todos a un 4.1] T El pera Salas 4.2] T & quand 5.1] T A aquel ome 5.2] T ata q*ue* 5.3] T mẽores & o 6.1] T Queixa*n*do sse muito 6.2] T do gra*n* rei 6.3] T & dizian como 7.1] T E un judeu 7.2] T q*ue* lle dissessen 8.1] T e por esto 8.2] T ca uos sodes 8.4] T ymos enuiar 9.1] T Quand esto disse fugiu 9.2] T diabres p*er* com 10.1] T Daquesto deron 10.2] T por que sabor

Rubric

Como Santa Maria de Salas livrou un ome de cinco demonios que avia en si.

T Ind *missing* E, **E Ind** cinquo diaboos que o querian levar e matar

Captions (T)

1. Como fillaron cinco diaboos a un ome polo fazer perder. 2. Como os diaboos non o leixavan ir a Santa Maria de Salas en romeria. 3. Como veeron i dos frades e o levaron aa egreja apesar dos diaboos. 4. Como os frades o meteron na egreja e rogaron a Santa Maria por ele. 5. Como os diaboos deron todos sinal e fogiron a omagen de Santa Maria. 6. Como todalas gentes loaron muito a Santa Maria polos muitos bẽes que faz.

19. *The Talking Sheep*

R *A madre do que a bestia | de Balaam falar fez*
ar fez pois ũa ovella | ela falar ũa vez.

Just as God made Balaam's ass speak,
so did his mother give speech to a sheep.

1 Esto fez Santa Maria
por ũa pobre moller
que a de grado servia
come quen ben servir quer,
e por end' ela un dia | valeu ll' u lle foi mester
e mostrou i seu miragre | que vos non foi mui rafez.
R *A madre do que a bestia | de Balaam falar fez …*

Our Lady did this
for a poor woman
who served her willingly,
and wanted only to give good service.
And so one day she helped her in her need,
and performed one of her miracles which
you will not think meagre.

2 Aquesta moller mesquĩa
de quanto pod' achegar
comprou ũa ovellĩa
e foi a dar a guardar
a un pegureir' agĩa | e pois ao trosquiar
foi en demandar a lãa | pola vender por seu prez.
R *A madre do que a bestia | de Balaam falar fez …*

That wretched woman
put together every penny she had
and bought a little sheep
and at once entrusted it to a
shepherd to look after and at shearing time
she went to ask for its wool, to sell it for
what she could get.

3 Mais o pegureir' astroso
a ovella ascondeu
e come cobiiçoso
diss': "O lobo a comeu."
A vella por mentiroso | o tev' end', e lle creceu
tal coita por sa ovella | que tornou tal come pez.
R *A madre do que a bestia | de Balaam falar fez …*

But the villainous shepherd
hid the sheep
and, greedy fellow,
said: "It was taken by wolves."
The old woman was sure that he was lying,
and was so distressed on account of her
sheep that her face turned black as pitch.

Cantiga 147 (T 147, E 147)

Metrics

15 [7' 7]	15 [7' 7]	|	7'	7	7'	7	15 [7' 7]	15 [7' 7]
A	A	|	b	c	b	c	c	a

R.1] bes·tia; Ba·la·am 1.5] =ende‿ela 1.6] =lle‿u 2.2] =pode‿achegar 2.5] =pegureiro‿agĩa; a·o 3.1] =pegureiro‿astroso 3.3] co·bi·i·ço·so 3.4] =disse‿o 3.6] =teve‿ende‿e 4.1] Gro·ri·o·sa 4.2] mia (*single syllable*) 4.3] =ende‿es 4.5] ja·zi·a 4.6] =disse‿Ei me‿acá 4.7] =aquesto‿engano 5.2] tros·qui·ou 5.3] =se‿a·o 5.4] =pode‿andou 5.7] =dizendo‿Esto

Editorial variants

2.1] M1 mesq[u]ỹa V mesquynna 2.3] V ouellynna 2.5] V agynna 3.1] V Mas 5.3] V et meteuss' ao camynno 5.5] V uellocynno

Manuscript variants

R.2] T Balaan (2–3R) 2.1] E mesqỹa 2.2] E pud 2.3] T ouellỹna 3.1] E Mas 5.1] T, E festỹno 5.5] T uelocỹno

4 1 E disse: "Ai, Groriosa,
2 a mia ovella me dá,
3 ca tu end' es poderosa
4 de o fazer." E dalá
5 du jazia a astrosa | ovella diss': "Ei m' acá."
6 E assi Santa Maria | aquest' engano desfez.
R *A madre do que a bestia | de Balaam falar fez ...*

And she cried: "Glorious Virgin
Give me back my sheep
for you have the power
to do it." And forthwith
the poor sheep spoke from where it lay hidden
and said: "Here I am." Thus did Our Lady
undo that deceit.

5 1 E a vella mui festĩo
2 sa ovella trosquiou,
3 e meteu s' ao camĩo
4 e quanto mais pod' andou
5 a costas seu vellocĩo. | A Rocamador chegou
6 dizend': "Esto fez a Virgen | que sempre teve belmez."
R *A madre do que a bestia | de Balaam falar fez ...*

And the old woman made haste
and sheared her sheep.
She set off and walked
as fast as she could,
carrying her fleece on her back. And she came
to Rocamadour, saying: "This is the work of
Our Lady, who has always been gracious."

Rubrics

T Como ũa moller pobre deu sa ovella a guardar a un ovelleiro e quando ao trosquiar das ovellas ascondeu lla o pastor e disse que a comera o lobo, enton falou a ovella du jazia e disse: "aquei m' acá".

T **Ind** ũa moller de[u] ũa ou[el]la a un ouelleiro e quando uẽo ao [tro]s[quia]r ascondeu lla e a ouella fallou e disse aqueimaca, *text badly rubbed*

E Como ũa moller pobre deu sa ovella a guardar a un ovelleiro e quando ao trosquiar das ovellas vẽo a vella demandar a sua e o ovelleiro disse que a comera o lobo e ela chamou Santa Maria de Rocamador e a ovella braadou u la tĩia o ovelleiro asconduda e disse: "ei me acá, ei m' acá".

E trasquiar E **Ind** bradou u lla tijna; eimaca ei-

Captions (T)

1. Como ũa vella pobre comprou ũa ovella de sa lazeira. 2. Como a vella deu a ovella ao pastor que lla guardasse. 3. Como o pastor ascondeu a ovella e diss' aa vella que o lobo a comera. 4. Como a vella se começou a queixar a Santa Maria e a ovella diss': "aquei m' acá". 5. Como a vella trosquió sa ovella e levou o vellocinno a Santa Maria de Rocamador. 6. Como chegou a vella a Rocamador e pos o vellocinno ant' o altar.

4] dis

20. *Cantiga de loor*

R 1 *Eno nome de Maria*
2 *cinque letras non mais i á.*

1 1 M mostra madr’ e maior
2 e mais mansa e mui mellor
3 de quant’ al fez Nostro Sennor
4 nen que fazer poderia.
R *Eno nome de Maria …*

2 1 A demostra avogada
2 aposta e aorada
3 e amiga e amada
4 da mui santa compannia.
R *Eno nome de Maria …*

3 1 R mostra ram’ e raiz
2 e reĩ’ e emperadriz
3 rosa do mundo e fiiz
4 quen a visse ben seria.
R *Eno nome de Maria …*

4 1 I nos mostra Jesucristo
2 justo joiz e por isto
3 foi por ela de nos visto,
4 segun disso Isaía.
R *Eno nome de Maria …*

5 1 A ar diz que averemos
2 e que tod’ acabaremos
3 aquelo que nos queremos
3 de Deus pois ela nos guia.
R *Eno nome de Maria …*

Cantiga 70 (**To** 80, T 80, E 70)

Metrics

8!	8!	|	8!	8!	8!	8!
A	A	|	b	b	b	a

This poem is in strict syllabic metre, using lines of exactly 8 syllables, stressed either on the final syllable (=8 in conventional notation) or the penultimate syllable (=7’) The rhyme of *Maria - i á* suppresses the difference in stress, rather than indicating an anomalous stress pattern *Mariá.*

1.1] =Eme mostra madre‿e 1.3] =quanto‿al 2.2] a·o·ra·da 3.1] =Erre mostra ramo‿e ra·iz 3.2] =re·ĩ·a‿e 3.3] fi·iz 4.2] jo·iz 4.4] I·sa·í·a 5.2] =todo‿acabaremos

Editorial variants

R.1] **Fid** Enno **V** En o R.2] **M2** no-mais **V** no máis ý-a **A, RL** no mais 1.1] **A** Eme 1.2] **M1** mais MELLOR **V** máis mellor 2.4] **M2** conpannia **M1** conpan[n]ia **V** conpanía **A** compania **RL** conpan[h]ia 3.2] **M** REYNN’ **Fid** reinn’ **V** Reynn’ **RL** Reynh’ 3.3] **M1, RL** mund[o] **V** mund’; e fijz 3.4] **Fid, V** quen a 4.1] **Fid** Jesocristo

Just five letters are in the name of Maria.

M is for Mother, and the greatest, mildest and best of everything Our Lord created or ever could create.

A declares her Advocate, fair and adored, dear and beloved of the company of saints.

R is Root and branch, queen and empress, rose of the world — happy is he who would see her.

I gives us Iesus Christ, the Just Judge, he was clothed in human flesh by her, as Isaiah said.

A says that we will Achieve and Attain all that we ask of God, as she is our guide.

Manuscript variants
R.2] **To**, T no*n* mais E no mais 1.2] E mais mellor 2.4] E co*m*pania 3.2] **To** reĩn T reỹ E reyn 3.3] **To** fiiz E mu*nd* e fijz 4.2] E iuyz

Rubric
De loor de Santa Maria das cinco leteras que á no seu nome e o que queren dizer.

T (80) cinquo T *rubric is repeated at cantiga 60* T **Ind** *missing* E çinque E **Ind** an o nome seu

Captions (T)
missing

21. *The Pilgrims to Rocamadour whose Meat was Stolen*

R *Non sofre Santa Maria | de seeren perdidosos*
os que as sas romarias | son de fazer desejosos.

Holy Mary will not allow any loss to be suffered by those who wish to go on her pilgrimages.

1 E dest' oid' un miragre | de que vos quero falar
que mostrou Santa Maria | per com' eu oí contar
a ũus romeus que foron | a Rocamador orar
como mui bõos crischãos | simplement' e omildosos.
R *Non sofre Santa Maria | de seeren perdidosos …*

On this, hear ye a miracle of which I will tell you, which Holy Mary revealed, as it was told to me, to pilgrims who went to pray at the shrine of Rocamadour, in simple humility, like good Christians.

2 E pois entraron no burgo | foron pousada fillar
e mandaron comprar carne | e pan pera seu jantar
e vinno, e entre tanto | foron aa Virgen rogar
que a seu fillo rogasse | dos seus rogos piadosos
R *Non sofre Santa Maria | de seeren perdidosos …*

As soon as they arrived in the town, they went to find lodgings, and sent for meat and bread for their dinner, and also wine, and meanwhile they went to beseech the Blessed Virgin to intercede with her son, with her merciful intercessions,

3 por eles e non catasse | de como foran errar
mais que del perdon ouvessen | de quanto foran pecar.
E pois est' ouveron feito | tornaron non de vagar
u seu jantar tĩian | ond' eran cobiiçosos.
R *Non sofre Santa Maria | de seeren perdidosos …*

on their behalf, asking him not to pay heed to how they had erred but to forgive them for all the sins they had committed. And when they had finished this intercession they returned promptly to where their dinner awaited them, which they eagerly desired.

4 E mandaran nove postas | meter, asse Deus m' ampar,
na ola ca tantos eran | mais poi-las foron tirar
acharon end' ũa menos | que a serventa furtar
lles fora, e foron todos | por en ja quanto queixosos.
R *Non sofre Santa Maria | de seeren perdidosos …*

And, as God is my witness, they gave orders for nine cuts of meat to be put in the cooking pot, for that was their number, but when they took them out they found that one was missing, for the serving girl had stolen it, and they all complained bitterly about it.

Cantiga 159 (T 159, E 159)

Linguistic notes

1.4] 'simplement' e': an alternative reading 'simplemente omildosos' is excluded by the plica over the final 'e' in both manuscript readings, and is a modern usage. The adverb is only found in two *cantigas*, 151 ('simpremente') and 159, in each case qualifying a verb of prayer.

3.4] 'u seu' could be edited 'u o seu' to avoid dieresis of 'seu'. See *cantiga* 32 (anthology 7), 5.7 for a case of 'u' interpreted as 'u‿o'.

Metrics

15' [7' 7']	15' [7' 7']	|	15 [7' 7]	15 [7' 7]	15 [7' 7]	15' [7' 7']
A	A	|	b	b	b	a

R.1] se·e·ren 1.1] =desto‿o·ide‿un 1.2] =como‿eu o·i 1.3] ũ·us ro·meus 1.4] =simplemente‿e, *see Linguistic note above*
2.3] *necessary elision* a‿a 3.3] =esto‿ouveron 3.4] =onde‿eran; se·u (*dieresis, see Linguistic note above*); tĩ·i·an; co·bi·i·ço·sos
4.1] =me‿ampar 4.3] =ende‿ũa 5.3] =ũa‿arca; o·i·ron 5.4] =de‿ir 6.1] =logo‿a 6.3] sa·i·ron a·a 7.1] =fezesse‿en 7.3] =ante‿o

5 1 E buscaron pela casa | pola poderen achar
2 chamando Santa Maria | que lla quisesse mostrar
3 e oiron en ũ' arca | a posta feridas dar
4 e d' ir alá mui correndo | non vos foron vagarosos.
R *Non sofre Santa Maria | de seeren perdidosos ...*

And they went through the house looking for it, calling on Holy Mary to show them where it was; and in a chest they heard the piece of meat knocking, and they did not waste any time in running to find it.

6 1 E fezeron log' a arca | abrir e dentro catar
2 foron, e viron sa posta | dacá e dalá saltar
3 e sairon aa rua | muitas das gentes chamar
4 que viron aquel miragre | que foi dos maravillosos
R *Non sofre Santa Maria | de seeren perdidosos ...*

And they had the chest opened and looked inside, and saw their piece of meat jumping up and down and they went out into the street to call many people to come and see that miracle, which was one of most wondrous

7 1 que a Virgen groriosa | fezess' en aquel logar.
2 Des i fillaron a posta | e foron a pendorar
3 per ũa corda de seda | ant' o seu santo altar
4 loando Santa Maria | que faz miragres fremosos.
R *Non sofre Santa Maria | de seeren perdidosos ...*

deeds that the Blessed Virgin Mary performed in that place. And then they took the piece of meat and hung it on a silken rope, before Holy Mary's altar, giving praise to her for her fine miracles.

Editorial variants

R.1] **M2** sofre (0R), soffre (1–7R) **V** de sereen (6R) **A** [Santa] (1R) 1.3] **V** a uuns 3.2] **M** ouves[s]en; peccar **V** ouuessen 3.4] **V** tijnnan 4.2] **V** poil-as 4.3] **M1** furtar- 5.3] **M** un' arca 7.2] **V** et fóron-a

Manuscript variants

R.1] **T** soffre; sofre (1–7R) **E** sofre; soffre (1–7R) 3.2] **E** ouuese*n*; peccar 5.3] **T E** un arca 6.2] **E** sartar

Rubric

Como Santa Maria fez descobrir ũa posta de carne que furtaran a ũus romeus na vila de Rocamador.

T Ind furtara ũa manceba a

Captions (T)

1. Como os romeus deron aa manceba nove postas de carne que llis adobasse. 2. Como os romeus foron fazer oraçon ant' o altar de Santa Maria. 3. Como os romeus acharon mẽos ũa posta de carne que furtara a manceba. 4. Como os romeus acharon a posta que andava faltando en ũa arca. 5. Como os romeus chamaron muita gente que vẽessen veer aquel miragre. 6. Como colgaron a posta ant' o altar e loaron muito Santa Maria.

1] adobas 3] furtará manceba

22. *The Moors of Faro who Threw a Statue of the Virgin into the Sea*

R *Pesar á Santa Maria | de quen por desonra faz*
dela mal a sa omagen | e caomia llo assaz.

Holy Mary is deeply grieved by those who harm and defile her image, and makes them pay a heavy price.

1 Desto direi un miragre | que fezo en Faaron
a Virgen Santa Maria | en tempo d' Aben Mafon
que o reino do Algarve | tĩi' aquela sazon
a guisa d' om' esforçado | quer en guerra, quer en paz.
R *Pesar á Santa Maria | de quen por desonra faz …*

On this theme I will tell a miracle which the Blessed Virgin Mary performed in Faro in the time when Ben Mafon ruled over the kingdom of the Algarve, being a valiant man in war or peace.

2 En aquel castel' avia | omagen, com' apres' ei,
da Virgen mui groriosa | feita como vos direi
de pedra ben fegurada | e, com' eu de cert' achei,
na riba do mar estava | escontra ele de faz.
R *Pesar á Santa Maria | de quen por desonra faz …*

In the castle of Faro there was, as I was told, a very beautiful statue of the Virgin Mary, carved, as I will recount, very finely in stone, which, as I truly found, stood on the seashore facing the water.

3 Ben do tempo dos crischãos | a sabian i estar
e por ende os cativos | a ian sempr' aorar,
e Santa Mari' a vila | de Faaron nomẽar
por aquesta razon foron. | Mas o poboo malvaz
R *Pesar á Santa Maria | de quen por desonra faz …*

From Christian times it was known to have been there, and so the Christian slaves would go there to worship it, and for that reason they called the town of Faro Mary's town. But the wicked Moorish

Cantiga 183 (T 183, E 183)

Metrics
15 [7' 7] 15 [7' 7] | 15 [7' 7] 15 [7' 7] 15 [7' 7] 15 [7' 7]
A A | b b b a

R.2] ca·o·mia 1.1] Fa·a·ron 1.2] =de‿Aben 1.3] =tĩ·i·a‿aquela 1.4] =de‿ome‿esforçado 2.1] =castelo‿avia; como‿apreso‿ei 2.3] =como‿eu; certo‿achei 3.1] sa·bi·an 3.2] =i·an sempre‿a·o·rar 3.3] =Maria‿a; Fa·a·ron 3.4] po·bo·o 4.3] =sobre‿esto 4.4] =mundo‿en 5.1] ni·un 5.2] =enquanto‿aquela 5.4] =ontre‿as 6.2] =tanto‿i; como‿a; o·i 6.3] a·os

Editorial variants
R.2] **M1** [dela] 1.3] **V** tijnn' 3.3] **V** María uila 4.2] **V** et en o 4.4] **V** soberuia 5.2] **V** en quant' 5.3] **M** fórona **V** fóron-a 5.4] **M** posérona **V** et poséron-a

Manuscript variants
R.1–2] E faz mal | mal a 3.3] T nomear 4.2] T sanudos 4.4] T soberuia 5.4] T entr

Rubric
Dun miragre que mostrou Santa Maria en Faaron quando era de mouros.

T, T **Ind** quand E **Ind** en saton quand

Captions (T)
1. Como ũa omagen de Santa Maria estava en Faaron na riba do mar. 2. Como os mouros deitaron a omagen de Santa Maria no mar por desonra-la. 3. Como nunca poderon tomar pescado en Faaron enquant' a omagen jouve no mar. 4. Como os mouros sacaron a omagen do mar e a poseron no muro. 5. Como des que a poseron no muro foron provar se poderian pescar. 6. Como deitaron sas redes e sacaron tanto pescado que as non podian tirar.

1] omgen

4 1 dos mouros que i avia | ouveron gran pesar en
2 e eno mar a deitaron | sannudos con gran desden
3 mas gran miragre sobr' esto | mostrou a Virgen que ten
4 o mund' en seu mandamento | a que soberva despraz.
R *Pesar á Santa Maria | de quen por desonra faz ...*

people who lived there were very angry at this and threw the statue into the sea, in wrath and with great scorn, but at this a great miracle was performed by the Blessed Virgin, who holds the world in her sway, and who is not pleased by pride.

5 1 Ca fez que niun pescado | nunca poderon prender
2 enquant' aquela omagen | no mar leixaron jazer.
3 Os mouros, pois viron esto | foron a dali erguer
4 e poseron a no muro | ontr' as amẽas en az.
R *Pesar á Santa Maria | de quen por desonra faz ...*

For she ordained that the Moors could take no fish while they left the statue lying in the water. When they realised this, the Moors brought it out of the sea and placed it on the walls of the castle, lined up with the battlements.

6 1 Des i tan muito pescado | ouveron des enton i
2 que nunca tant' i ouveran | per com' a mouros oí
3 dizer e aos crischãos | que o contaron a mi,
4 por en loemos a Virgen | en que tanto de ben jaz.
R *Pesar á Santa Maria | de quen por desonra faz ...*

As soon as they did this, they caught more fish than they had ever had before, so I was told by Moors and Christians who all recounted this; and so let us praise the Blessed Virgin, in whom there is so much goodness.

23. The Muslim Servant

R *Muitas vegadas o dem' enganados*
ten os omes, por que lles faz creer
muitas sandeces, e taes pecados
desfaz a Virgen por seu gran saber.

1 E desto contado
vos será per mi
miragr' e mostrado
quant' end' aprendi,
fremos' aficado,
e ben ascuitado
será, per mẹu grado,
e dev' a seer,
que o muit' onrado
Deus, e acabado
pola de que nado
foi, quiso fazer.
R *Muitas vegadas o dem' enganados …*

2 En Consogr' avia
un bon om' atal
que Santa Maria
amava mais d' al,
e mui gran perfia
por ela prendia
sempre cada dia,
com' oí dizer,
con un d' Almaria
mouro, que dizia
que ren non valia
o seu gran poder.
R *Muitas vegadas o dem' enganados …*

3 Aqueste mour' era
daquel ome seu
cativo, e fera-
ment' era encreu
e ja o quisera
de grad' e fezera
crischão e dera
lle de seu aver.
Mais non o podera
macar lo dissera
con el ca tevera
sempr' en descreer
R *Muitas vegadas o dem' enganados …*

4 ena Groriosa,
e a razõar
mal e soberviosa-
ment' e desdennar
que era enganosa
muit' e mentirosa
sa fe e dultosa
e sen prol tẽer
e tal revoltosa
cous' e embargosa
e d' oir nojosa
non é de caber.
R *Muitas vegadas o dem' enganados …*

Time after time the Devil has men deceived, and makes them believe many foolish things. Such sins as these the Blessed Virgin undoes by her great wisdom.

[1] On this I will show you and tell a great miracle, which was, as I heard, a really fine one which our noble bounteous Lord saw fit to perform for that Lady of whom he was born. It deserves to be carefully heard, and so it will be, as it pleases me.

[2] In Consuegra there lived a good man who loved the Blessed Virgin Mary above all others and every day, as I heard tell, argued for her with a Moor from Almeria, who held that her great power was worth nothing.

[3] The Moor belonged to the man and was his slave, and was a fierce unbeliever, and the man had dearly wanted to make him a Christian, and had given him part of his wealth. But he had got nowhere with him, for all his good will, for the Moor had persisted in denigrating

[4] our glorious Lady, and would proudly argue against her and belittle her, saying that to believe in her was deceitful and false and without virtue — such repugnant and obstinate things, an offence to the ear, cannot be borne.

5 O om' entendudo
foi e de bon sen
e apercebudo
de guardar mui ben
o mouro barvudo
fals' e descreudo
e come sisudo
o mandou meter
en logar sabudo
d' aljub' ascondudo
e dentr' estendudo
o fezo jazer.
R *Muitas vegadas o dem' enganados …*

6 El ali jazendo
o demo chegou
e logo correndo
en ele travou
mais se defendendo
o mour', e tremendo
muit' e contendendo
ll' o dedo coller
na boc' e gemendo
e fort' estrengendo
tod' e desfazendo
llo fezo perder.
R *Muitas vegadas o dem' enganados …*

7 Daquesta maneira
duas noites fez
mais aa terceira
a Sennor de prez
a mui verdadeira
e virgen enteira
come lumẽeira
se lle fez veer
e deu lle carreira
per que na fogueira
d' inferno que cheira
non podess' arder.
R *Muitas vegadas o dem' enganados …*

8 E disse: "Pagão
se queres guarir
do demo de chão
t' ás a departir
e do falso vão
mui louco vilão
Mafomete cão
que te non valer
pode, e crischão
te faz e irmão
nosso, e loução
sei e sen temer."
R *Muitas vegadas o dem' enganados …*

9 Poi-lo castigara
el lle respondeu
que en quant' andara
todo faleceu
e que mal mercara
de que non fillara
batism', e errara
en seu connocer
por quanto viltara
a fii tan cara
mais "mannãa crara
querrei receber
R *Muitas vegadas o dem' enganados …*

10 a fe dos Romãos
ca connosco ben,"
diss' el, "que pagãos
andan con mal sen
a guisa de vãos
ca non son certãos
d' a lei dos crischãos
per ren mantẽer
non come loução
mais con antivãos
contra Mec' as mãos
punnan de tender."
R *Muitas vegadas o dem' enganados …*

[5] The man was wise and clever, and realised that he should closely guard that false infidel, the bearded Moor, and being of good counsel he had him shut away in a secret place, a hidden prison, and left him languishing there.

[6] And as the Moor lay there, the Devil burst in to seize him by force, but the Moor defended himself, shaking with terror and groaning as he fought back, biting the Devil's finger and crushing and battering him so that he let him go.

[7] In this way he fought for two nights, but on the third that worthy Lady, the true and perfect virgin, appeared to him in a blaze of light, and showed him the way to save himself from burning in the reeking fires of hell.

[8] She said: "Pagan, if you really want to be saved, you must openly renounce the Devil, and that vain false wicked dog Mahomet, who cannot help you; and you must become a Christian and our brother, and be bold and fearless."

[9] Once she had instructed him, he replied that he had failed in everything he had done, and had made a bad choice when he refused baptism, and he had shown bad judgement when he had spoken ill of her precious faith. But "Tomorrow morning I will gladly take

[10] the Roman faith," he said, "for I know that pagans are foolish vain folk, for they do not know any way to accept in joy the Christian faith but rather raise their arms and sing hymns to Mecca."

11 Quando foi mannãa
dali o sacou
seu dono e chãa-
mente lle contou
que viu da louçãa
Virgen que nos sãa
e nos da maçãa
fez perdon aver:
"Por end' aa crischãa,
comprida, certãa
lee, e non vãa,
quero m' atẽer."
R *Muitas vegadas o dem' enganados …*

12 Sa razon fiida,
fez lo batizar
seu don', e comprida-
ment' e muit' onrar.
E de bõa vida
foi pois, e servida
del a que convida
nos a gran prazer
de dar sen falida
qual non foi oida
d' avermos guarida
sen nunca morrer.
R *Muitas vegadas o dem' enganados …*

Cantiga 192 (T 192, E 192, E 397)

Linguistic note
9.10] 'fii': this otherwise unattested word is assumed to be a variant of *fe* 'faith' < FIDEM, selected or constructed to provide the two-syllable form demanded by the metre.

Metrics

10'	10	10'	10	|	5'	5	5'	5	5'	5'	5'	5	5'	5'	5'	5
A	B	A	B	|	c	d	c	d	c	c	c	b	c	c	c	b

R.1] =demo‿enganados *and subsequent refrains* R.2] cre·er R.3] ta·es 1.3] =miragre‿e 1.4] =quanto‿ende‿aprendi 1.5] =fremoso‿aficado 1.8] =deve‿a se·er 1.9] =muito‿onrado 2.1] =Consogra‿avia 2.2] =ome‿atal 2.4] =de‿al 2.8] =como‿o·í 2.9] =de‿Almaria 3.1] =mouro‿era 3.4] =mente‿era 3.6] =grado‿e 3.9] *editorial* 'o' *avoids hypometry* 3.12] =sempre‿en des·cre·er 4.4] =mente‿e 4.5] *necessary elision* era‿enganosa 4.6] =muito‿e 4.10] =cousa‿e 4.11] =de‿o·ir 5.1] =ome‿entendudo 5.6] =falso‿e des·cre·u·do 5.10] =de‿aljube‿ascondudo 5.11] =dentro‿estendudo 6.6] =mouro‿e 6.7] =muito‿e 6.8] =lle‿o 6.9] =boca‿e 6.10] =forte‿estrengendo 6.11] =todo‿e 7.3] a·a 7.8] ve·er 7.11] =de‿inferno 7.12] =podesse‿arder 8.4] =te‿ás 9.3] =quanto‿andara 9.7] =batisme‿e 9.10] fi·i, *see Linguistic note above* 10.3] =disse‿el 10.7] =de‿a 10.11] =Meca‿as 11.9] =ende‿a‿a (*for another example of editorially restored elision of* a‿a, *see cantiga 11 [anthology 5]), 9.6*) 11.11] le·e 11.12] =me atẽer 12.1] fi·i·da 12.3] =dono‿e 12.4] =mente‿e muito‿onrar 12.10] o·i·da 12.11] =de‿avermos

Editorial variants
R.1] V(397) enganadas R.2] M lle[s] V(397) ten as gentes 1.2] V(397) min A(397) mi 1.12] V(397) quisso 3.1] V(397) mouro 3.2] M om' e V ome seu 3.7] M1 dera- V(192) déra- V(397) creschão et déra- 3.9] M non podera (*hypometric*) 3.10] V(397) ll' o 4.1] V En a 4.5] M era 'ng[an]osa V(192) era engannosa 4.8] V(397) e sem 4.10] V(397) embargosa 5.7] V(397) sessudo 5.12] V(397) iacer 6.4] M, V(192) entrou 6.5] M mais defendendo 6.6] M ss' o mour' V(192) ss' o V(397) s' o 6.9] M boqu' 7.7] V(192) lumeeira 8.9] V(397) creschão 9.1] V Poil-o 9.2] M respondeo 9.4] M, V(192) falleceo V(397) faleçeo 9.7] M, V(192) bautism' V(397) batism' e pecara 9.8] V(397) connosçer 9.11] M "Mais mannãa crara …" V(192) mannáá V(397) clara 10.1] V romãos 10.3] V(397) dis' él 10.7] M, V(192) d' a lee V(397) da ley 10.9] M, V(192) nen 10.11] M Mec' a[s] V(192) Meca mãos 11.5] V(397) vió 11.9] M Porend' a 11.12] M mantẽer 12.1] M ffiida 12.2] M, V(192) bautizar

Manuscript variants
R.1] E397 enganadas (0–11R); uegasdas (1R) R.2] E192 per que lle E397 te*n* as gentes 1.2] E397 min 1.9] T que muit; *a superscript* o *has been added above the* m *in a later hand* 1.10] T de uos; *the* o *has a subscript point indicating erasure* 1.12] E397 foi u quisso 3.1] E397 mouro 3.7] E397 creschão 3.8] T do 3.9] T, E non podera 3.10] E397 llo 4.5] T era enga*n*nosa E192 era ngosa E397 era enganosa 4.8] E397 e sem 4.10] E397 embargosa 5.2] E397 foi de 5.7] T sesudo E397 sessudo 5.9] E397 e logar 6.4] T, E192 entrou 6.5] T, E mais defendendo 6.6] T, E192 ss o mour E397 s o mou 6.9] T, E boqu 7.7] E192 lumeeira E397 lumeeyra 7.9] E397 careyra 8.1–2] E397 pagão se q*ue*res | guarir. se 8.9] E397 creschão 8.10] T de faz 9.2] E respondeo 9.4] E192 falleceo E397 faleçeo 9.5] T, E397 errara 9.7] T babtism e mercara E192 bautism e E397 batisme e pecara 9.8] E397 co*n*nosçer 9.11] E192 ma*n*naa E397 manãa clara 10.3] E397 dis el 10.7] T, E192 da lee dos 10.9] E192 nen 10.11] T, E192 Mec a mãos 11.5] E397 uio 11.9] T, E a 11.12] T, E192 mantẽer E397 manteer 12.1] E192 fijda 12.2] T batiçar E192 bautizar

[11] When morning came the Moor's master took him out of the prison and he clearly retold how he had seen the fair Virgin who heals us and brings us forgivenesses for Adam's sin: "And so I mean to hold to the true certain Christian faith, which is not vain."

[12] When he had finished his testimony, his master had him baptised, and gave him honour and reward. And from then on he lived a good life, and served the Lady who invites us to share her bliss, given without fail, such as man has never heard, so that we might be saved and have life eternal.

Rubrics

T Como Santa Maria tirou un mouro que era cativo en Consogra de poder do demo.

E Como Santa Maria livrou ũu mouro a que queria fillar o demo e feze o tornar crischão.

E **Ind** un

Captions (T)

1. Como o ome boo contendia con seu mouro polo tornar crischão. 2. Como o mouro luitava com o demo e lli mordeu no polegar. 3. Como Santa Maria livrou o mouro do demo e lli disse que se tornasse crischão. 4. Como o mouro o contou a seu sennor e lli disse que o tornasse crischão. 5. Como o ome boo fez tornar ao mouro logo crischão. 6. Como o mouro foi mui boo crischão e loou sempre Santa Maria.

3] tornas 4] tornass

24. The Rabid Man

R *Todolos coitados que queren saude*
demanden a Virgen e a sa vertude.

All the afflicted who wish for good health should seek out the Virgin and her great power.

1 Ca ela poder á de saude dar
e vida por sempr' a quen lla demandar
de coraçon, e desto quer' eu contar
un mui bon miragre, assi Deus m' ajude.
R *Todolos coitados que queren saude …*

For she has the power to give health and life everlasting to whoever asks for it with a pure heart. And on this I will tell a very good miracle, as God is my help.

2 Per todo o mund' ela miragres faz,
mais dũa sa casa, cabo Monsarraz,
que chaman Terena, sei ben que assaz
faz muitos miragres a quen i recude.
R *Todolos coitados que queren saude …*

Throughout the world she performs miracles, but I know for sure that in a place of hers called Terena, near Monsarraz, she performs many miracles for those who seek refuge there.

3 E por end' un ome bõo, Don Mateus,
qu' en Estremoz mora, prougu' assi a Deus
que raviou mui fort', e os parentes seus
alá o levaron, ca muit' ameude
R *Todolos coitados que queren saude …*

And so when it pleased God for a good man by the name of Mateus, who lived in Estremoz, to be taken by a fearful madness, his family took him to Terena, for it is common

Cantiga 223 (F 55, E 223)

Metrics

11'	11'	|	11	11	11	11'
A	A	|	b	b	b	a

R.1] sa·u·de 1.1] sa·u·de 1.2] =sempre‿a 1.3] =quero‿eu 1.4] =me‿ajude 2.1] =mundo‿ela 3.1] =ende‿un, *Mettmann assumes elision*: ende‿ũu‿ome; bõ·o 3.2] =que‿en, *alt. avoiding elision of* que: que en 'Stremoz = que en‿Estremoz; prougue‿assi 3.3] =forte‿e; ra·viou 3.4] =muito‿a·me·u·de 4.1] vẽ·en 4.3] =como‿aprendi 4.4] =lle‿ante; a·ta·u·de 5.2] tẽ·er 5.3] =podesse‿esta 5.4] =se‿escude

Editorial variants

3.1] M ũu V uun 3.2] M Estre[moz] mora, proug' V Estre mora proug' 5.3] M podes[s]' V podes'

Manuscript variants

R.2] E uer *with* tude *added in right-hand margin in later hand*; odolos (1R), *missing decorated initial* 3.1] F, E ũu 3.2] E estre mora; F, E proug 5.3] E podes

Rubric

Como Santa Maria sãou en Monsarraz un ome bõo que cuidava morrer de ravia.

E sãou ũu; coidava E Ind sãou un; coidava

Captions (F)

missing

4 1 de todalas terras gentes vẽen i.
2 E pois i foron, quis a Virgen assi
3 que foi logo são e, com' aprendi,
4 ja ll' ante fazian os seus ataude
R *Todolos coitados que queren saude …*

for people to go there from all around. And when they arrived, the Virgin was pleased for him to be healed — and as I heard it, his family were already having his coffin made

5 1 en que o metessen por morto de pran.
2 Por en non devia tẽer por afan
3 quen servir podess' esta de bon talan
4 e contra o demo daquesta s' escude.
R *Todolos coitados que queren saude …*

to bury him, and they were sure he was dead. So whoever thinks to serve Our Lady of great virtue should not think it folly, but should seek shelter with her from the Devil.

25. *The Priest who Swallowed a Spider*

R 1 *Muito bon miragr' a Virgen | faz estranno e fremoso*
2 *porque a verdad' entenda | o neicio perfioso.*

1 1 E daquest' un gran miragre | vos será per mi contado
2 e d' oir maravilloso | pois oide o de grado,
3 que mostrou a santa Virgen | de que Deus por nos foi nado,
4 dentro en Cidad Rodrigo | e é mui maravilloso
R *Muito bon miragr' a Virgen | faz estranno e fremoso ...*

2 1 ontr' os outros que oistes. | E tenn' eu que atal éste
2 o que vos contarei ora | que avẽo a un preste
3 que dizia sempre missa | da madre do Rei celeste
4 e porque a ben cantava | era en mui desejoso
R *Muito bon miragr' a Virgen | faz estranno e fremoso ...*

3 1 o poblo de lla oiren. | Mas un dia, sen falida,
2 ena gran festa d' Agosto | desta Sennor mui comprida
3 estava cantando missa | e pois ouve consumida
4 a osti' ar quis o sangui | consomir do grorioso
R *Muito bon miragr' a Virgen | faz estranno e fremoso ...*

4 1 Jesucrist'. E viu no caliz | jazer ũa grand' aranna
2 dentro no sangui nadando | e teve o por estranna
3 cousa, mais mui grand' esforço | fillou, a foro d' Espanna,
4 e de consomir lo todo | non vos foi mui vagaroso.
R *Muito bon miragr' a Virgen | faz estranno e fremoso ...*

5 1 E pois aquest' ouve feito | non quis que ll' empeecesse
2 Deus o poçon da aranna | nen lle no corpo morresse
3 e pero andava viva | non ar quis que o mordesse
4 mas ontr' o coir' e a carn' ia | aquel bestigo astroso.
R *Muito bon miragr' a Virgen | faz estranno e fremoso ...*

6 1 E andava muit' aginna | pelo corp' e non fazia
2 door nen mal, por vertude | da Virgen Santa Maria
3 e se s' ao sol parava | log' a aranna viia
4 e mostrando a a todos | dizend': "O Rei piadoso
R *Muito bon miragr' a Virgen | faz estranno e fremoso ...*

7 1 quis que polos meus pecados | aqueste marteir' ouvesse.
2 Por en rogo aa Virgen | que se a ela prouguesse
3 que rogass' ao seu fillo | que cedo mi a morte desse
4 ou me tolless' esta coita | ca ben é en poderoso."
R *Muito bon miragr' a Virgen | faz estranno e fremoso ...*

The Virgin performs many fine strange and handsome miracles, to reveal the truth to stubborn fools.

[1] To show this I will tell you a great miracle, wondrous to hear, which the Blessed Virgin, of whom God was born, revealed in Ciudad Rodrigo — hear it and rejoice! It is a most wondrous tale

[2] compared with others you have heard — and I am sure that this is true of what I will now recount, which befell a priest who would always sing the mass of the mother of our heavenly King, and he sang it so well that the people were always eager

[3] to hear him sing it. But one day, fatefully, on the high feast of that worthy Lady in August, he was singing mass; and having eaten the host, he then prepared to drink the blood of our glorious

[4] saviour Jesus Christ. And he saw a huge spider there in the chalice, swimming around, and he was greatly surprised, but he summoned up his courage, as a good Spaniard, and wasted no time in consuming everything.

[5] And once he had done this, it was God's will that the poisonous spider did not harm him, nor that it should die in his body; but instead that noxious insect walked alive in him, and did not bite him, but passed between his skin and his flesh.

[6] And the spider moved quickly through his body, causing him no pain or harm, by the power of the Blessed Virgin. And if he stood still in the light, the spider could be seen, and he showed it to all the people, saying: "Our merciful Lord

[7] wished me to suffer this torment for my sins; and so I entreat the Virgin, if she sees fit, to ask her son to take my life soon or relieve me of this grief, for he has the power to do it."

8 Esta aranna andando | per cima do espîaço
e depois pelos costados | e en dereito do baço
des i ia ll' aos peitos | e sol non leixava braço
per que assi non andasse. | E o corpo mui veloso
R *Muito bon miragr' a Virgen | faz estranno e fremoso ...*

9 avia esta aranna. | E un dia, el estando
ao sol, ora de nõa | foi ll' o braç' escaentando,
e el a coçar fillou s' e | non catou al se non quando
lle saiu per so a unlla | aquel poçon tan lixoso.
R *Muito bon miragr' a Virgen | faz estranno e fremoso ...*

10 E tan toste que saida | foi, o crerigo fillou a
e fez logo dela poos | e en sa bolsa guardou a
e quando disse sa missa | consumiu a e passou a
e disse que lle soubera | a manjar mui saboroso.
R *Muito bon miragr' a Virgen | faz estranno e fremoso ...*

11 As gentes que i estavan | quand' ouveron esto visto
loaron muito a madre | do santo rei Jesucristo
e des ali adeante | foi o crerigo por isto
mui mais na fe confirmado | e non foi luxurioso.
R *Muito bon miragr' a Virgen | faz estranno e fremoso ...*

Cantiga 225 (F 67, E 225)

Linguistic note
The edition follows the main text of F in the systematic alternation of 'consomir' (3.4, 4.4), 'consumida' (3.3), and 'consumiu' (10.3).

Textual note
The duplication of introductory formulae in the first two strophes suggests that strophe 1 was added to create the geographical location which distinguishes this narrative from its counterpart in *cantiga* 222. 'Atal' (2.1) logically refers to 'estranno e fremoso' in the refrain. See Parkinson 2013 for an extended textual commentary.

Metrics
15' [7' 7'] 15' [7' 7'] | 15' [7' 7'] 15' [7' 7'] 15' [7' 7'] 15' [7' 7']
A A | b b b a

R.1] =miragre‿a *and subsequent refrains* R.2] =verdade‿entenda; nei·ci·o per·fi·o·so 1.1] =daquesto‿un 1.2] =de‿o·ir; o·i·de 2.1] =ontre‿os; tenno‿eu 3.1] o·i·ren 3.2] =de‿Agosto 3.4] =ostia‿ar; quis o E *variant suggests alt.* quis' o= quiso‿o 4.1] =Jesucristo‿E; grande‿aranna 4.3] =grande‿esforço; de‿Espanna 5.1] =aquesto‿ouve; lle‿em·pe·e·ce·sse 5.4] =on·tre‿o coi·ro‿e‿a car·ne‿i·a, *elision of* e‿a *necessary to avoid hypermetry*; *alt.* mas on·tre‿o coi·ro‿e a car·ne‿i·a‿|‿aquel bestigo astroso, *alt.* bestigoo‿astroso 6.1] =muito‿aginna; corpo‿e 6.3] =se‿a·o; logo‿a; vi·i·a 6.4] =dizendo‿O 7.1] =marteiro‿ouvesse 7.2] a·a 7.3] =rogasse‿a·o; mi‿a 7.4] =tollesse‿esta 8.3] =lle‿a·os 9.2] =lle‿o braço‿es·ca·en·tan·do; a·o 9.3] =se‿e 9.4] sa·iu 10.1] sa·i·da 10.2] po·os 11.1] =quando‿ouveron

Editorial variants
R.2] V verdat 3.1] V fallida 3.2] V en a 3.4] **M1**, V Sangui 4.2] **M1**, V Sangui 4.3] V esforzo 5.4] **M2** coir' e [a] carn' **M1**, V coir' e carn' 7.3] M rogas[s]' V rogas' 7.4] M tolles[s]' V tolles' 8.1] V espinaço 8.3] **M2** ya-ll **M1**, V ya-ll'; V leixaba 10.2] M guardo[u]-a V guardó-a 11.4] V luixurioso

Manuscript variants
R.2] E uerdat 2.3] F celestre E celeste *with* r *added above the line* 3.1] E fallida 3.3] E *con*somida 3.4] E quisó; glorioso 4.3] F cousa & mui, *with the* & *added above the line* 5.2] F moriese 5.4] E coir e carn 6.1] F, E agỹna 6.3] F ueya 7.2] F prouguese 7.3] E rogas 7.4] E tolles 8.4] E andassa 9.3] F si no*n* 10.3] E consumiu 11.4] E luixurioso

[8] And the spider went on crawling, over his backbone, and along his ribs, right through his spleen and thence to his chest, and neither arm was spared for its wandering; and most hairy

[9] was the spider's body. And one day, as he was outside at None, his arm began to itch and he began to scratch it, and before he knew it out came that poisonous filth from under his fingernail.

[10] And as soon as it came out, the priest seized it and ground it to a powder which he kept in his purse and the next time he said her mass, he ate and consumed it, and said that it was a very tasty morsel.

[11] All the people who were present, when they saw all this, gave praise to the mother of our Lord Jesus Christ and from that day on the priest was strengthened in his faith, and was cured of lust.

Rubrics

F Como un crerigo estava cantando missa e viu jazer ũa aranna no caliz e consomiu a e depois saiu lle viva pela unlla do dedo da mão.

E Como ũu clerigo ena missa consomiu ũa aranna que lle caeu no caliz e andava lle ontr' o coiro e a carne viva e fez Santa Maria que lle saisse pela unna.

E calez; fez santa que E **Ind** hun clerigo; arana; andoulle

Captions (F)
missing

26. *The Imprisoned Squire*

R 1 *Quen os pecadores guia | e aduz a salvaçon*
2 *ben pode guiar os presos | poi-los saca de prijon.*

1 1 Esta é Santa Maria, | madre do Rei de vertude,
2 que fez un mui gran miragre | que creo, se Deus m' ajude,
3 e que sacou un cativo | de prijon e deu saude
4 a que muito mal fezeran | os mouros por sa razon.
R *Quen os pecadores guia | e aduz a salvaçon …*

2 1 Este foi un escudeiro | de Quintanela d' Osonna
2 que ia a Vilasirga | cada ano sen vergonna
3 tẽer a festa d' Agosto | mas pois foi por sa besonna
4 a Sevilla ena guerra | caeu en cativ' enton.
R *Quen os pecadores guia | e aduz a salvaçon …*

3 1 E en gran coita jazendo | cada noit' e cada dia
2 mui de coraçon rogava | a Virgen Santa Maria
3 de Vilasirga, u ele | ia sempr' en romaria,
4 que o tirass' de cativo | sen dano e sen lijon.
R *Quen os pecadores guia | e aduz a salvaçon …*

4 1 E el aquesto fazendo | chegou d' Agosto a festa
2 da Virgen mui groriosa | que aos coitados presta
3 e el nembrou s' end' e logo | chorou, baixando a testa.
4 E os mouros que o viron | preguntaron o enton
R *Quen os pecadores guia | e aduz a salvaçon …*

5 1 por que siia tan trist' e | tan muit' e assi chorava.
2 E el respondeu lles logo | de como xe lle nembrava
3 da gran festa que fazian | na terra u el morava
4 en tal dia, e por ende | quebrava ll' o coraçon.
R *Quen os pecadores guia | e aduz a salvaçon …*

6 1 Quand' oiu esto seu dono | foi tan brav' e tan irado
2 que logo a un seu mouro | o fez açoutar privado
3 que lle deu d' açoutes tantos | que non ficou no costado
4 neno corpo coiro são | ata eno vargallon.
R *Quen os pecadores guia | e aduz a salvaçon …*

7 1 Pois mandou o en un carcer | deitar fond' e tẽevroso
2 mas el rogou aa Virgen, | madre do Rei grorioso,
3 que dele s' amerceasse | ca por ela tan astroso
4 o fezeran a açoutes | os mouros, e por al non.
R *Quen os pecadores guia | e aduz a salvaçon …*

8 1 E el aquesto dizendo, | pareceu ll' a Groriosa
2 que alumẽou a carcer, | tan muito vẽo fremosa,
3 e disse ll': "Oí ta coita | e non fui mui vagarosa
4 en vĩir pera livrar te | daquesta perseguçon."
R *Quen os pecadores guia | e aduz a salvaçon …*

A saint who guides sinners and leads them to salvation, can also lead captives after freeing them from captivity.

[1] Such is Holy Mary, mother of the King of goodness who wrought a fine miracle, which I truly believe, so help me God, and released from prison and restored to health a captive who had been ill used by the Moors on her account.

[2] This man was a squire from Quintanella de Osoña, who proudly went every year to Vilasirga to celebrate her August feast day; but after duty led him to go to Seville for the war, he was taken into captivity.

[3] And as he lay in great distress, every night and every day he would pray with all his heart to the Blessed Virgin Mary of Vilasirga, where he always used to go on pilgrimage, asking her to free him from captivity without harm or injury.

[4] And while he was in this plight, there came the August feast day of the most glorious Virgin, who aids the afflicted, and he was mindful of this, and at once lowered his head and wept. And the Moors who saw him asked him

[5] why he was so sad and wept so bitterly in that way. And he told them how he remembered the high festival which was being celebrated on that day in the land where he lived, and how this was breaking his heart.

[6] When his master heard this he was so wildly enraged that he instantly had one of his Moorish servants flog him, giving him so many cuts that there was not a scrap of his skin left unharmed, on his back or his body, from his neck to his groin.

[7] And he had him cast into a deep dark prison. But he implored the Virgin, mother of the glorious King, to have pity on him, as it was for her sake, and none other, that the Moors had whipped him into such a wretched state.

[8] And as he made this plea, the Glorious Virgin appeared to him, coming in such beauty that she lit up the whole prison, and she said to him: "I have heard your distress, and I have not delayed in coming to free you from this oppression."

9 1 E quando ll' est' ouve dito | logo s' os ferros partiron
2 e caeu ll' a meadade | deles, que o non oiron
3 e passou perant' os mouros | e viu os, mas non o viron
4 que estavan assũados | por fazer sa oraçon.
R *Quen os pecadores guia | e aduz a salvaçon ...*

10 1 E pois deles foi partido | fillou en seu col' agĩa
2 a meadade dos ferros | que ena perna tĩia
3 e a Vilasirga logo | a cas da santa reĩa
4 os aduss' en testimõia | que é preto de Carron.
R *Quen os pecadores guia | e aduz a salvaçon ...*

11 1 E entrou pela eigreja | dando mui grandes braados
2 dizend': "Esto fez a Virgen | que acorr' aos coitados."
3 E pois que contou seu feito | a quantos i viu juntados
4 loaron Santa Maria | chorando con devoçon.
R *Quen os pecadores guia | e aduz a salvaçon ...*

Cantiga 227 (F 87, E 227)

Linguistic note
6.4] 'neno corpo': a contraction of 'nen no corpo'

Textual note
10.4] 'Carron': Carrión de los Condes, close to Vilasirga in the province of Palencia.

Metrics

15 [7' 7]	15 [7' 7]	|	15' [7' 7']	15' [7' 7']	15' [7' 7']	15 [7' 7]
A	A	|	b	b	b	a

1.2] =me‿ajude 1.3] sa·u·de 2.1] =de‿Osonna 2.2] i·a 2.3] =de‿Agosto 2.4] =cativo‿enton; ca·eu 3.1] =noite‿e 3.3] =i·a sempre‿en 3.4] tirass' *apocopated form of* tirasse (*for another example see cantiga 159 [anthology 7]*) 3.6]; *alt. elision* =que‿o tirasse 4.1] =de‿Agosto 4.2] a·os 4.3] =se‿ende‿e 5.1] =triste‿e; muito‿e; si·i·a 5.4] =lle‿o 6.1] =Quando‿o·iu; bravo‿e 6.3] =de‿açoutes 7.1] =fondo‿e 7.2] a·a 7.3] =se‿a·mer·ce·a·sse 8.1] =lle‿a 8.3] =lle‿O·í 9.1] =lle‿esto‿ouve; se‿os 9.2] =ca·eu ll‿a me·a·da·de; o·i·ron 9.3] =perante‿os 10.1] =colo‿agĩa 10.2] me·a·da·de; tĩ·i·a 10.3] re·ĩ·a 10.4] =adusse‿en tes·ti·mõ·ia 11.1] =bra·a·dos 11.2] =dizendo‿Esto; acorre‿a·os

Editorial variants
R.1] V aos (1–11R) R.2] M, A pois o[s] V pois o 2.1] M1 [E]ste foi V Esto foi 2.3] M mais 2.4] V en a 4.2] M cuitados 4.3] V neubrou 5.1] V triste 6.4] V nen o; en o 7.1] M mandó-o V teneuroso 7.3] M1, V amercẽasse 8.4] V uijr 9.1] M quand' esto ouve 10.1] V agynna 10.2] M mea[da]de V meade; en a; tiynna 10.3] M Reynna 10.4] M adus[s] V adus' en testimonya 11.1] M ygreja

Manuscript variants
R.1] F aos (0R, 1R, 4R) E aos (1–11R) E pois o 2.1] F Quintanela Do, *incomplete line* E sto, *decorated initial missing* 2.3] E mais; *the last four words,* foi por sa besonna, *written on a strip of parchment, pasted in place; the remainder of the line is written over an erasure* 4.2] E cuitados 7.1] F, E mando o 7.3] F, E amercẽasse 9.1] E quand esto ouue, *the* o *of* esto *is a later superscript addition* 10.2] E meade; tiỹa 10.3] E reỹna 10.4] E adus; testimoỹa 11.1] E ygreia

Rubrics
F Como Santa Maria livrou un escudeiro que jazia en cativo da prijon en que o tĩan.
E Como Santa Maria sacou un escudeiro de cativo de guisa que o non viron os que guardavan o carcer en que jazia.

Captions (F)
1. *missing.* 2. Como o sennor foi mui bravo e feze o açoutar. 3. Como Santa Maria vẽo a ele e lli britou os ferros e o sacou da carcer. 4. Como saiu ant' os mouros que lli non disseron nulla ren. 5. Como entrou na eigreja de Santa Maria de Vilasirga con seus ferros. 6. Como contou todo o feito aa gente e loaron por end muit' a Santa Maria.

3] saco 5] igreja

[10] And when she had said these words, his fetters immediately broke, and half of them fell from him, without a sound. And he walked right past the Moors — he could see them but they did not see him, as they were gathered together to say their prayers.

[10] And as soon as he had escaped from them, he threw onto his shoulder the half of the fetters that were still on his leg, and he went at once to the house of the heavenly queen at Vilasirga, which is close to Carrión, bringing the fetters with him as evidence.

[11] And he went into the church, crying out at the top of his voice: "This is the work of the Virgin, who aids the afflicted." And when he had told his tale to all whom he found assembled there, they all wept devoutly and gave thanks to Holy Mary.

27. The Woman who could not Enter a Church

R *A que as portas do ceo | abriu pera nos salvar*
poder á nas deste mundo | de as abrir e serrar.

1 Desto direi un miragre | segundo que aprendi
que avẽo en Alcáçar | e creo que foi assi
dũa mui bõa crischãa | moller que morava i
que sabia ena Virgen | mais doutra cousa fiar.
R *A que as portas do ceo | abriu pera nos salvar …*

2 Onde por amor da Virgen | ao sabado sempr' ir
punnav' a ũa eigreja | sua oraçon oir
e levava sa oferta | sigo pera oferir,
mas un sabado ll' avẽo | que foi aquest' obridar
R *A que as portas do ceo | abriu pera nos salvar …*

3 por fazendas de sa casa | muitas que ouv' a fazer.
Mais aa tarde ll' en mente | vẽo como falecer
fora, e arrepentiu se | e por esto correger
foi ja tard' aa eigreja | e cuidou i dentr' entrar.
R *A que as portas do ceo | abriu pera nos salvar …*

4 Esta eigrej' alongada | da vila ja quant' está
mas quando chegou a ela | cuidou log' entrar alá,
mas as portas ben serradas | achou, e fillou s' acá
de fora fazer sas prezes | e começou de chorar.
R *A que as portas do ceo | abriu pera nos salvar …*

5 E pois aquest' ouve feito | e compriu sa oraçon
viu log' as portas abertas | e foi en seu coraçon
muit' ende maravillada | porque moller nen baron
non vira que llas abrisse. | E foi log' ao altar
R *A que as portas do ceo | abriu pera nos salvar …*

6 e pos i sa oferenda | des i logo se saiu
da eigreja. E pois fora | foi, as portas serrar viu
e con gran medo que ouve | logo dali recodiu
e foi se pera a vila | mas non de mui gran vagar.
R *A que as portas do ceo | abriu pera nos salvar …*

7 E quando foi aas portas | da vila e entrar quis,
achou as assi serradas | que des ali foi ben fis
de non entrar, e coitada | foi en muit', par San Denis,
mas rogou enton a Virgen | que llas abriu log' en par.
R *A que as portas do ceo | abriu pera nos salvar …*

She who opened the gates of heaven for our salvation, has power to open and close all earthly doors.

[1] On this I will tell a miracle, just as I heard it, which befell in Alcazar, and this is how I believe it happened for a very virtuous Christian woman who lived there, and who trusted in the Blessed Virgin above all others.

[2] And so for love of the Virgin every Saturday she took pains to go to a church of hers and hear the prayers, and she would take with her a gift as an offering; but one Saturday it so happened that she forgot this

[3] because of a great amount of work that she had to do in her house. But in the evening she realised her mistake, and she was most penitent, and to put it right she went late at night to the church and tried to get in.

[4] This church is a very long way from the town, and when she arrived there she tried to get inside but found the doors fast closed, and went outside to say her prayers, and began to weep.

[5] And when she had wept and made her devotions she suddenly saw the doors were open, and in her heart she was amazed for she had not seen man or woman opening them. And she hastened to the altar

[6] and left her offering there, and straight away she went out of the church, and when she had departed she saw the doors closing, and in great fear she departed from the place and returned to the town, in no little haste.

[7] And when she got to the gates of the town and tried to come back in, she found that they were closed, and she was convinced that she would not be able to get in, and was most grieved at this, by Saint Denis; but she prayed to the Virgin, who opened them wide for her.

8 1 Enton ũa dona bela | e nobre ll' apareceu,
2 que a fillou pela mão | e na vila a meteu
3 e levou a a sa casa | ond' ela prazer prendeu
4 mas ante que i chegasse | começou ll' a preguntar
R *A que as portas do ceo | abriu pera nos salvar …*

9 1 dizendo: "Sennor, quen sodes, | que a tan pobre moller
2 com' eu tan gran ben fezestes?" | Respos ll' ela volonter:
3 "Eu sõo a que nas coitas | acorr' a quen m' á mester
4 en que Deus por sa mercee | quis de mi carne fillar."
R *A que as portas do ceo | abriu pera nos salvar …*

10 1 Quand' a bõa moller esto | oiu, logo se deitou
3 a seus pees por beijar llos | mas non a viu e ficou
5 ende mui desconortada | e en sa casa entrou
7 e aqueste feit' a todos | outro dia foi contar.
R *A que as portas do ceo | abriu pera nos salvar …*

Cantiga 246 (F 1, E 246)

Linguistic note

2.2] 'eigreja': the form with 'ei-' is given here despite both manuscript witnesses having 'igreia'/'ygreja', because this is clearly an exception to the otherwise consistent preference for 'eigreja' in F, and 'ygreja' in E, evident here (4.1 and 6.2) and elsewhere (for example *cantiga* 249 [anthology 27], 2.1). See Parkinson & Barnett 2013: 469–70 and 475–77 on the word profile showing the distribution of variants of 'eigreja' throughout the *CSM*.

Metrics

15 [7' 7] 15 [7' 7] | 15 [7' 7] 15 [7' 7] 15 [7' 7] 15 [7' 7]
A A | b b b a

2.1] =sempre‿ir 2.2] =punnava‿a; *alt.* sua‿e oraçon 2.4] =lle‿avẽo; aquesto‿obridar 3.1] =ouve‿a 3.2] =lle‿en 3.4] =tarde‿aa; dentro‿entrar 4.1] =eigreja‿alongada; quanto‿está 4.2] =logo‿entrar 4.3] =se‿acá 5.1] =aquesto‿ouve 5.2] =logo‿as 5.3] =muito‿ende 5.4] =logo‿ao 6.1] sa·iu 7.3] =muito‿par, *alt.* foi muito 7.4] =logo‿en 8.1] =lle‿apareceu 8.3] =onde‿ela 8.4] =lle‿a 9.2] =como‿eu; lle‿ela 9.3] =acorre‿a; me‿á 10.1] =Quando‿a; o·iu 10.4] =feito‿a

Editorial variants

R.1] V ce (4R) 1.4] V en a 2.2] M ygreja; sua e 2.3] M por a 3.2] M Mas 3.3] **M2** ar[r]epenti[u]-sse **M1** ar[r]epenti-sse V arrepentisse 4.1] M ygrej' 6.2] M ygreja 7.3] M no[n] entrar V no entrar; M, V cuitada; Dinis 8.3] M levó-a a 9.2] **M1** Respos-ll' era 9.3] V Eu soon M cuitas 10.3] V cassa

Manuscript variants

R.1] E do ce (4R) 2.2] F igreia E ygreia, *see Linguistic note above*; sua & 2.3] E por a 3.2] E mas 3.3] F arrepenti E arepenti 4.1] E ygrei 4.3] F sarrada*s* 6.2] F e[.]g[.]ja, *partially legible due to damage to folio* E ygreia 6.3] F *first hemistich missing* 7.3] E no; cuitada; Dini*s* 8.3] F leuou a E leuo a a 9.3] E cuitas 10.3] E cassa

Rubric

Dũa bõa moller que ia cada sabado a ũa eigreja que chaman Santa Maria das Martires e obridou xe lle e depois foi ala de noite e abriron xe lle as portas da eigreja.

F *missing* E obrido E **Ind** chamavan; dos Martires e oblidouxelle

Captions (F)

missing

[8] Then a fair and noble lady appeared to her and took her by the hand and brought her into the town and took her back to her house, which gave her great joy, but before they arrived there, she asked the lady

[9] "Madam, who are you, to do such kindness for as poor a woman as I?" And the lady replied freely: "I am she who comes to the aid of those who call on me in their distress, for God by his grace saw fit to take flesh in me."

[10] When the good woman heard this, she at once fell at the lady's feet to kiss them; but saw her no more, which left her most bereft, and she returned to her house and the next day told everyone of the Virgin's great deed.

28. *The Stonemason who Survived a Great Fall*

R 1 *Aquel que de voontade | Santa Maria servir*
2 *d' ocajon será guardado | e doutro mal sen mentir.*

Whosoever gladly serves Our Lady will surely be protected from accidents and other ills.

1 1 E de tal razon com' esta | un miragre vos direi
2 que en Castroxeriz fezo | a madre do alto Rei
3 a Virgen Santa Maria | per com' eu aprix e sei
4 e por Deus meted' i mentes | e querede o oir.
R *Aquel que de voontade | Santa Maria servir …*

On this kind of theme I will tell a miracle which the mother of our high King, the Blessed Virgin Mary, performed in Castroxeriz, as I know because I heard it. By Our Lord take heed and listen to this tale.

2 1 Quand' a eigreja fazian | a que chaman d' Almaçan
2 que é en cabo da vila | muitos maestres de pran
3 ian i lavrar por algo | que lles davan como dan
4 aos que tal obra fazen. | Mas un deles ren pedir
R *Aquel que de voontade | Santa Maria servir …*

When they were building the church called Almanzano, which is close to the town, many fine builders came to work there for the wages that were given, as they are now, to those who do such work. But one of them would not ask

3 1 non queria, mas lavrava | ali mui de coraçon
2 pora gaannar da Virgen | mercee e gualardon.
3 E por end' or' ascuitade | o que ll' avẽo enton
4 e sempr' averedes ende | que falar e departir.
R *Aquel que de voontade | Santa Maria servir …*

for any money, but worked there willingly to earn the grace and favour of the Blessed Virgin. And so give ear to what then happened to him, so that you will always be able to speak of it and tell the tale.

4 1 El maestr' era de pedra | e lavrava ben assaz
2 e quadrava ben as pedras | e poĩa as en az
3 eno mais alto da obra | como bon maestre faz.
4 E un dia fazend' esto | foron ll' os pees falir
R *Aquel que de voontade | Santa Maria servir …*

He was a stonemason, and worked hard to square off the stones and lay them out in a row at the highest part of the construction, as a good mason does. And one day as he was at his work, he lost his footing

Cantiga 249 (F 69, E 249)

Linguistic note

4.2] 'poĩa': there is no evidence from rhymes to distinguish between 'põia' and 'poĩa'. Corresponding forms of the verbs 'tẽer' and 'vĩir' overwhelmingly rhyme with '-ĩa' and '-inna'.

Metrics

15 [7' 7] 15 [7' 7] | 15 [7' 7] 15 [7' 7] 15 [7' 7] 15 [7' 7]
A A | b b b a

R.2] =de‿ocajon 1.1] =como‿esta 1.3] =como‿eu 1.4] =metede‿i 2.1] =Quando‿a; de‿Almaçan 2.2] ma·es·tres 2.4] a·os 3.2] ga·a·nnar; mer·ce·e 3.3] =ende‿ora‿ascuitade; lle‿avẽo 3.4] =sempre‿averedes 4.1] =maestre‿era 4.2] po·ĩ·a 4.4] =fazendo‿esto; lle‿os 5.1] ca·eu; ca·en·do 6.1] ca·e·ra; *hypermetric line; alt.* recebeu ne·un mal *or* prendeu en ne·un mal 6.2] =se‿ergeu; teve‿ollo 6.3] a·o 7.1] lo·o·res 7.2] a·a 7.3] =sempre‿ajamos 7.4] =gãa‿o, *alt.* gaann' (*see* 3.3); re·mi·ir

Editorial variants

2.1] M ygreja 3.2] V ganar 3.3] M ascoitade 4.2] M2 põyas-as M1 põya-as 4.3] M eno ma[i]s V en o más 5.3] V sobe los 7.4] M gaann' V ueno

Manuscript variants

2.1] E ygreia 3.1] F mais 3.2] F, E gãar, *giving a hypometric line* 3.3] E ascoitade 4.3] E mas 5.1] F cau 6.3] F fois ao, *the superscript* s *may be a later addition*; esperital 7.2] E aos 7.4] F gaann E gãan; ueno

5 1 e caeu ben do mais alto | e en caendo chamou
2 a Virgen Santa Maria | que o mui toste livrou.
3 Ca pero que da cabeça | sobelos cantos topou
4 assi o guardou a Virgen | que sol non se foi ferir
R *Aquel que de voontade | Santa Maria servir …*

and fell right from the top of the works, and as he fell he called upon the Blessed Virgin Mary, who very quickly rescued him; and even though he struck his head on the masonry, the Virgin protected him so that he came to no harm

6 1 nen sentiu sol se caera | nen recebeu en neun mal
2 ante s' ergeu mui correndo | que non tev' ollo por al
3 mas foi ao altar logo | da Virgen espirital
4 por loar a sa mercee | e os seus bẽes gracir.
R *Aquel que de voontade | Santa Maria servir …*

and did not even realise that he had fallen, nor was he injured in any way, but rather he got up and ran for his life, without looking at anything else, and went at once to the altar of the holy Virgin to praise her goodness and give thanks for her bounty.

7 1 E quantos ali estavan | deron loores por en
2 aa Virgen groriosa | que os seus val e manten.
3 E por ende lle roguemos | que sempr' ajamos seu ben
4 e nos gã' o de seu fillo | que nos vẽo remiir.
R *Aquel que de voontade | Santa Maria servir …*

And all who were there gave thanks therefore to the Glorious Virgin, who helps and guards her own. And so let us beseech her to give us her bounty and to secure for us the bounty of her son, who came to redeem us.

Rubrics

F Como Santa Maria livrou de morte en Castroxeriz un maestre que lavrava na eigreja e que caeu de cima e non se feriu.

E Como un maestro que lavrava na eigreja que chaman Santa Maria d' Almaçan en Castroxeriz caeu de cima en fondo e guardou o Santa Maria que se non feriu.

E guardoo **E Ind** egreja; guardoo; *final word*, feriu, *missing*

Captions (F)

missing

29. *The Girl who was Captivated by an Image of the Christ Child*

R *Mui gran dereito faz | d' o mund' avorrecer*
o que pode amor | da Virgen ben aver.

1 En terra de Proença | un gran miragr' achei
escrito que fezera | a madre do gran Rei
e des que o oirdes | ben sõo fis e sei
que non oistes doutro | nunca tal retraer.
R *Mui gran dereito faz | d' o mund' avorrecer …*

2 Un burges i avia | mui rico e que ben
casad' era, mas fillos | non podia per ren
aver, ca lle morrian | e prometeu por en
ũa que lle nacera | de en orden na meter.
R *Mui gran dereito faz | d' o mund' avorrecer …*

3 Por end' a un convento | de donas que dali
mui pret' era, sa madre | levou a, com' oí,
e a moça na claustra | per com' eu aprendi
viu ũa majestade | enos braços tẽer
R *Mui gran dereito faz | d' o mund' avorrecer …*

4 seu fillo. E de pedra | eran ambos non d' al
mas eran tan ben feitos | que a moça atal
amor colleu con eles | que des ali sen al
niun sabor avia | doutra cousa veer.
R *Mui gran dereito faz | d' o mund' avorrecer …*

5 Sempre quando a madre | aa eigreja orar
ia e a levava | sigo ant' o altar
logo ela s' esfurtava | e ia se parar
ant' aquela omagen | ond' avia prazer.
R *Mui gran dereito faz | d' o mund' avorrecer …*

6 E levava lle sempre | rosa ou outra fror
ou fruita que achasse | de mui bõa odor
e con est' aa omagen | colleu tan grand' amor
que outra ren do mundo | non sabia querer.
R *Mui gran dereito faz | d' o mund' avorrecer …*

7 Quando chegou seu tempo | que en religion
meteron a minĩa | vẽo ll' a coraçon
de pedir o seu fillo | da omagen enton
que faagar podesse | e en braços coller.
R *Mui gran dereito faz | d' o mund' avorrecer …*

8 Porque a moça tantas | vezes viian ir
as donas aa claustra | e delas se partir
por en a asseitaron | e viron lle pedir
o fill' aa omagen | e viron lle tender
R *Mui gran dereito faz | d' o mund' avorrecer …*

9 os braços que llo désse. | E ela ar tendeu
os seus braços e deu llo | e poi-lo recebeu
a moça faagou o | e tal amor colleu
con el, que des i "fillo" | começou a dizer
R *Mui gran dereito faz | d' o mund' avorrecer …*

10 e mui leda cantando | nos braços o fillou.
E aquesto fazendo | o convento chegou
e a omagen logo | seu fill' a si tirou
assi que todas elas | ben llo viron fazer.
R *Mui gran dereito faz | d' o mund' avorrecer …*

11 Mantenent' o convento | levaron manaman
logo dali a moça | pero con grand' afan
chorando e dizendo: | "Monjas, de mal talan
sodes, porque meu fillo | mi fezestes perder."
R *Mui gran dereito faz | d' o mund' avorrecer …*

12 Quando a abadessa | a assi falar oiu
tan aficadamente | preguntou lle que viu
mas chorando a moça | assi lle recodiu:
"Rogo vos que meu fillo | me querades render."
R *Mui gran dereito faz | d' o mund' avorrecer …*

13 Sobr' est' a madre vẽo | e preguntou ll' assaz
que vira, e a moça | lle diss': "A mi non praz
d' al se non de meu fillo | e dade mio en paz."
E ergeu se mui toste | e fillou s' a correr
R *Mui gran dereito faz | d' o mund' avorrecer …*

14 e foi se aa omagen | e disse: "Dá me meu
fill'", e tendeu os braços | como se fosse seu.
Quand' esto viu a madre | en ela salto deu,
cuidando que queria | por el ensandecer.
R *Mui gran dereito faz | d' o mund' avorrecer …*

Whoever earns the love of the Virgin
does well to renounce the world.

[1] In the land of Provence I found in writing a great miracle which the mother of the great King had performed there. And once you hear it I am sure and certain that you will not hear anyone else tell such a tale.

[2] A burgher lived there who was very rich and happily married, but he could not manage to have sons, for all of them died, and so he made a vow to send one of his daughters to a convent.

[3] And so the girl's mother took her, as I heard, to a nunnery which is very close by. And the girl, as I was told, saw in the cloister a statue of the Blessed Virgin in majesty with her son

[4] in her arms. Both were carved in stone, but so well wrought that the girl was so taken with them that from then on they were the only thing she delighted in seeing.

[5] Whenever the mother went to pray in the church and took her with her to the altar, the girl would always run off and go and stand before that statue, which gave her such joy

[6] and she would always bring her a rose or some other flower or any fruit she could find of sweet taste, and in this she grew such love for the statue that there was nothing else in the world she loved so much.

[7] When the time came for the girl to enter the nunnery, she had the idea of asking the statue if she could take the child in her arms and caress it.

[8] As the nuns saw the girl so often go into the cloister and escape from them, they spied on her and saw her ask the statue to give her the child, and they saw her

[9] stretch out her arms to receive him. And the statue reached out to her and gave her the child, and when she took him, she caressed him and became so fond of him that she called him "my son"

[10] and singing joyfully she took him in her arms. As she did this, the nuns came into sight, and the statue at once took back her child, so that all the nuns could see.

[11] Meanwhile the nuns at once led the girl away from there, though she cried in distress saying: "You are wicked, you nuns, for you have taken my son away from me."

[12] When the abbess heard her speak so wildly in this way, she asked her what she had seen. But the girl tearfully replied: "I just ask you to give me back my son."

[13] Then her mother came and asked her at length what she had seen, and the girl replied: "I want nothing except my son, give him to me and leave me be." And she arose quickly and ran off

[14] and went to the statue, saying "Give me my son" and she reached out as though it was hers. When her mother saw this she leapt on her, thinking that she was going mad.

15 1 E sobr' est' ao papa | que ten logar de Deus
2 que dali mui pret' era | a madre e os seus
3 parentes a levaron | dia de San Mateus
4 dizendo: "Padre santo | que pod' esto seer
R *Mui gran dereito faz | d' o mund' avorrecer …*

16 1 desta moça que fillo | chama, e al non diz,
2 por un da majestade | pintad' e con verniz?
3 Mas vos que sedes padre | da lee e joiz
4 rogad' a Deus que desto | a quera guarecer."
R *Mui gran dereito faz | d' o mund' avorrecer …*

17 1 O papa, que sant' ome | era, respos lles: "Cras
2 mandarei cantar missa." | " E tu a levarás,"
3 diss' aa ama da moça, | "e se de Satanas
4 ven aquesta sandece | pode se desfazer."
R *Mui gran dereito faz | d' o mund' avorrecer …*

18 1 A missa foi cantada | logo depo-la luz
2 a grand' onra da madre | do que morreu na cruz
3 e quando foi na sagra | áque a madr' aduz
4 ant' o altar sa filla | polo feito saber.
R *Mui gran dereito faz | d' o mund' avorrecer …*

19 1 A moça teve mentes | e dacá e dalá,
2 e pois viu a ostia | alçar, disso: "Ahá,
3 aquel é o meu fillo | e dade mio acá."
4 E o papa fez logo | a ostia trager
R *Mui gran dereito faz | d' o mund' avorrecer …*

20 1 e meteu lla nas mãos | e diss' ela: "Est' é
2 o meu amado fillo, | fillo meu, a la fe
3 e por ende me quero | ir con el ca temp' é."
4 E meteu a na boca | e leixou se morrer.
R *Mui gran dereito faz | d' o mund' avorrecer …*

21 1 Quand' esto viu o papa | que sant' ome fiel
2 era, loou por ende | o gran Deus d' Irrael
3 e a Santa Maria | que miragre tan bel
4 mostrara, e tan toste | o mandou escrever.
R *Mui gran dereito faz | d' o mund' avorrecer …*

Cantiga 251 (E 251)

Linguistic note
2.4] 'en orden na meter': 'na' represents an assimilated form of the feminine direct object pronoun 'a'.

Metrics

12 [6 6]	12 [6 6]	|	13 [6' 6]	13 [6' 6]	13 [6' 6]	13 [6' 6]
A	A	|	b	b	b	a

Note that the *vuelta* reprises the rhyme but not the metre of the refrain.

R.1] =de‿o mundo‿avorrecer *and subsequent refrains* 1.1] =miragre‿achei 1.3] o·ir·des 1.4] =o·is·tes 2.2] =casado‿era 2.4] *necessary elision* de‿en 3.1] =ende‿a 3.2] =preto‿era; como‿o·í 3.3] =como‿eu 4.1] =de‿al 4.4] ni·un; ve·er 5.1] aa eigreja orar, *hypermetric line:* eigreja‿orar *or* a‿a *or* aa‿eigreja. *The manuscript reading* quand a *may be a misplaced attempt to rectify the hypermetry over the whole line* 5.2] =ante‿o; i·a 5.3] =se‿esfurtava; i·a; *necessary elision* logo‿ela 5.4] =ante‿aquela; onde‿avia 6.3] =esto‿aa; *necessary elision* esto‿aa‿omagen *or* esto‿a‿a omagen; grande‿amor 7.2] =lle‿a 7.4] fa·a·gar 8.1] vi·i·an 8.2] a·a 8.4] =fillo‿a·a 9.3] fa·a·gou 10.3] =fillo‿a 11.1] =Mantenente‿o 11.2] =grande‿afan 12.1] *necessary elision* a‿assi; oi·u 13.1] =Sobre‿esto‿a; lle‿assaz 13.2] =disse‿A 13.3] =de‿al; da·de·mio 13.4] =se‿a 14.1] *necessary elision* se‿aa 14.3] =Quando‿esto 15.1] =sobre‿esto‿a·o 15.2] =preto‿era 15.4] =pode‿esto se·er 16.2] =pintado‿e 16.3] le·e e jo·iz 16.4] =rogado‿a 17.1] =santo‿ome 17.3] *necessary elision of restored* aa: disse‿a‿a (*see* 6.3) 18.2] =grande‿onra 18.3] =madre‿aduz 18.4] =ante‿o 19.2] *trisyllabic* os·ti·a *would need to be accented on the penultimate syllable to fit the cadence before the caesura; alt.* vi·u (*dieresis*) 19.3] da·de·mio 19.4] os·ti·a 20.1] =disse‿ela Este‿e 20.3] =tempo‿e 21.1] =Quando‿esto; santo‿ome fi·el 21.2] =de‿I·rra·el; lo·ou

Editorial variants
1.3] V et desque; ben soon 2.4] M orden-na meter V órden na meter 3.4] V en os 5.1] M quand[o] M2 à M1 aa V quand'; aa 5.4] V aquella 6.3] M con' est' à omagen 7.2] V mjinyna 9.2] V deu-ll'o e poil-o 9.3] M faagó-o 9.4] V que de sí fillo 10.1] M canta[n]do M2 *undivided line* V cantado 11.1] M Ma[n]tenent' V Matenent' 12.1] M abadess' a assi V abadessa assi 13.3] V et dáde-my-o 14.1] M foi-sse à omagen 16.2] M Magestade 17.3] M diss' à ama V diss' á ama 18.1] V depol-a 19.3] V et dáde-mi-o 20.1] V Est é

[15] And at this her mother and her family took her on St Matthew's day to the Pope, who is closest to God, and who lived nearby, and said: "Holy Father, what can be the matter

[16] with this girl who does nothing but address as her son the infant in the arms of a painted and varnished statue of Our Lady? You who are father and judge of our creed, pray to God that he frees her from this ailment."

[17] The Pope, who was a holy man, replied: "Tomorrow I will have a mass said." "And you will bring her to it," he said to the girl's nurse, "and if this madness comes from Satan, it can be undone."

[18] The mass was sung straight after dawn, to the great honour of the mother of he who died on the cross, and when they came to the sacrament, then the mother brought her daughter to the altar, to see what would ensue.

[19] The girl looked around her and when she saw the host being elevated, she said: "Ah, there is my son, give him to me now." And the Pope had the host brought to him

[20] and placed it in her hands and she said: "This is my beloved son, my child, indeed and so I wish to follow him, for now is the time." And she put the host in her mouth, and passed away.

[21] When the Pope beheld this, as the faithful holy man he was, he gave thanks to the great God of Israel and to Holy Mary, who had shown such a fine miracle, and at once he had it written down.

Manuscript variants

R.1] E grand (15R) 2.4] E orden na meter 5.1] E quand a 5.4] E aquella 6.3] E esta omagen 9.3] E faagoo 10.1] E cantado 11.1] E Matenent 12.1] E abadessa assi 14.1] E foisse a omagen 16.2] E magestade 17.3] E diss á ama

Rubric

Como Santa Maria levou consigo a menĩa de Proença que pedia o fillo aa sa majestade.

E **Ind** menina

30. *Cantiga de loor*

1 1 Quen bõa dona querrá
2 loar, lo' a que par non á
R *Santa Maria.*

2 1 E par nunca ll' achará
2 pois que madre de Deus foi ja
R *Santa Maria.*

3 1 Pois madre de Deus foi ja
2 e virgen foi e seerá
R *Santa Maria.*

4 1 E virgen foi e será
2 por ende cabo del está
R *Santa Maria.*

5 1 Por en cabo del está
2 u sempre por nos rogará
R *Santa Maria.*

6 1 U por nos lle rogará
2 e del perdon nos gãará
R *Santa Maria.*

7 1 E perdon nos gãará
2 e ao demo vencerá
R *Santa Maria.*

8 1 E o demo vencerá
2 e nos consigo levará
R *Santa Maria.*

Cantiga 160 (T 160, E 160)

Metrics
This is an example of *leixa-pren*, where line 2 of each strophe is reused as line 1 of the subsequent strophe, in this case in a subtly shortened form. MS E (followed by Mettmann in his first edition) misrepresents the structure of this non-*zajal*, presenting the first strophe as a refrain, despite musical indications to the contrary.

7 8 | 4'
a a | B

1.2] =loa‿a 2.1] =lle‿achará 3.2] se·e·rá 6.2] gã·a·rá 7.1] gã·a·rá 7.2] a·o

Editorial variants
1.1] **M1** *S1 given as refrain throughout* 2.R] **A** Quen bõa dona | Santa Maria *given as refrain* 4.1] **M1** seerá 8.R] **V** *refrain omitted*

Manuscript variants
2.R] E Quen bõa dona (*and* 5R) 3.R] E Que*n* bona dona 4.1] E seera 4.R] E Que*n* bõa dona querra 5.1] T Por ende 6.R] E Quen bona dona 7.R] E Quen bona 8.R] E *missing*

Rubric
De loor de Santa Maria.

E Ind *missing*

Captions (T)
missing

[1] If you would praise a virtuous lady,
praise the one who has no peer
Holy Mary.

[2] You will never find her peer
since she was the mother of God
Holy Mary.

[3] Since she was the mother of God
and was and ever will be a virgin
Holy Mary.

[4] She was and ever will be a virgin
and so she sits at his [God's] side
Holy Mary.

[5] And so she sits at his side,
where she will ever plead for us
Holy Mary.

[6] Where she will plead to him for us
and win mercy for us
Holy Mary.

[7] And she will win mercy for us
and defeat the Devil
Holy Mary.

[8] And she will defeat the Devil,
and take us with her [to heaven]
Holy Mary.

31. *The Merchant who Fell Overboard*

R *Na que Deus pres carne e foi dela nado*
ben pode valer a todo perigoado.

She in whom God took flesh and of whom he was born, clearly can help anyone who is in danger.

1 Ca per ela foi a morte destroida
e nossa saude cobrada e vida
tod' est' avemos pola Sennor comprida.
Pois un seu miragre vos direi de grado
R *Na que Deus pres carne e foi dela nado …*

For through her was death destroyed, and our health and life restored, and all this we have through our worthy Lady. So I will gladly tell a miracle

2 que fez esta Virgen santa e reĩa
que é dos coitados todos meezĩa
contar-vo-lo-ei brevement' e agĩa
quant' end' aprendi a quen mio á contado.
R *Na que Deus pres carne e foi dela nadoo …*

wrought by this holy Virgin, Queen of Heaven, who is medicine for all afflicted. I will tell briefly and quickly the story I heard from those who told it.

3 Ontre Doir' e Mĩ' en Portugal morava
un mercador rico muito que amava
Santa Maria e por ela fiava
e ena servir sempr' era seu cuidado.
R *Na que Deus pres carne e foi dela nado …*

Between the Douro and the Minho in Portugal there lived a very rich merchant, who loved Holy Mary and trusted in her, and whose desire was to serve her.

4 Como quer que el pelas terras mercasse
se dõa fremos' e aposta achasse
que pera o seu altar lle semellasse
de lla aduzer era muit' entregado.
R *Na que Deus pres carne e foi dela nado …*

Although he traded in many different lands, if he came across a rich and beautiful gift which seemed right for her altar, he would devote himself to bringing it to her.

5 Porque amava muito Santa Maria
de coraçon, disse ca en romaria
a Rocamador de bõa ment' iria
tanto que o el podess' aver guisado.
R *Na que Deus pres carne e foi dela nado …*

And because he loved Holy Mary with all his heart, he pledged that he would go gladly on a pilgrimage to Rocamadour, as soon as he could arrange it.

6 Assi foi que el sa nav' ouve fretada
pera ir a Frandes, e essa vegada,
pois que ouve ben sa fazenda guisada,
foi se con quant' aver avia mercado.
R *Na que Deus pres carne e foi dela nado …*

And it happened that he had his boat loaded to go to Flanders, and on this occasion, as his affairs were well in hand, he set off with all the gifts he had bought.

7 Mais pela costeira do gran mar d' Espanna
ind' aquela nave con mui gran companna
levantou s' o mar con tormenta tamanna
que muito per foi aquel dia irado.
R *Na que Deus pres carne e foi dela nado …*

But as that boat, with a great company on board, passed by the coast of the great Spanish sea, the sea rose up in such a great storm that raged all that day.

8 1 Levantou sas ondas fortes feramente
2 sobr' aquela nave, que aquela gente
3 cuidou i morrer, e logo mantenente
4 chorou e coidou enton i seu pecado.
R *Na que Deus pres carne e foi dela nado …*

Its waves rose up with fearsome strength over that ship, so that the people on board expected to die, and at once began to weep and reflect on their sins.

9 1 E o mercador eno bordo da nave
2 estava enton encima dũa trave
3 e ũa onda vẽo fort' e mui grave
4 que lle deu no peit' e no mar foi deitado.
R *Na que Deus pres carne e foi dela nado …*

And the merchant on board the ship was standing on a spar, and a great and mighty wave swept over and struck him in the chest, and he was cast into the sea.

10 1 A nav' alongada foi, se Deus me valla
2 del ũa gran peça pelo mar, sen falla,
3 mai-lo demo que sempre nosco traballa
4 quisera que morress' i log' afogado.
R *Na que Deus pres carne e foi dela nado …*

The ship, so help me God, sailed a long way away from him over the sea, but the Devil, who ever causes us trouble, wanted him to be drowned there.

11 1 El andand' assi en aquela tormenta
2 nembrou se da Virgen que sempr' acrecenta
3 eno nosso ben, ca pero que nos tenta
4 o demo, non pode nosc', a Deus loado.
R *Na que Deus pres carne e foi dela nado …*

As he went through this trouble he remembered the Blessed Virgin who always does us good, for even though the Devil tempts us, he cannot prevail over us, God be praised.

12 1 "Ai, Madre de Deus," diss' el, "teu ben m' ajude,
2 tu que es Sennor santa de gran vertude
3 pois a todolos coitados dás saude
4 nembra te de mi que ando tan coitado.
R *Na que Deus pres carne e foi dela nado …*

"O Mother of God," he said, "may your grace help me, you who are our Holy Lady of great virtue, as you give health to all the afflicted, remember me in my distress.

13 1 Sennor, por mercee non me desampares
2 por algũu tempo t' eu fazer pesares
3 e se m' ora daquestas ondas tirares
4 servir-t'-ei eu sempr' e farei teu mandado.
R *Na que Deus pres carne e foi dela nado …*

My Lady, by your mercy do not abandon me, on account of any sadness I have once given you, and if you now rescue me from these waves, I will always serve you and do your will.

14 1 Nembra te, Sennor, que t' ei eu prometudo
2 d' ir aa ta casa, est' é ben sabudo,
3 mais tu, dos coitados esforç' e escudo,
4 val-me, Sennor, ca muit' and' atormentado."
R *Na que Deus pres carne e foi dela nado …*

Remember, my Lady, that I have made you a promise to go to your church, as is well known; and so, my Lady, strength and shield of the afflicted, help me, for I am in great distress."

15 1 El esto dizendo, log' a Virgen santa
2 vẽo, que o dem' e seus feitos quebranta
3 come sennor bõa que os seus avanta
4 fora d' ontr' as ondas o ouve tirado.
R *Na que Deus pres carne e foi dela nado …*

As he said this, the Holy Virgin, who destroys the Devil and his works, came at once, as the good lady she is who supports her own, and she soon plucked him out of the waves.

16 1 E fez enton i gran maravilla fera
2 ca tornou o mar manso de qual ant' era.
3 Se ll' el algun tempo serviço fezera
4 mui ben llo per ouv' ali gualardõado.
R *Na que Deus pres carne e foi dela nado …*

And she performed a great and mighty miracle, for she made the sea as calm as it had been before. If the merchant had served her well before, she there gave him a very rich reward for his service.

17 1 E levou o salvo a terra segura
2 que sol non sentiu coita nen rancura
3 esto fez a da virgĩidade pura
4 que por nos viu seu Fillo crucifigado.
R *Na que Deus pres carne e foi dela nado …*

And she brought him safe to dry land, and he felt no pain nor trouble; this was the work of the Virgin most pure, who saw her son crucified for us.

18 1 E ante dez dias, oí por verdade,
2 que a nave foss' a aquela cidade
3 u portar avia, pola piadade
4 de Santa Maria foi el i chegado.
R *Na que Deus pres carne e foi dela nado …*

And ten days before the ship arrived in the city for which it was bound, this is a true tale, he arrived there by the mercy of the Blessed Virgin Mary.

Cantiga 267 (F 53, E 267, E 373)

Textual notes

R.1] The original reading 'Na que Deus pres carne e foi dela nado' was copied into E267 (or its exemplar) with an unnecessary elision of 'carne' with the following 'e'. The decorated initial 'N' was not present at this stage. The music copyist assigned four figures to 'Na que de-' and the remaining two to 'pres carn' e'. An additional 'de' was then added to the first line to restore text-music congruency, tacitly replacing the construction 'prender carne en' with the alternative 'prender carne de'. This version was regularised to 'A de que Deus pres carn(e)' in subsequent copies. E373 retained the unelided 'carne e', in a hypermetric line which had to be resolved by leaving the final 'e' without a corresponding musical figure (Parkinson 2001).

R.2] The original reading is likely to have been 'valer todo'. The hypermetry resulting from the addition of 'a' needed to be resolved by syneresis of '-goa-' in 'perigoado', represented graphically in F by 'periguado'.

Metrics

11' 11' | 11' 11' 11' 11' [NB Many lines are divided 5' 5']
A A | b b b a

R.2] pe·ri·goa·do 1.2] sa·u·de 1.3] =todo‿esto‿avemos 2.1] re·ĩ·a 2.2] me·e·zĩ·a 2.3] brevemente‿e 2.4] =quanto‿ende‿aprendi; mio (*single syllable*) 3.1] =Doi·ro‿e Mĩo‿en 3.4] =sempre‿era 4.2] =fremosa‿e 4.4] =muito‿entregado 5.3] =mente‿iria 5.4] =podesse‿aver 6.1] =nave‿ouve 6.4] =quanto‿aver 7.1] =de‿Espanna 7.2] =indo‿aquela 7.3] =se‿o 8.2] =sobre‿aquela 9.3] =forte‿e; ũ·a 9.4] =peito‿e 10.1] =nave‿alongada 10.4] =morresse‿i logo‿afogado 11.1] =andando‿assi 11.2] =sempre‿acrecenta 11.4] =nosco‿a 12.1] =disse‿el; me‿ajude 12.3] sa·u·de 13.1] mer·ce·e 13.2] =te‿eu; al·gũ·u 13.3] =me‿ora 13.4] =servir-te‿-ei eu sempre‿e 14.1] =te‿ei 14.2] =de‿ir a·a; esto‿e 14.3] =esforço‿e 14.4] =muito‿ando‿atormentado 15.1] =logo‿a 15.2] =demo‿e 15.4] =de‿ontre‿as 16.2] =ante‿era 16.3] =lle‿el 16.4] =ouve‿ali 17.2] *necessary dieresis* sen·ti·u 17.3] vir·gĩ·i·da·de 18.1] o·í 18.2] =fosse‿a 18.3] pi·a·da·de 19.1] =nave‿ali 19.4] =quanto‿avia 20.4] =sempre‿ouve‿Ei

Editorial variants

R.1] M A [de] que V(267) Na de que V(373) A de que; carne e A(373) carn' e RL A de que; carne e R.2] A(267 & 373) pe-ri-goa-do 1.1] V(373), RL destruida 2.1] M Reynna V(373), RL Raynna 2.2] V(267 & 373), RL meezynna 2.3] M agynna V contar-uol-o-ei; agynna RL agyn[h]a 2.4] V mi-o-á RL mi o á 3.1] M Entre; Mynn' V(373) Min' RL Min[h]' 3.2] M [rico] 3.4] V en a 4.3] M V(267) e que pera o altar RL que pera o seu altar lhe 5.4] V(373), RL guissado 6.1] RL nau 6.2] V(373), RL en essa 7.2] V(267) qued' aquela 8.1] V(373) Leuáron-s' as; ferament RL Leváron-s' as; ferament[e] 8.3] M, V(267) que logo 8.4] V(373) chorou cada un enton ý se pecado RL chorou cada un enton y se[u] pecado 9.1] V(267) E o marcador en o; (373) O mercador en o RL O mercador 9.3] M2 ua 9.4] M [no] peit' 10.1] RL nau 10.3] V(267) mail-o; (373), RL mais o 10.4] V(373), RL morresse alí 11.2] V(373), RL nenbró-sse 11.3] V en o 11.4] V(373) nosco a Deus RL nosco, Deus 12.4] V(373), RL min 13.2] V(267) alguun; (373) algun 13.3] M se mi ora V(373), RL se m' ora 14.2] V(267) este é 14.3] M mas 14.4] V(373), RL ando tormentado 15.2] V(373), RL demo e 16.4] V(267) ll'-o 17.1] V(373) leuó-o RL levô-o 17.3] V(267) virgijndade 17.4] V(373), RL croçifigado 18.2] V(373), RL foss' en aquela çibdade 18.3] V(373), RL piedade 19.1] V(373), RL naue chegaron 19.3] V pertornaron 20.4] V Ei-uol-o

19 1 E tanto que os da nav' ali chegaron
2 poi-lo viron todos se maravillaron
3 e os seus enton mui ledos per tornaron
4 e contou lles el quant' avia passado.
R *Na que Deus pres carne e foi dela nado …*

And as soon as the people on the boat arrived at port, when they saw him they were all amazed, and his men were then most exceedingly joyful, and he told them what had happened to him.

20 1 E o mercador pois se tornou de França
2 e foi en sa terra sen longa tardança
3 a Rocamador se foi e confiança
4 na Virgen sempr' ouv'. Ei-vo-lo acabado.
R *Na que Deus pres carne e foi dela nado …*

And when the merchant returned from France and went back to his country, with little delay he set off to Rocamadour, and ever put his faith in the Virgin Mary. And so my tale ends.

Manuscript variants

R.1] E267 Na de que, *the* de *is a later superscript addition*; Na que (1–19R); carné foi; da nado (4R) E373 carne e (*and* 3R, 9–10R, 12–17R, 19–20R) R.2] F periguado E373 perigõado (18R) 1.1] E373 destruida 1.4] E373 pois un seu, *the* un *is a later superscript addition* 2.1] F Reynna E267 Reỹna E373 rayña 2.2] F, E373 meezynna 2.3] F agynna E267 agỹna E363 agyna 3.1] E267 Entre E373 doir emin 3.2] E267 mercador muito 4.2] F se dona 4.3] F que pera o altar E267 & q*ue* pera o altar 5.4] E373 guissado 6.1] F nauuoue 6.2] E373 e*n* essa 7.1] F Mas 7.2] F que daq*u*ela E267 q*ue* daq*u*ela 7.3] F lauа*n*tou 8.1] E373 Leuaron; ferament 8.3] E267 q*ue* logo 8.4] F cuidou E373 chorou cada un enton y se pecado 9.1] E373 O mercador 9.4] E267 deu peit 10.3] E373 mais o 10.4] E373 morresse ali afogado 11.2] F nembrou E373 nenbro 11.4] F, E373 nosco a 12.1] F be*n* miude 12.4] F nembra E373 mi*n* 13.2] F, E373 algun 13.3] E267 mi ora 14.1] E Nenbra 14.2] E267 este e 14.3] E267 mas 14.4] E373 ando torme*n*tado 15.2] E373 demo e 16.3] E373 ell algun 17.1] E373 leuo o 17.3] E373 uirgijdade 17.4] F crocifigado 18.2] F fosse aquela E373 foss en aquela cibdade 18.3] F, E373 piedade 19.1] E373 naue chegaron 19.2] F pois o

Rubric

Como Santa Maria livrou un mercador do perigoo do mar en que andava u caera da nave.

E das ondas do; que cuidava; dũa E **Ind** das ondas do; que cuidava morrer; *final two words,* da nave, *missing*

Captions (F)

missing

32. *The Huntsman whose Skull was Crushed by a Bell*

R *Quen a Virgen por sennor*
tever, de todo mal guarrá.

Whoever owns the Virgin as his lady, will recover from all ill.

1 Ond' un miragre que fez
vos direi saboroso
en Prad' a Sennor de prez
en un logar viçoso u á
R *Quen a Virgen por sennor …*

Of which I will tell you of a choice miracle which our worthy Lady performed in Prado, in a pleasant spot where there stands

2 ũa sa eigrej' ali
mui fremosa capela
en que fez, com' aprendi,
esta que nos caudela e dá
R *Quen a Virgen por sennor …*

a church of hers, a most fair chapel, in which, as I heard, the wonder was wrought by the Lady who protects us and gives

3 saude e salvaçon,
que deu a un monteiro
que na sa eigreja enton
entrou mui deanteiro alá
R *Quen a Virgen por sennor …*

health and salvation, as she gave to a huntsman, who on that occasion came rashly into her church

4 u viu os sinos estar
e foi que os tangesse
mais un deles se britar
foi e caeu sobr' esse. "Ahá"
R *Quen a Virgen por sennor …*

and saw the bells and went to ring them; but one of them broke free and fell on him. "O ho"

5 disseron todos, "par Deus
mort' é sen nulla falla
por end' a que val os seus
mester á que lle valla ja
R *Quen a Virgen por sennor …*

said all that saw it, "by Our Lord, he is surely a dead man; he needs help now from Our Lady who rescues her own,

Cantiga 276 (F 80, E 276)

Linguistic note

7.2] 'pera fole': a ripe pear hollowed out by insects (Parkinson 1992).

Metrics

7	8	|	7	6'	7	8 [=6' 1]
A	B	|	c	d	c	b [d b]

For correct scansion of the composite line 4 (8 [6' 1]), elision is required in strophes 1 ('viçoso‿u'), 2 ('caudela‿e'), 3 ('deanteiro‿alá'), 4 ('esse‿Ahá'), 7 ('mole‿alá'), 8 ('e‿a'), 11 ('fremosa‿e'), and 12 ('loada‿e').

1.1] =Onde‿un 1.3] =Prado‿a 1.4] 2.1] =eigreja‿ali 2.3] =como‿aprendi 3.1] sa·u·de 3.3] *necessary elision* eigreja‿enton 3.4] de·an·tei·ro 4.4] =ca·eu sobre‿esse 5.2] =morto‿e 6.1] =ferido‿e 6.4] =pode‿andar 7.1] =mole‿a 8.1] =ante‿o 8.2] va·a·mos 8.4] =como‿en verdade‿achamos 9.1] =ante‿essa 9.3] =ante‿a 10.1] =se‿ergesse 10.4] =muito‿enteiros 11.1] lo·ou 12.1] mer·ce·e 12.2] grã·a·da 12.4] lo·a·da; *note deliberate hypermetry, a metrical 'ritardando'* (see Parkinson 2010b).

6 ca de guisa ferid' é
que non á osso são
na cabeça, a la fe,
nen pod' andar per chão ca
R *Quen a Virgen por sennor …*

for he is so badly hurt that there is not a sound bone in his whole skull; he will never get up from this, as

7 mais mol' a cabeça ten
ca non é pera fole
nen manteiga e por en
pois que a ten tan mole alá
R *Quen a Virgen por sennor …*

his head is like a wasp-blown pear, it's soft as butter; so if that's the way it is,

8 ant' o seu altar põer
da Virgen o vaamos."
E foron assi fazer
com' en verdad' achamos e a
R *Quen a Virgen por sennor …*

let's go and lay him at the Virgin's altar." And they did, so the story runs, and that

9 noite ant' essa sennor
jouve tal come morto
mais ant' a luz gran sabor
lle deu a que conforto dá
R *Quen a Virgen por sennor …*

night he lay before her, seemingly dead; but before daybreak she who comforts her own gave him the will

10 que s' ergesse pera ir
con os outros monteiros
e tan toste foi sentir
os ossos muit' enteiros da
R *Quen a Virgen por sennor …*

to get up and go along with the other huntsmen; and at that moment he found all the bones of his skull

11 testa, e por en loou
muito a Groriosa
porque en ele mostrou
sa vertude fremosa e sa
R *Quen a Virgen por sennor …*

mended. And so he gave hearty praise to the Glorious Virgin, who had shown her marvellous power in him, and

12 mercee que nunca fal
de que é mui grãada
por en de todos sen al
sempre é mui loada e será.
R *Quen a Virgen por sennor …*

the boundless goodness with which she is so richly endowed; for which reason she is highly praised, and ever will be.

Editorial variants

2.3] M fez', com 3.3] M eigreja 'nton 5.3] M2 òs 6.4] M por 8.4] V uerdat 9.1] M Noit[e] ant' V Noit' ant' 9.3] M2 mai M1, V mais 12.2] V granada

Manuscript variants

3.3] F Eigreia*n*ton E eigreianto*n* 4.3] F ũu 7.1] F Mas 8.4] E u*e*rdat 9.1] F, E noit, *hypermetric line without reversal of false elision of* noite 9.3] F mas

Rubric

Como Santa Maria do Prado, que é cabo Segovia, guariu un monteiro del rei dũa campãa que lle caeu de suso.

E *missing* E **Ind** Prado cabo Segobia; dun badalo da campãa que lle dera na cabeça

Captions (F)

missing

33. *King Alfonso is Healed by the Virgin's Book*

R *Muito faz grand' erro e en torto jaz,*
a Deus quen lle nega o ben que lle faz.

1 Mas en este torto per ren non jarei
que non cont' o ben que del recebud' ei
per sa madre virgen a que sempr' amei,
e de a loar mais doutra ren me praz.
R *Muito faz grand' erro e en torto jaz ...*

2 E como non devo aver gran sabor
en loar os feitos daquesta Sennor
que me val nas coitas e tolle door
e faz m' outras mercees muitas assaz?
R *Muito faz grand' erro e en torto jaz ...*

3 Por en vos direi o que passou per mi,
jazend' en Bitoira enfermo assi
que todos cuidavan que morress' ali
e non atendian de mi bon solaz.
R *Muito faz grand' erro e en torto jaz ...*

4 Ca ũa door me fillou atal
que eu ben cuidava que era mortal,
e braadava: "Santa Maria, val,
e por ta vertud' aqueste mal desfaz."
R *Muito faz grand' erro e en torto jaz ...*

5 E os fisicos mandavan me põer
panos caentes, mas non o quix fazer
mas mandei o livro dela aduzer
e poseron mio, e logo jouv' en paz
R *Muito faz grand' erro e en torto jaz ...*

6 que non braadei nen senti nulla ren
da door, mas senti me logo mui ben
e dei ende graças a ela por en,
ca tenno ben que de meu mal lle despraz.
R *Muito faz grand' erro e en torto jaz ...*

7 Quand' esto foi, muitos eran no logar
que mostravan que avian gran pesar
de mia door e fillavan s' a chorar,
estand' ante mi todos come en az.
R *Muito faz grand' erro e en torto jaz ...*

8 E pois viron a mercee que me fez
esta Virgen santa, Sennor de gran prez
loaron a muito todos dessa vez
cada ũu põend' en terra sa faz.
R *Muito faz grand' erro e en torto jaz ...*

Cantiga 209 (F 95, E 209)

Note

The identification of the miraculous book as a manuscript of the *CSM* is found only in the rubric of E and the caption of panel 3 of the F miniature. It is unlikely that any of the extant codices, except perhaps To or its exemplar, was complete at the time of Alfonso's illness (1276/7).

Metrics

The refrain shows a consistent accent on the 5th syllable, which could be interpreted as regular division of the line into two hemistichs: 11 [= 5'+5]. This pattern is found in less than half the lines of the strophes.

11	11	|	11	11	11	11
A	A	|	b	b	b	a

R.1] =grande‿erro *and subsequent refrains* 1.2] =conto‿o; recebudo‿ei 1.3] =sempre‿amei 2.1] *alt.* devo‿a‿aver 2.3] do·or 2.4] =me‿outras mer·ce·es 3.2] =jazendo‿en Bi·toi·ra 3.3] =morresse‿ali 4.1] *hypometric, resolved either by dieresis* fi·llo·u *or by paragogic extension of* door = do·o·re 4.3] bra·a·da·va 4.4] =vertude‿aqueste 5.4] =jouve‿en; mio (*single syllable)* 6.1] bra·a·dei 6.2] do·or 7.1] =Quando‿esto 7.3] =se‿a; mia (*single syllable*) do·or 7.4] =estando‿ante 8.1] mer·ce·e 8.4] =põendo‿en

Editorial variants

4.1] M fillou [y] atal V fillou atal 5.4] V et poséron-mi-o 8.3] M loárona V loáron-a 8.4] V uun; M põendo 8.R] M Mu[i]to

Great is the error, and great is the wrong,
of whoever denies the good things God does for him.

[1] But this is an error I will not fall into, for I cannot number the good things he has done for me, by his mother the Blessed Virgin, who I have always loved, and who I love to praise above all other joys.

[2] And how could I not take great pleasure in praising the great deeds of that Lady who succours me in my sorrows and takes away my pain and gives me so many other blessings.

[3] And so I will tell you what happened to me, as I lay in Vitoria in such great affliction, that everyone thought I was going to die there, and none expected comfort for me.

[4] For I was seized by such a pain that I truly thought it was fatal, and I cried out: "O Holy Mary, help me and by thy great power remove this illness."

[5] And the doctors called for warm cloths to be placed on me, but I would not have it, but called for her book to be brought, and they laid it on me, and at once I was at peace

[6] and I did not cry out nor did I feel any pain, but at once I felt very well, and I gave thanks to her therefore, for I am sure that she is not pleased that I should be ill.

[7] When this happened, there were many around me who were showing how much my illness grieved them, and were weeping, as they lined up in front of me.

[8] And when they saw the grace that was given me by this holy Virgin, our most worthy Lady, they all gave thanks to her at that time, each one kneeling and bending their head.

Manuscript variants

1.R] F uito; torto (1R): *the underlaid first line of this refrain, at the foot of the first column, is missing the initial* M *and the final word* jaz; *the refrain is repeated in full in running text at the top of the second column* E Muto (8R) 1.1] E Mas e ẽste: *the first two words,* Mas e, *are probably overwritten in slightly larger letters; thus, the macron that should be over the first* e *has been displaced to the right, almost over the first* e *of* este 3.3] F morres 8.4] F poendo E põendo

Rubric

Como el rei don Afonso de Castela adoeceu en Bitoria e ouv' ũa door tan grande que coidaron que morresse ende e poseron lle de suso o livro das Cantigas de Santa Maria e foi guarido.

F *missing* E Castella; posseron E **Ind** Castella; Bitouria; morressende; foi logo guarido

Captions (F)

1. Como al rei don Afonso fillou un door atal que todos cuidaron que morresse. 2. Como os fisicos lli querian põer panos caentes e el non quis. 3. Como el rei mandou que lli trouxessen o libro das cantigas que el fez de Santa Maria. 4. Como abriron o libro de Santa Maria e llo poseron sobelo door. 5. Como el rei foi logo são e non sintiu ningun door e loou Santa Maria. 6. Como el rei e todolos outros que i estavan loaron muito Santa Maria poend' en terra sas fazes.

1] morres

34. *King Alfonso is Healed*

R 1 *Santa Maria, valed', ai Sennor*
2 *e acorred' a vosso trobador*
3 *que mal lle vai.*

1 1 A tan gran mal e a tan gran door
2 *Santa Maria, valed', ai Sennor*
3 como sofr' este vosso loador
4 *Santa Maria, valed', ai Sennor*
5 e sã' é ja, se vos en prazer for
6 do que diz "ai".
R *Santa Maria, valed', ai Sennor …*

2 1 Pois vos Deus fez doutra cousa mellor
2 *Santa Maria, valed', ai Sennor*
3 e vos deu por nossa rezõador
4 *Santa Maria, valed', ai Sennor*
5 seede mi ora bõ' ajudador
6 en est' ensai
R *Santa Maria, valed', ai Sennor …*

3 1 que me faz a mort', ond' ei gran pavor
2 *Santa Maria, valed', ai Sennor*
3 e o mal que me ten tod' en redor,
4 *Santa Maria, valed', ai Sennor*
5 que me fez mais verde mia coor
6 que dun cambrai.
R *Santa Maria, valed', ai Sennor …*

4 1 Que fez enton a galardõador
2 *Santa Maria, valed', ai Sennor*
3 de todo ben e do mal sãador?
4 *Santa Maria, valed', ai Sennor*
5 Tolleu ll' a fever e aquel umor
6 mao e lai.
R *Santa Maria, valed', ai Sennor …*

Cantiga 279 (**To** App 10, **E** 279)

Note

Both manuscript witnesses and all editions omit the repetition of R.1 in lines 2 and 4 of strophes 2, 3, and 4. All previous textual editions reproduce the inconsistency of the manuscripts. This edition assumes that the copyists did not appreciate that the pattern in stophe 1 was to be replicated in strophes 2–3. The only alternative is to assume that the interpolations in strophe 1 are a kind of false refrain (Parkinson 1987).

Metrics

10	10	4	|	10	10	10	10	10	4
A	A	B	|	a	A	a	A	a	b

R.1] =valede‿ai *and subsequent refrains* R.2] =acorrede‿a 1.1] do·or 1.2] =sofre‿este 1.3] =são‿é 2.3] =bõa‿ajudador; se·e·de 2.4] =este‿ensai 3.1] =morte‿onde‿ei 3.2] =todo‿en 3.3] co·or 4.2] sã·a·dor 4.3] =lle‿a 4.4] ma·o

Editorial variants

R.3] **M** mal le **V** ma-lle 1.5] **V** et são iá 2.5] **V** bõa 'iudador 3.3] **M1** enredor

Manuscript variants

R.3] **To**, **E** malle 2.5] **E** boa iudador 3.5] **To** fezo 4.1] **To** ue, *missing decorated initial*

Rubric

Como el rei pediu mercee a Santa Maria que o guarecesse dũa grand' enfermidade que avia, e ela como sennor piadosa oiu lle seu rogo e deu lle saude.

E pidiu; enfmidade; sennor poderosa guarecé o **E Ind** e ela guarecé o

O Holy Mary, my Lady, come to my aid;
help your troubadour,
for he is in sore distress.

[1] In this great trouble and pain
O Holy Mary, my Lady, come to my aid
that afflicts the singer of your praises
O Holy Mary, my Lady, come to my aid
and if you will, he can be cured of the ill
that makes him cry aloud.
O Holy Mary, my Lady, come to my aid …

[2] Since God made you finer than all others
O Holy Mary, my Lady, come to my aid
and gave you to be our advocate
O Holy Mary, my Lady, come to my aid
now be my strong support
in this trial
O Holy Mary, my Lady, come to my aid …

[3] this trial of death, that I so greatly fear
O Holy Mary, my Lady, come to my aid
and of the evil that is all around me
O Holy Mary, my Lady, come to my aid
which leaves me as green
as Cambrai cloth.
O Holy Mary, my Lady, come to my aid …

[4] What then did she do, she who rewards
O Holy Mary, my Lady, come to my aid
all good and heals all ill?
O Holy Mary, my Lady, come to my aid
She took away his fever and that
evil sickness.
O Holy Mary, my Lady, come to my aid …

35. *The Priest who Scorned the Virgin*

R 1 *Quen vai contra Santa Maria*
2 *con sobervia, faz mal a si.*

1 1 Ca sobervia non dev' aver
2 ome contra a que vencer
3 foi ao demo per saber
4 ser omildosa e fazer
5 per que Deus quis dela nacer,
6 ca doutra guisa non querria
7 ser Deus ome, nen si nen si.
R *Quen vai contra Santa Maria ...*

2 1 E por esto vos contarei
2 un gran miragre que achei
3 que fez a madre do gran Rei
4 en Terena, e mui ben sei
5 que outros i, com' apres' ei,
6 fez muitos e faz cada dia
7 aos que os van buscar i.
R *Quen vai contra Santa Maria ...*

3 1 Mui pret' un crerigo morar
2 fora daquel santo logar
3 desta Groriosa sen par,
4 e un dia quis preegar
5 en sa eigreja e mostrar
6 aas gentes que "Gran folia
7 será" diss' el "creed' a mi,
R *Quen vai contra Santa Maria ...*

4 1 de quantos vos fordes partir
2 de vossas eigrejas e ir
3 a Terena por i servir
4 nen dar do voss' e oferir
5 e juro vos eu sen mentir
6 que por est' escomungaria
7 quantos alá fossen daqui.
R *Quen vai contra Santa Maria ...*

Whoever is so proud as to oppose Our Lady,
does harm to himself.

[1] For no man's pride should set them against the Lady who defeated the Devil by being able to be humble and behave so that God wished to be born of her, for had it not been so, God would not have wished to become man, in any way.

[2] And so I will tell you a great miracle that I discovered, which the mother of the high King performed in Terena, and I know well that she performed many there, and still does so every day, to those who come there to seek her.

[3] A priest lived close by the holy place dedicated to the matchless Virgin, and one day he thought to give his sermon in his church, and explain to the people that "It will be great folly," he said "believe you me,

[4] for any of you to abandon your churches and go off to Terena to worship or to give of your goods as an offering. And I truly swear to you that for this reason I would excommunicate everyone who went there from here.

5 E se per ventura aven
que en esta festa que ven
d' Agosto per vosso mal sen
fordes i per nen ũa ren,
escomungar-vos-ei por en."
E u esto dizer queria,
torceu xe ll' a boca, assi
R *Quen vai contra Santa Maria …*

6 que nulla cousa non falou
nen a missa non ar cantou,
e de guisa torto ficou
que pe nen mão non mudou
per poder da que despreçou
por aquelo que dit' avia.
E foi tolleito log' ali
R *Quen vai contra Santa Maria …*

7 que u quis descomungaçon
dizer, non disse si nen non,
nen ar pode mostrar razon,
mais braadou come cabron.
Enton todos de coraçon
loaron muit' a que nos guia
e temeron a mais des i.
R *Quen vai contra Santa Maria …*

8 Mas quando se atal sentiu
que tolleit' era e se viu
tan maltreito, ben se partiu
daquel err' e se repentiu,
assi que logo ben guariu
e fez assi que todavia
deu i do seu, com' aprendi.
R *Quen vai contra Santa Maria …*

Cantiga 283 (F 8, E 283)

Note

1.7] 'nen si nen si': emphatic negative. Attested in the secular lyric [courtesy of Manuel Ferreiro]:
'verdad' é que dar / non lhi poden esta nen si nen si.'
Gil Perez Conde, 'Tantas minguas achan a Don Foan' (B1517) l. 18.

Metrics

8'	8	|	8	8	8	8	8	8'	8
A	B	|	c	c	c	c	c	a	b

The repetition of the same rhyme in five successive short lines is a case of 'insistent rhyme' (Parkinson 1999: 28–29). For another example see *cantiga* 192 (anthology 23).

R.2] so·ber·via 1.1] =deve‿aver *or* deve‿a‿aver 1.3] a·o 2.5] =como‿apreso‿ei 2.7] =a·os 3.1] =preto‿un 3.3] Gro·ri·o·sa 3.4] pre·e·gar 3.6] a·as 3.7] =disse‿el cre·ede‿a 4.4] =vosso‿e 4.5] =esto‿escomungaria 5.3] =de‿Agosto 5.7] =lle‿a 6.6] =dito‿avia 6.7] =logo‿ali 7.1] des·co·mun·ga·çon 7.4] bra·a·dou 7.6] =muito‿a 8.2] =tolleito‿era 8.4] =erro‿e 8.7] =como‿aprendi

[5] And if by any chance, on the feast day which is to come in August, you should be unwise enough to go there for any reason, I will excommunicate you for it." And as he went to say this, his mouth was twisted, so that

[6] he could not utter a word, nor could he sing mass, and thus he was struck down and could not move hand nor foot, by the power of the Lady whom he insulted by what he had said. And he was so quickly paralysed

[7] that as he tried to say "excommunicate" he could not say yes or no, nor even form a sentence, but just bleated like a goat. And so everyone heartily praised the Lady who guides us, and feared her all the more for it.

[8] But when the priest realised that he was paralysed and saw himself in such a poor state, he truly repented of the mistake he had made, and so was immediately restored, and he even gave of his own goods to Terena, as I heard in the tale.

Editorial variants
3.1] **M1** ũu **V** uun 3.4] **M** p[r]eegar **M1** ũu **V** et uun; peegar 5.6] **M1** u el esto 6.2] **M** nena **V** nen a 7.7] **M** temérona **V** et teméron-a 8.1] **M** ss[e] atal **V** ss'atal

Manuscript variants
R.1] E Que uai (6R) 1.1] F a soberuia 3.1] E uũ cl*er*igo 3.4] E uũ; peegar 5.1] E Et se 5.4] E ne hũa 5.6] E u el esto 8.1] F, E ssatal

Rubrics
F Como un crerigo que defendia aas gentes que non fossen a Santa Maria de Terena fazer oraçon se tolleu do corpo e da fala e tanto que se repentiu foi guarido.

E Como Santa Maria de Terena sãou un clerigo da boca que se lle torcera mui feramente.

E se lle mui

Captions (F)
missing

36. *The Dying Friar who was Tormented by the Devil*

R *Quen ben fiar na Virgen | de todo coraçon*
guarda-lo-á do demo | e de sa tentaçon.

1 E daquest' un miragre | mui fremoso direi
que fez Santa Maria | per com' escrit' achei
en un livr' e d' ontr' outros | traladar o mandei
e un cantar en fige | segund' esta razon.
R *Quen ben fiar na Virgen | de todo coraçon …*

2 Un frade foi doente | dun mõesteiro mal
e todos ben cuidavan | que mort' era sen al
e se non foss' a Virgen | reĩa esperital
a sa alma levara | o dem' a perdiçon.
R *Quen ben fiar na Virgen | de todo coraçon …*

3 Ca ante que morresse | un sinal lle mostrou
que contra ũa porta | mui de rijo catou,
mas un frad' i estava | que o empreguntou
por que esto fazia | que llo dissess' enton.
R *Quen ben fiar na Virgen | de todo coraçon …*

4 E aquel frad' enfermo | enton non respondeu
mas muita de paravla | sobeja lle creceu
com' en desasperando | e todo se torceu
e aa cima disse | mui trist' e en mal son
R *Quen ben fiar na Virgen | de todo coraçon …*

5 que quantos bẽes feitos | avia, nulla ren
prestar non lle poderan, | e tal era seu sen,
e tan gran prol ll' avia | fazer mal come ben.
E quand' est' ouve dito, | disse ll' o compannon
R *Quen ben fiar na Virgen | de todo coraçon …*

6 que aquesto o demo | fazia, sen dultar,
que lle metia medo | polo desasperar
mas se ele quisesse | ũu vesso rezar
da Virgen groriosa, | log' o demo felon
R *Quen ben fiar na Virgen | de todo coraçon …*

7 se partiria dele. | E o frade rezou
o vesso muit' agĩa | que ll' o frad' ensinou
e atan tost' o demo | se foi e o leixou,
que o non viu pois nunca | e vedes por que non.
R *Quen ben fiar na Virgen | de todo coraçon …*

8 Porque en aquel vesso | aa Virgen assi
dezia: "Con ta graça, | Sennor, acorr' a mi,
ca tu de piadade | madr' es, por end' aqui
me guarda do diabo | chẽo de traiçon."
R *Quen ben fiar na Virgen | de todo coraçon …*

9 E quand' est' ouve dito, | começou de riir
e disso aos frades: | "Non veedes vĩir
a Virgen groriosa? | Con ela me quer' ir."
E logo ante todos | fezo sa confisson
R *Quen ben fiar na Virgen | de todo coraçon …*

10 e repentiu se muito | do que foi descreer
e comungou. E logo | começou a dizer
que o do leit' ergessen, | e mandou se põer
en terra, e a alma | foi dar a Deus en don.
R *Quen ben fiar na Virgen | de todo coraçon …*

Cantiga 284 (F 66, E 284)

Metrics

13 [6' 6]	13 [6' 6]	|	13 [6' 6]	13 [6' 6]	13 [6' 6]	13 [6' 6]
A	A	|	b	b	b	a

1.1] =daquesto‿un 1.2] =como‿escrito‿achei 1.3] =livro‿e de‿ontre‿outros 1.4] =segundo‿esta 2.2] =morto‿era 2.3] =fosse‿a; *necessary elision* re·ĩ·a‿esperital 2.4] =demo‿a 3.3] =frade‿i 3.4] =dissesse‿enton 4.1] =frade‿enfermo 4.3] =como‿en 4.4] =triste‿e; a·a 5.1] bẽ·es 5.3] =lle‿avia 5.4] =quando‿esto‿ouve; lle‿o 6.3] ũ·u 6.4] =logo‿o 7.2] =muito‿agĩa; lle‿o frade‿ensinou 7.3] =toste‿o 8.1] a·a 8.2] =acorre‿a 8.3] =pi·a·da·de madre‿es; ende‿aqui 8.4] chẽ·o; tra·i·çon 9.1] =quando‿esto‿ouve; ri·ir 9.2] a·os; ve·e·des vĩ·ir 9.3] =quero‿ir 10.1] des·cre·er 10.3] =leito‿ergessen

Editorial variants

R.2] V guardal-o-á 1.3] M ontr' 2.3] M Reynna 2.4] V a dem' 3.2] V rrijo 3.3 V que o en preguntou 4.4] M1 triste e en 5.4] V disse-lle 6.3] V uun 7.2] V agynna 7.4] V nunqua

Whoever truly trusts in the Virgin with all his heart,
she will protect from the Devil and his temptations.

[1] And on this theme I will tell a very fine miracle which Our Lady performed, which I found recorded in a book, and from among the others there I had it copied and turned it into a song, with these words.

[2] A monk in a monastery was gravely sick, and everyone thought that he was dead and gone, and had it not been for the Blessed Virgin, our heavenly queen, the Devil would have taken his soul to hell.

[3] For before he died, the Devil appeared to him and he looked fixedly at a door. But a monk was with him, and asked him to tell him then why he was doing that.

[4] The sick monk did not reply at once, but then came out with many wild words, as if in despair, and he writhed wildly and finally said, very sadly and in sorrowed tones

[5] that none of the good things he had done could aid him now, or so he saw it, and he might just as well have done wrong as good. And when he had said this, his companion told him

[6] that the Devil was making him say it, without doubt, and was frightening him to bring him to despair, but if he wished to say a prayer to the Glorious Virgin, then the wicked Devil

[7] would leave him. And the monk quickly said the prayer which the other monk taught him, and at once the Devil departed and left him, and was not seen again, and this is why.

[8] For in that prayer the monk said to the Virgin: "Come to my aid, my Lady, with your grace, for you are the mother of all mercy, and so protect me here from the Devil who is full of deceit."

[9] And when the monk had said this, he began to smile and said to the other monks: "Can you not see the Virgin coming to me? I will gladly go with her." And before them all he made his confession

[10] and showed deep repentance for having doubted, and took communion. And then he asked them to lift him from the bed, and had them lay him on the ground, and he gave up his soul as a gift to God.

Manuscript variants

1.3] F entr 2.3] F, E Reynna 2.4] E a dem 3.2] E rrijo 5.2] E podian 5.4] F, E disselle 6.3] F mais 7.4] E nu*n*q*ua* 8.2] E dizia

Rubric

Como Santa Maria livrou un monge do poder do demo que o tentava.

F *missing*

Captions (F)

missing

37. *The Fire at the Convent of Carrizo*

R 1 *Atan gran poder o fogo | non á per ren de queimar*
2 *como á Santa Maria, | quando quer, de o matar.*

1 1 Ca macar grand' elemento | foi Deus do fogo fazer
2 e de queimar toda cousa | lle foi dar tan gran poder,
3 maior o deu a sa madre, | de que ele quis nacer
4 e pois ena carne dela | foi os infernos britar.
R *Atan gran poder o fogo | non á per ren de queimar …*

2 1 Ond' un mui maravilloso | miragre vos contarei
2 que avẽo en Carriço | per com' en verdad' achei
3 un mõesteiro que éste | preto de Leon, e sei
4 que o fez Santa Maria | por sa vertude mostrar.
R *Atan gran poder o fogo | non á per ren de queimar …*

3 1 Aquel mõesteiro éste | desta ordin de Cistel
2 e á i ũa omagen | que ten seu fillo, mui bel
3 menĩo, ontre seus braços | e sé en ũu chapitel
4 fremos' e mui ben lavrado | posto sobelo altar.
R *Atan gran poder o fogo | non á per ren de queimar …*

4 1 As donas daquel convento | todas mui gran devoçon
2 an en aquesta omagen | e van i de coraçon
3 cada noit' e cada dia | e fazen grand' oraçon
4 e vẽen con sas candeas | por o log' alumear.
R *Atan gran poder o fogo | non á per ren de queimar …*

5 1 Onde foi ũa vegada | que palla deitaron i
2 muita na eigreja toda | e era mester assi
3 por gran frio que fazia | e ar deitaron log' i
4 estadaes encendudos | como soian deitar.
R *Atan gran poder o fogo | non á per ren de queimar …*

6 1 E un estadal daqueles | ũa monja encendeu
2 ontr' o altar e o coro | e o fogo s' aprendeu
3 del aa palla e logo | tan feramente correu
4 a chama del que s' ouvera | ao altar a chegar.
R *Atan gran poder o fogo | non á per ren de queimar …*

7 1 Mais a Virgen groriosa | non quis esto consentir
2 nen quis que aquele fogo | podesse adeant' ir
3 e por end' a sa omagen | fillou logo, sen mentir,
4 o veo da sa cabeça | e ant' o fogo lançar
R *Atan gran poder o fogo | non á per ren de queimar …*

Great as the power is of fire to consume, so is the power of Holy Mary to extinguish it, when she wishes.

[1] For though God created a powerful element in fire, and gave it great power to burn all things, greater power did he give to his mother, of whom he was born, for once he had taken flesh of her he broke the gates of hell.

[2] And so I will tell you a most wonderful miracle which befell in Carrizo, as I heard to be the truth, which is a monastery close to León, and I know well that Holy Mary performed it to display her great power.

[3] That monastery is of the Cistercian order, and in it there is a statue of her son, a fair child, in her arms, and it stands in a finely carved canopy placed above the altar.

[4] The nuns of that convent are all devoted to that statue, and gladly go there every night and every day, and pray at length and come with candles to light it up.

[5] In this way on one occasion when they spread a lot of hay throughout the church, which was necessary because of the very cold weather, they set out lit candles, as they always did.

[6] And a nun lit one of those candles between the altar and the choir, and the straw caught fire and the flames spread so fiercely that they would have reached the altar.

[7] But the Glorious Virgin would not allow this, nor would she permit the fire to spread any further, and so her statue, truth to tell, took the veil from off her head and cast it onto the fire.

8 1 o foi. E depois o fogo | sol non queimou nulla ren
2 ante foi tan toste morto | polo prazer da que ten
3 en poder os elementos | ca nen ũu non vai nen ven
4 se non quanto o seu fillo | quer en eles ordĩar
R *Atan gran poder o fogo | non á per ren de queimar …*

9 1 que ordĩou que o veo | delgado mais ca cendal
2 podess' amatar o fogo | e non sofrer que mais mal
3 fezesse do que fezera | por vertud' esperital
4 da Virgen, ond' a omagen | avia o semellar.
R *Atan gran poder o fogo | non á per ren de queimar …*

10 1 Entonce a sancreschãa | que dormia s' espertou
2 e para tanger os sinos | duas consigo levou
3 monjas e aa eigreja | foi e pois que dentr' entrou
4 viu tod' esto que ja dixe | e foi o logo contar
R *Atan gran poder o fogo | non á per ren de queimar …*

11 1 ao convent' u durmia, | e disse: "Por esto vin,
2 por vos mostrar gran miragre | que ora conteu a min
3 e sei que poi-lo oirdes, | diredes, par San Martin
4 que doutro maior daqueste | nunca oistes falar."
R *Atan gran poder o fogo | non á per ren de queimar …*

12 1 Log' enton a abadessa | que era bõa moller
2 foi ala e o convento | ar foi i mui volonter
3 e pois viron o miragre | disseron: "Muit' é mester
4 que dest' a Santa Maria | sabiamos loores dar."
R *Atan gran poder o fogo | non á per ren de queimar …*

13 1 Enton começaron todos | cantando a dar loor
2 aa Virgen groriosa | madre de Nostro Sennor
3 e pois deitaron s' a prezes | cab' o altar en redor
4 rezando per seus salteiros | quanto podian rezar.
R *Atan gran poder o fogo | non á per ren de queimar …*

Cantiga 332 (E 332)

Metrics

15 [7' 7]   15 [7' 7] | 15 [7' 7]   15 [7' 7]   15 [7' 7]   15 [7' 7]
A   A | b   b   b   a

1.1] =grande‿elemento 2.1] =Onde‿un 2.2] =como‿en verdade‿achei 2.3] sei (*single syllable*) 3.2] ũ·a 3.3] me·nĩ·o 3.4] =fremoso‿e 4.3] =noite‿e; grande‿oraçon 4.4] =logo‿alumear 5.1] ũ·a 5.3] =logo‿i 5.4] es·ta·da·es; so·i·an 6.1] ũ·a 6.2] =ontre‿o; se‿aprendeu 6.3] a·a 6.4] =se‿ouvera; a·o 7.2] =adeante‿ir 7.3] =ende‿a 7.4] =ante‿o 8.3] ũu (*single syllable*) 8.4] or·dĩ·ar 9.1] or·dĩ·ou 9.2] =podesse‿amatar 9.3] =vertude‿esperital 9.4] =onde‿a 10.1] =se‿espertou 10.3] =dentro‿entrou; a·a 10.4] =todo‿esto 11.1] =convento‿u; a·o 11.3] sei (*single syllable*); o·ir·des 11.4] o·is·tes 12.1] =Logo‿enton 12.3] =Muito‿é 12.4] =desto‿a; sa·bia·mos lo·o·res 13.2] a·a 13.3] =se‿a; cabo‿o

Editorial variants

1.4] V en a 1.R] M [A]tan V Atan 2.1] M maravil[loso] V marauil 3.3] V menynno; uun 8.3] V uun 8.4] V ordynar 9.1] V ordynou; uẽo 10.3] V et pera 11.3] V poil-o 12.4] M1 sábiamos V sabiámos

[8] After this the fire did not consume anything but was quickly put out at the behest of the Lady who holds sway over the elements, for nothing comes nor goes save that her son ordains it,

[9] and he ordained that her veil, finer than lace, could extinguish fire and stop it from doing more harm than it had done, by the great power of the Virgin, whose likeness that statue was.

[10] And so the sacristan who was asleep, awoke and took two other nuns with her to ring the bells and went to the church. And when she went in, she beheld all that I have told, and went to recount it

[11] to the rest of the sleeping convent, saying: "I have come here to show you a great miracle, which has just come about in my presence, and I know that once you have heard it, by St Martin, you will say that you have never heard speak of any greater than this."

[12] Then the abbess, who was a good woman, went to the church, and the convent also went very willingly, and when they beheld the miracle they said: "It is truly right that we should give thanks for it to Holy Mary."

[13] And so they all began to sing the praise of the Glorious Virgin, mother of Our Lord, and then they knelt in prayer around the altar, singing all the psalms of the psalter.

Manuscript variants

1.R] tan gran 2.1] E marauil 9.1] E uẽo 10.2] E pera

Rubric

Como en ũu mõesteiro en reino de Leon levantou se fogo de noite e matou o a omage de Santa Maria con o veo que tĩina na cabeça.

E levatou **E Ind** moesteiro; omagem; tiina

38. *The Woman who was Healed of a Swollen Arm*

R *Com' a grand' enfermidade | en sãar muito demora*
assi quen guarec' a Virgen | é guarid' en pouca d' ora.

1 Onde desta razon grande | miragre contar vos quero
que fezo Santa Maria | a madre do gran Deus vero
que no dia do joizo | verrá mui brav' e mui fero
e juigará o mundo | tod' en mui pequena ora.
R *Com' a grand' enfermidade | en sãar muito demora …*

2 En Estremoz, ũa vila | de Portugal, foi aquisto
que guariu ũa enferma | a madr' onde Jesucristo
naceu por salvar o mundo | que foi connosçud' e visto
ond' o sol, quand' el pres morte, | tornou mais negro ca mora.
R *Com' a grand' enfermidade | en sãar muito demora …*

3 Aquesta moller manceba | era e grand' e fremosa
mais ũa enfermidade | ouve mui perigoosa
ca o braço ll' inchou tanto | de que foi temerosa
de o perder e o corpo. | Mais a inchaçon foi fora
R *Com' a grand' enfermidade | en sãar muito demora …*

4 e en mui pequeno tempo | foi o braço tan inchado
que mais seer non podia | e vermell' e ampolado
muit' e de maa maneira | e sol carne nen pescado
non comia, nen al nada. | Mais aquela que sempr' ora
R *Com' a grand' enfermidade | en sãar muito demora …*

5 a Deus, s' amercẽou dela | ca pois foi ena eigreja
sua a que a levaron | log' a que bẽeita seja
a guariu ben daquela | enfermidade sobeja
por mostrar a sa vertude | que muito toste lavora.
R *Com' a grand' enfermidade | en sãar muito demora …*

6 Quand' esto viron as gentes | deron loores grãadas
aa Virgen groriosa | a que sempre sejan dadas
que as portas do iferno | ten por noss' amor sarradas
e o dem' avezimao | eno avisso ancora.
R *Com' a grand' enfermidade | en sãar muito demora …*

Cantiga 346 (E 346)

Metrics

15' [7' 7']	15' [7' 7']	|	15' [7' 7']	15' [7' 7']	15' [7' 7']	15' [7' 7']
A	A	|	b	b	b	a

R.1] =Como‿a grande‿enfermidade R.2] =guarece‿a; guarida‿en; de‿ora 1.3] =bravo‿e; jo·i·zo 1.4] =todo‿en; ju·i·ga·ra 2.2] =madre‿onde; gua·riu 2.3] =connosçudo‿e 2.4] =onde‿o; quando‿el 3.1] =grande‿e 3.2] pe·ri·go·o·sa 3.3] =lle‿inchou; *hypometric line, necessary dieresis*: fo·i 4.2] =vermello‿e; se·er; po·di·a 4.3] =muito‿e; ma·a 4.4] =sempre‿ora; co·mi·a 5.1] =se‿amercẽou 5.2] =logo‿a; bẽ·ei·ta 5.3] *hypometric line, necessary dieresis*: gua·ri·u 5.4] *hypometric line in MS* 6.1] =Quando‿esto; lo·o·res grã·a·das 5.2] a·a 6.3] =nosso‿amor 6.4] =demo‿avezimao

Just as great illnesses take a long time to heal,
so whoever the Virgin heals is restored in little time.

[1] So on this theme I will tell you a great miracle which was performed by Holy Mary, the mother of the great true God, who will come in wrath and power on the Day of Judgement, and will quickly judge the whole world.

[2] This miracle took place in Estremoz, a town in Portugal, where a sick woman was healed by the mother in whom Jesus Christ was born to save the world, and when he died, it was witnessed and observed, the sun turned black as a sloe.

[3] That woman was a strong and beautiful young woman, but suffered from a very grave illness, for her arm swelled up so much that she feared to lose it and her whole body. But the swelling increased

[4] and very soon her arm was swollen as large as could be, and was red and covered with foul blisters, and she could not eat anything, neither fish nor meat. But the Lady who always prays

[5] to Our Lord took pity on her; and when the woman arrived at the church of the Virgin, where her friends had carried her, she whose name is blessed at once healed her of that monstrous illness, to display her power which works so speedily.

[6] When people saw this, they gave hearty thanks to the Glorious Virgin, who is always worthy of praise, and who for love of us has closed the gates of hell and bound the evil Devil in the pit.

Editorial variants

R.2] M2 guareç M1, V guarez' 3.3] M foi [mui] temerosa V foi temerosa 5.1] V en a 5.4] M mui toste 6.1] V granadas 6.3] M inferno 6.4] V en o

Manuscript variants

R.2] E guarez 1.4] E iuygaria, *the* y *is a later alteration to the original* i 3.3] E foi temerosa 5.3] E guariu ben 5.4] E mui toste, *a reduction of* muito toste *creating a hypometric line* 6.3] E jnferno

Rubric

Como Santa Maria guariu ũa moller d' Estremoz do braço e da garganta que ll' inchara.

39. *The King’s Ferret*

R 1 *Eno pouco e eno muito | en todo lles faz mercee*
2 *aos seus servos a Virgen | madre do que todo vee.*

1 1 Desto direi un miragre | grande que fez a reĩa,
2 madre de Deus Jesucristo | a un rei que muito tĩa
3 en ela sa asperança | ca lle fez veer agĩa
4 pesar e prazer mui grande | dũa ren por sa mercee.
R *Eno pouco e no muito | en todo lles faz mercee …*

2 1 Este pesar foi por ũa | bestiola que muit’ amava
2 el rei, que sigo tragia | e a que mui ben criava
3 a que chaman donezĩa | os galegos, e tirava
4 con ela aves das covas | e de taes ome vee.
R *Eno pouco e no muito | en todo lles faz mercee …*

3 1 Pero esta outras cousas | muitas e bõas fazia
2 trebellando e saltando | onde gran prazer avia
3 aquel rei, e por aquesto | atan gran ben lle queria
4 que tĩia que fezera | Deus en dar lla gran mercee.
R *Eno pouco e no muito | en todo lles faz mercee …*

4 1 E por esto lle fezera | de fust’, en que a guardava,
2 ũa arca mui ben feita | e dentro a enserrava
3 porque mal non recebesse, | ca muito se receava
4 do gato, que ena noite | mellor ca no dia vee.
R *Eno pouco e no muito | en todo lles faz mercee …*

5 1 Onde ll’ avẽo un dia | indo per ũa carreira
2 que a quis tirar da arca | e com’ ela é ligeira
3 caeu ontr’ os pes das bestas | e foi en atal maneira
4 que el rei con coita disse: | “Santa Maria, mercee!
R *Eno pouco e no muito | en todo lles faz mercee …*

6 1 Guarda me mia donezĩa | que a non perça per morte.”
2 E quantos ali estavan | ouveron gran desconorte
3 ca lle pose o cavalo | del rei o pe atan forte
4 sobr’ ela, e el rei disse: | “Ai, varões, quen a vee?
R *Eno pouco e no muito | en todo lles faz mercee …*

7 1 Dade mia qual quer que seja | sequer viva sequer morta
2 e conortar m’ ei con ela | come quen se mal conorta.”
3 Enton fez Santa Maria, | a que é dos ceos porta,
4 que de so o pe saisse | viva pola sa mercee.
R *Eno pouco e no muito | en todo lles faz mercee …*

The Virgin mother of all-seeing God grants favours to all her servants, both in great matters and small ones.

[1] Whereof I will tell you of a great miracle, which the heavenly queen, mother of our Lord Jesus Christ, performed for a king who put great trust in her, for she brought him great sorrow and gladness on one occasion by her favours.

[2] The sorrow was for a small creature which the king loved dearly and took everywhere with him and cared for with great love. It was a ferret, which the Galicians call "little lady", and the king set it to catching birds, hidden in their holes, or in plain view.

[3] But this ferret could do many other clever things, playing and jumping, which gave the king great pleasure so that he loved it so dearly that he thanked God for his favour in giving it to him.

[4] And for its sake he made a very strong box for it made of solid wood, to keep it in, and shut it inside to keep it from harm, for he was in great fear of cats, those beasts who can see better in the dark than in daylight.

[5] And it befell one day, that, as he travelled on the highway, he went to take the ferret out of its box; but as it was so light, it fell between the hooves of the horses, so that the king cried out in anguish: "Holy Mary, help me!

[6] Protect my little lady for me, lest it die and I lose it." All those who were there were greatly distressed for the king's horse was treading over it so heavily and the king cried out "Men, who can see it?

[7] Bring it back to me, be it alive or dead, and I will be comforted by it in my distress." Then Holy Mary, our gateway to heaven, by her mercy made the ferret come out unharmed from under the horse's hooves.

8 1 Enton quantos ali eran | e viron tal maravilla
2 que fezo a Groriosa, | que é de Deus madr' e filla,
3 en fazer que o cavalo | que con seu pe tan mal trilla
4 non a matasse. E esto | fez aquel que todo vee
R *Eno pouco e no muito | en todo lles faz mercee ...*

9 1 per prazer da Groriosa | sa madr', a que comendada
2 a ouv' el rei, u do pee | do cavalo foi trillada.
3 Por en seja el bẽeito | e ela seja loada
4 e sempr' ambos de nos ajan | piedade e mercee.
R *Eno pouco e no muito | en todo lles faz mercee ...*

Cantiga 354 (E 354)

Metrics

15' [7' 7'] 15' [7' 7'] | 15' [7' 7'] 15' [7' 7'] 15' [7' 7'] 15' [7' 7']
A A | b b b a

R.1] *necessary elision* e‿eno; mer·ce·e *and subsequent refrains and strophe endings* R.2] a·os; ve·e *and subsequent strophe endings* 1.1] re·ĩ·a 1.2] tĩ·a 1.3] ve·er a·gĩ·a 2.1] =muito‿amava; bes·tio·la 2.4] ta·es 3.4] tĩ·i·a 4.1] =fuste‿en 4.3] re·ce·a·va 4.4] di·a 5.1] =lle‿avẽo; ũ·a 5.2] =como‿ela 5.3] =ca·eu ontre‿os 6.1] mia (*single syllable*) 6.4] =sobre‿ela 7.1] mia (*single syllable*) 7.2] =me‿ei 7.3] ce·os 7.4] sa·i·sse 8.2] =madre‿e 9.1] =madre‿a 9.2] =ouve‿el; pe·e 9.3] bẽ·ei·to 9.4] =sempre‿ambos

Editorial variants

R.1] **V** En o 1.2] **M** ũu **V** a uun Rey que muito tijnna **A** 'uun' *treated as one syllable*; 'tii-nna' 2.3] **V** donezynna 3.4] **M2** tiia **M1** tĩia **V** tijnna 4.4] **V** en a 5.1] **M** ũu **V** uun 5.2] **V** arça 6.1] **V** donezynna 6.4] **V** ¿quén a uee? 7.1] **V** Dade-mi-a; se que uiua, se quer morta 8.4] **V** non a

Manuscript variants

R.1] E & no mujto 1.1] E Reynna 1.2] E ũu; tĩja 1.3] E agynna 5.1] E ũu

Rubric

Como Santa Maria guardou de morte ũa bestiola que chaman donezĩa.

[8] And all who were there witnessed this wonder performed by the Virgin, mother and daughter of God, through whom the ferret was not hurt by the horse whose hooves do such harm. And this miracle was ordained by our all-seeing Lord

[9] for the sake of the Glorious Virgin, his mother, to whom the king had entrusted his ferret, when it fell under the horse's hooves. And so let us bless Our Lord and praise Holy Mary, and may they both always have pity and mercy on us.

40. *Cantiga de loor*

R *Muito deveria*
ome sempr' a loar
a Santa Maria
e seu ben rezõar.

1 Ca ben deve razõada
seer a que Deus por madre
quis, e seend' el seu padre
e ela filla e criada
e onrada
e amada
a fez tanto que sen par
é preçada
e loada
e será quant' el durar.
R *Muito deveria …*

2 Outrossi loar devemos
a por que somos onrados
de Deus e ar perdõados
dos pecados que fazemos
ca têemos
que devemos
por aquesto lazerar
mas creemos
e sabemos
que nos pod' ela guardar.
R *Muito deveria …*

3 Razõa-la ben sen falla
devemos ca nos razõa
ben ante Deus e padrõa
é noss' e por nos traballa
e baralla
e contralla
o dem' e faz lo estar
que non valla
nemigalla
nen nos possa mal buscar.
R *Muito deveria ….*

4 E por esto lle demando
que lle non venna emente
do que diz a maa gente
porque sõo de seu bando
e que ando
a loando
e por ela vou trobar
e cuidando
e buscando
como a possa onrar
R *Muito deveria …*

5 mas que lles dé galardões
ben quaes eles merecen
porque me tan mal gradecen
meus cantares e meus sões
e razões
e tenções
que por ela vou fillar
ca felões
corações
me van por ende mostrar.
R *Muito deveria …*

6 E ar aja piadade
de como perdi meus dias
carreiras buscand' e vias
por dar aver e herdade
u verdad' e
lealdade
per ren nunca puid' achar
mais maldad' e
falsidade
con que me cuidan matar.
R *Muito deveria ….*

Cantiga 300 (E 300)

Metrics

5'	6	5'	6	|	7'	7'	7'	7'	3'	3'	7	3'	3'	7
A	B	A	B	|	c	d	d	c	c	c	b	c	c	b

R.2] =sempre‿a 1.2] se·er 1.3] =se·en·do‿el 1.4] *necessary elision* filla‿e 1.10] =quanto‿el 2.5] tê·e·mos 2.8] cre·e·mos 2.10] =pode‿ela 3.4] =nossa‿e 3.7] =demo‿e 4.3] ma·a 4.4] sõ·o 5.2] qua·es 6.3] =buscando‿e 6.5] =verdade e 6.7] =puide‿achar 6.8] =maldade‿e

Everyone should praise the Virgin and proclaim her goodness.

[1] For it should certainly be proclaimed that she is the one whom God chose as his mother, and as he was her father and she is daughter and handmaiden, he gave her such honour and love that she is matchless in worth and praise, and so she shall be until the world ends.

[2] We should also praise the Lady by whom we have honour from God and forgiveness for the sins we commit; for we believe that we should rightly suffer for them, but we believe and know that she can protect us.

[3] We should proclaim her truly, no doubt, for she takes our part before God, and she is our patron and strives for us and she fights and contests the Devil and through her he has no power at all over us, and cannot seek to harm us.

[4] And so I beseech her not to pay heed to what evil folk say, for I am of her company and I go about praising her and writing poetry for her, thinking and searching for ways of honouring her.

[5] And may she give them the rewards that they richly deserve, when they show so little gratitude for my songs and my melodies, and the refrains and arguments that I create for her, for what they show to me are evil hearts.

[6] And may she also be merciful of how I misspent my days seeking ways and means to give my wealth and my property to those in whom however much I tried I could not find truth and loyalty, but rather wickedness and falsehood, with which they seek my death.

Editorial variants
1.4] **A** fill' et **C** filla‿e *in underlaid version* 1.R] **V** Mvito *and subsequent refrains* 2.3] **M** [O]utrossi **V** Ovtrossí 2.2] **Mo** õrrados 2.5] **Mo** tẽmos 2.7] **V** lacerar 3.1] **V** Razõal-a **Fid** Razóala 4.1] **M** [de]mando **V** mando **C** demando 4.2] **Mo** vẽna ẽmente 4.3] **Mo** gẽte 4.4] **V** soon **Mo** bãdo 4.8] **Mo** cuidãdo 4.9] **Mo** buscãdo 5.3] **Mo** tã 5.8] **Mo** cafelões 5.10] **M** porende **Fid**, **C** por ende **Mo** por ẽde 6.3] **Mo** buscãd' 6.7] **Mo** nũca

Manuscript variants
2.1] E vtrossi, *missing decorated initial* 4.1] E lle mando

Rubric
De loor de Santa Maria.

41. *Epilogue (Petiçon)*

1 Macar poucos cantares | acabei e con son
Virgen, dos teus miragres, | peço ch' ora por don
que rogues a teu fillo | Deus que el me perdon
os pecados que fige | pero que muitos son
e do seu paraiso | non me diga de non
nen eno gran joizo | entre mig' en razon
nen que polos meus erros | se me mostre felon
e tu mia sennor, roga | ll' agora e enton
muit' aficadamente | por mi de coraçon
e por este serviço | dá m' este galardon.

2 Pois a ti, Virgen, prougue | que dos miragres teus
fezess' ende cantares, | rogo te que a Deus,
teu fillo, por mi rogues | que os pecados meus
me perdõ' e me queira | receber ontr' os seus
no santo paraiso | u éste San Mateus
San Pedr' e Santiago | a que van os romeus
e que en este mundo | queira que os encreus
mouros destroir possa | que son dos filisteus
com' a seus ẽemigos | destroiu Macabeus
Judas, que foi gran tempo | cabdelo dos judeus.

3 E al te rog' ainda | que lle queiras rogar
que do diab' arteiro | me queira el guardar
que punna todavia | pera om' enartar
per muitas de maneiras, | por faze-lo pecar
e que el me dé siso | que me poss' amparar
dele e das sas obras | con que el faz obrar
mui mal a quen o cree | e pois s' en mal achar
e que contra os mouros | que terra d' ultramar
tẽen e en Espanna | gran part' a meu pesar
me dé poder e força | pera os en deitar.

4 Outros rogos sen estes | ti quer' ora fazer
que rogues a teu fillo | que me faça viver
per que servi-lo possa | e que me dé poder
contra seus ẽemigos | e lles faça perder
o que tẽen forçado | que non deven aver
e me guarde de morte | per oqueijon prender
e que de meus amigos | veja sempre prazer
e que possa mias gentes | en justiça tẽer
e que sempre ben sábia | empregar meu aver
que os que mio fillaren | mio sábian gradecer.

[1] Though I have finished these few songs, with their music, telling of your miracles, Mary, I now ask you as a reward that you pray God your son to forgive me the sins I have committed, though they are many, and not to deny me his heaven, nor speak against me at the Day of Judgement, nor take against me for my wrongdoing; intercede with him for me, my Lady, both now and again and again; give me this reward for my service.

[2] Virgin Mary, as you wished me to write songs about your miracles, I beg you to ask your son to forgive me my sins and receive me into his heaven, with St Matthew, St Peter, and St James to whom pilgrims go; ask him to let me destroy the Moorish infidels, our enemies, just as Judas Maccabeus, leader of the Jews, destroyed his foes the Philistines.

[3] And I also ask you to beg him to protect me from the wiles of the Devil, who ever strives by many means to entrap men and lead them into sin; ask him to give me wisdom to help me against the Devil and his works, by which he makes those who believe in him do ill and come to grief; ask him to give me strength to combat and cast out the Moors, who rule beyond the seas and over much of Spain, to my grief.

[4] I have other requests beside these; pray your son to let me live so that I may serve him, and to give me strength against his enemies to make them yield what they have taken by force; pray him to protect me from death and misfortune; may I have joy of my friends and give my people justice and use my wealth wisely, so that those who inherit from me may be grateful.

5 E ainda te rogo | Virgen, bõa sennor,
que rogues a teu fillo | que mentr' eu aqui for
en este mundo queira | que faça o mellor
per que del e dos bõos | sempr' aja seu amor
e pois rei me fez, queira | que rein' a seu sabor
e de mi e dos reinos | seja el guardador
que me deu e dar pode | quando ll' en prazer for
e que el me defenda | de fals' e traedor
e outrossi me guarde | de mal consellador
e d' ome que mal serve | e é mui pedidor.

6 E pois ei começado, | Sennor, de ti pedir
mercees que me gães | se o Deus por ben vir
roga lle que me guarde | de quen non quer gracir
algo que ll' ome faça | nen o ar quer servir
outrossi de quen busca | razon pera falir
non avendo vergonna | d' errar nen de mentir
e de quen dá joizo | sen o ben departir
nen outro gran consello | sen ant' i comedir
e d' ome mui falido | que outri quer cousir
e d' ome que mal joga | e quer muito riir.

7 Outrossi por mi roga, | Sennor de bon talan,
que me guard' o teu fillo | daquel que adaman
mostra sempr' en seus feitos | e daqueles que dan
pouco por gran vileza | e vergonna non an
e por pouco serviço | mostran que grand' afan
prenden u quer que vaan | pero longe non van
outrossi que me guardes | d' ome torp' alvardan
e d' ome que assaca | que é peior que can
e dos que lealdade | non preçan quant' un pan
pero que sempr' en ela | muito faland' estan.

8 E ainda te rogo, | Sennor espirital,
que rogues a teu fillo | que el me dé atal
siso, per que non caia | en pecado mortal
e que non aja medo | do gran fog' ifernal
e me guarde meu corpo | d' oqueijon e de mal
e d' amig' encoberto | que a gran coita fal
e de quen ten en pouco | de seer desleal
e daquel que se preça | muit' e mui pouco val
e de quen en seus feitos | sempr' é descomunal.
Esto por don cho peço | e ar pedir-ch'-ei al.

[5] And yet I ask you, Virgin, lady of goodness, to ask your son to help me do good while I am in this world, and win the love of God and good men; as he made me king, may he help me reign as he wishes, and guard me and the kingdoms which he gave me and can give when it pleases him; and may he protect me from traitors, false counsellors, and men who serve ill but seek favours.

[6] And since I have begun to ask you to win favours for me, my Lady, I pray you, if God wills, to guard me from those who will never be grateful for what is done for them, and never repay favours; from those who look for ways of doing wrong, and are not ashamed to lie and cheat; from those who give judgement without fairness, and give counsel without thought; from the wrongdoer who finds fault with others, and the cheat who is always merry.

[7] Again, O peerless Virgin, I ask you to protect me from those who are false in all they do; from those who are not noble enough to be generous, and feel no shame; those who give small favours and make a show of taking great pains wherever they go (not that they ever go far); also protect me from sly villains, from looters, worse than dogs; from those who do not give a jot for loyalty but talk of it without end.

[8] And I ask more, heavenly Lady; to pray your son to give me wit enough not to fall into mortal sin, so that I need not fear the eternal fires; may he guard my body from accident and illness, and keep me from false friends who abandon you in your distress, from those who make little of betrayal, from those of little worth who value themselves highly, and those who always look after themselves. All this I ask as a favour, and more:

9 Sennor Santa Maria | pois que começad' ei
de pedir che mercee | non m' en departirei.
Por en te rog' e peço | pois que teu fillo rei
me fez, que del me gães | siso, que mester ei,
con que me guardar possa | do que me non guardei
per que d' oj' adeante | non erre com' errei
nen meu aver empregue | tan mal com' empreguei
en algũus logares | segundo que eu sei
perdend' el e meu tempo | e aos que o dei
mas des oi mais me guarda | e guardado serei.

10 Tantas son as mercees, | Sennor, que en ti á
que por ende te rogo | que rogues o que dá
seu ben aos que ama | ca sei que o fará
se o tu ben rogares | que me dé o que ja
lle pedi muitas vezes | que quando for alá
no paraiso, veja | a ti sempr' e acá
mi acorra en mias coitas | por ti e averá
me bon galardon dado | e sempre fiará
en ti quen souber esto | e mais te servirá
por quanto me feziste | de ben e t' amará.

Cantiga 401 (To Petiçon, E Petiçon)

Notes

The more coherent version in **To** represents the original form of the poem as an epilogue to a collection of 100 poems:

1.1] 'Pois cen cantares feitos | acabei e con son ...'

2.1–2] 'Pois a ti, Virgen prougue | que dos miragres teus
fezess' eu cen cantares ...'

On the rewriting of this poem and Title (Prologue A), see Parkinson 2010a.

The *Petiçon* shows a regular distribution of the three second-person pronouns ('te', 'ti', 'che'). The dative 'ti' is used as an indirect object in double object constructions in 4.1 and 6.1. The alternative dative 'che' and the elided 'ch'' is used exclusively in such constructions with the verb 'pedir'. The accusative 'te' is used as a regular direct object with 'servir' (10.9) and in constructions with the verb 'rogar', which nevertheless takes the indirect object complements 'a teu fillo' (1.3, 4.2, 5.2, 8.2) and 'lle' (6.3).

1.3 and 2.4] 'perdõ/perdon': the verb 'perdõar' has two present subjunctive forms (given here in 3rd person sing.):

a) the regular 'perdõe' (as in *cantiga* 197, 7.3) which is reduced by elision to 'perdõ' e' in 2.4 (also in *cantiga* 253, 2.5);
b) 'perdon', usually found in the *CSM* in set phrases (such as 'se Deus me/vos perdon', as in *cantigas* 24, 8.1 and 31, R.1) and in rhyme position. The phrase 'que el me perdon' (1.3) is explicable as an extension of the normal use of 'perdon' to meet the demands of rhyme.

4.6 and 8.5] 'oqueijon': analysis of the occurrences of 'oqueijon' and 'ocajon' across the four manuscript witnesses does not indicate a preference for one or other form across the collection. Where there is variation between witnesses, preference is given to the form 'oqueijon' found in **To**.

9.1–2] 'Sennor Santa Maria | pois que começad' ei
de pedir che mercee | non m' en departirei.'

We interpret 'de pedir' in 9.2 as dependent on 'começar', making the reading 'm'en departirei' necessary to complete the construction 'departir de'. In Mettmann's edition, 'de pedir' is constructed with 'departir', making the 'en' superfluous.

[9] Blessed Lady Mary, as I have begun to ask favours, I will not cease; and so I beg and beseech you, since your son made me a king, to give me the wit, which I sorely need, to be strong where I have been weak, so that henceforth I may not fail where I have failed, nor use my wealth as badly as I have used it, sometimes, as I well know, wasting it and my time, and harming those to whom I have given; protect me and henceforth I will be well protected.

[10] There is so much grace in you, my Lady, that I beg you to ask him who gives favour to those he loves (for I know that he will do it if you approve) to give me what I have many times asked; that when I go hence to heaven I will always see you there, and you will help me in my distress and give me my reward; whosoever knows this will always trust you, and will serve you all the better for the favours you have given me; and will love you all the more.

Metrics

13 [6' 6]	13 [6' 6]	13 [6' 6]	13 [6' 6]	13 [6' 6]	13 [6' 6]	13 [6' 6]	13 [6' 6]	13 [6' 6]	13 [6' 6]
a	a	a	a	a	a	a	a	a	a

1.2] =che‿ora 1.5] pa·ra·i·so 1.6] =migo‿en; jo·i·zo 1.8] =lle‿agora; mia (*single syllable*) 1.9] =muito‿aficadamente 1.10] =me‿este 2.1] prou·gue 2.2] =fezesse‿ende 2.4] =perdõe‿e; ontre‿os 2.5] pa·ra·i·so 2.6] =Pedro‿e San·ti·a·go 2.8] des·tro·ir 2.9] =como‿a; des·tro·iu 3.1] =rogo‿ainda 3.2] =diabo‿arteiro 3.3] =ome‿enartar 3.5] =possa‿amparar 3.7] =se‿en 3.8] =de‿ultramar 3.9] =parte‿a 4.1] =quero‿ora 4.8] mias (*single syllable*) 4.10] mio sá·bian gra·de·cer 5.2] =mentre‿eu 5.4] =sempre‿aja 5.5] =reine‿a 5.7] =lle‿en 5.8] =falso‿e 5.10] =de‿ome 6.4] =lle‿ome 6.6] =de‿errar 6.8] =ante‿i 6.9] =de‿ome 6.10] =de‿ome 7.2] =guarde‿o 7.3] =sempre‿en 7.5] =grande‿afan 7.7] =de‿ome torpe‿alvardan 7.8] =de‿ome 7.9] =quanto‿un 7.10] =sempre‿en; falando‿estan 8.4] =fogo‿ifernal 8.5] =de‿oqueijon 8.6] =de‿amigo‿encoberto 8.8] =muito‿e 8.9] =sempre‿é 8.10] =pedir-che‿-ei 9.1] =começado‿ei 9.3] =rogo‿e 9.6] =de‿oje‿adeante; como‿errei 9.7] =como‿empreguei 9.9] =perdendo‿el 10.3] a·os 10.6] =sempre‿e 10.7] *necessary elision* mi‿a·co·rra; mias (*single syllable*) 10.10] =te‿amará

Editorial variants

1.6] M juyzio; migu' en A joyzio 1.7] M se me 1.8] A rogall' 2.4] V perdon', e 2.5] M Matheus 2.6] M Santi[a]go 2.8] M destruyr 2.9] V enemigos M destruyu Machabeus 3.4] V fazel-o M peccary 4.1] M te quer 4.3] V seruil-o 4.4] V enemigos 4.6] M ocajon 6.1] M te 6.2] V ganes 6.7] M e [de] quen dá juyzio V ioizo 6.9] M outro 7.1] V, RL Outrosí M Virgen de bon 7.6] M1 vaam V uáam RL vaam; M2 vam 8.4] M infernal 8.5] M ocajon 8.6] M encuberto 8.10] M pidir 9.2] M non me departirey C non m' ende partirei 9.4] V ganes 9.7] M tam 9.8] V en alguuns 10.3] M sey ca o 10.4] M tu por ben vires

Manuscript variants

1.1] To Pois ce*n* ca*n*tares feitos 1.6] E iuyzio; migu 1.7] To xe me 2.2] To eu cen cantares 2.4] To me perdõ é me queira receber m ontr E me perdon eme queira reçebir ontr 2.5] E matheus 2.6] E santigo 2.8] E destruyr 2.9] E destruyu machabe*us* 3.1] To q*u*eras 3.2] To q*u*era 3.3] E puna 3.4] E peccar 4.1] E te q*u*er 4.5] To teen 4.6] E ocaio*n* 4.8] E iustiça 6.1] E te 6.5] To do q*ue* busca 6.7] E & que*n* da iuyzio 6.9] E out*ro* 7.1] E Outrosi; uirgen do bon 7.4] E se*r*uico 7.6] E q*ue* uãam; non uam 7.8] E peor 8.4] E infernal 8.5] E ocaion 8.6] E encuberto 8.10] E pidir 9.2] E no*n* me 9.5] To guardar me 9.6] To erre se errei 9.7] E tam 10.3] E sey ca o 10.4] E tu por be*n* uires 10.10] To fiziste

Rubric

To Esta é la pitiçon que fez el rei don Afonso a Santa Maria por galardon destos cen cantares que ouve feitos dos seus miragres a loor dela.

E Ind Petiçon que fezo el rei a Santa Maria.

E *missing*

Festas and *Loores*

42. *Cantiga de festa* (*The Annunciation*)

R *Tan bẽeita foi a saudaçon*
per que nos vẽemos a salvaçon.

1 Esta troux' o angeo Gabriel
a Santa Maria come fiel
mandadeiro, por que Emanuel
foi logo Deus e pres encarnaçon.
R *Tan bẽeita foi a saudaçon …*

2 Ca ben ali u lle diss' el "Ave"
foi logo Deus ome feit', a la fe,
e macar el atan poderos' é
ena Virgen foi enserrad' enton.
R *Tan bẽeita foi a saudaçon …*

3 E u "Gracia plena" lle dizer
foi o angeo, nos fez connocer
a Deus, que non podiamos veer
ante, mais pois vimos ben sa faiçon.
R *Tan bẽeita foi a saudaçon …*

4 E u lle disse "Contigo é Deus"
enton foi prenne do que polos seus
salvar quis morte prender per judeus,
por nos tirar da ifernal prijon.
R *Tan bẽeita foi a saudaçon …*

5 E u lle disse "Bẽeita es tu
entr' as molleres" logo de Jesu
Cristo foi prenne, que naceu pois u
tres reis lle deron cada un seu don.
R *Tan bẽeita foi a saudaçon …*

6 E u lle disse: "Bẽeito será
aquel fruito que de ti naçerá"
ali nos deu carreira por que ja
ouvessemos sempre de Deus perdon.
R *Tan bẽeita foi a saudaçon …*

Cantiga 415 (**To** Festas de Santa Maria 2, E Festas 5)

Metrics

10	10	|	10	10	10	10
A	A	|	b	b	b	a

R.1] bẽ·ei·ta; sa·u·da·çon 1.1] =trouxe‿o an·ge·o Ga·bri·el 1.2] fi·el 1.3] E·ma·nu·el 2.1] =disse‿el 2.2] =feito‿a 2.3] =poderoso‿e 2.4] =enserrado‿enton 3.1] Gra·ci·a 3.2] an·ge·o 3.3] ve·er 3.4] fai·çon 5.1] Bẽ·ei·ta 5.2] =entre‿as 6.1] Bẽ·ei·to

Editorial variants
R.1] **M1** [foi] (2R) V saudaçion (3–4R) 1.1] **M2** tro[u]x' **M1**, V trox' 4.1] **M** Contig[o] é V Contigo é 6.1] **M2** Beeyto **M1**, V Bẽeyto

Manuscript variants
R.1] E beeita (1–5R); beeita a (2R); saudaçion (2–4R) R.2] E q*ue* uẽemos (2–3R); que ueemos (4R); q*ue* ueemos (5R) saluaçion (4–5R) 1.1] **To** trouxe E trox 2.1] E u disse lle 3.2] E con*n*osçer 3.4] **To** mas 4.1] E contig e 4.4] E infernal

Rubric
Como o angeo Gabriel vẽo saudar a Santa Maria e esta festa é no mes de março.

E festa no

So blessed was the angel's greeting
by which we came to salvation.

[1] This greeting the angel Gabriel brought to Holy Mary, as faithful messenger, and so Emmanuel became God and took human flesh.

[2] For when Gabriel said "Hail Mary" to her, God was at once made man, in faith, and even though he has such great power, he was enclosed in the Virgin's womb.

[3] And when the angel said "Full of grace" he let us know God, whom we would not have been able to see before, but now we clearly beheld his face.

[4] And when he said "The Lord is with thee" then was she pregnant with he who to save his own gladly died at the hands of the Jews, to bring us out of the captivity of hell.

[5] And when he said "Blessed art thou among women" then did she conceive Christ Jesus, who was born where three kings came each one to give him a gift.

[6] And when he said "Blessed is the fruit of thy womb" she showed us the way by which we could always gain God's forgiveness.

43. *May Song*

1	1	Ben vennas, maio, e con alegria	Welcome, May, with gladness
	2	por en roguemos a Santa Maria	so let us ask Our Lady
	3	que a seu fillo rogue todavia	ever to ask her son
	4	que el nos guarde d' err' e de folia.	to protect us from sin and folly.
	R	*Ben vennas, maio.*	*Welcome, May!*
2	1	Ben vennas, maio, con toda saude	Welcome, May, with all good health
	2	por en roguemos a de gran vertude	so let us ask the lady of great virtue
	3	que a Deus rogue que nos sempr' ajude	to ask God ever to help us
	4	contra o dem' e de si nos escude.	against the Devil, and to shield us from him.
	R	*Ben vennas, maio.*	*Welcome, May!*
3	1	Ben vennas, maio, e con lealdade	Welcome, May, with loyalty
	2	por en roguemos a de gran bondade	so let us ask the lady of great goodness
	3	que sempre aja de nos piadade	ever to have pity on us
	4	e que nos guarde de toda maldade.	and to protect us from all ill.
	R	*Ben vennas, maio.*	*Welcome, May!*
4	1	Ben vennas, maio, con muitas requezas	Welcome, May, with riches abundant
	2	e nos roguemos a que á nobrezas	so let us ask the lady whose nobility
	3	en si mui grandes que nos de tristezas	is very great, to guard us from
	4	guard' e de coitas e ar d' avolezas.	sadness and grief and even from mischief.
	R	*Ben vennas, maio.*	*Welcome, May!*
5	1	Ben vennas, maio, coberto de fruitas	Welcome, May, abundant in fruit
	2	e nos roguemos a que sempre duitas	so let us ask the lady whose mercies
	3	á sas mercees, de fazer en muitas	are always given abundantly
	4	que nos defenda do dem' e sas luitas.	to protect us from the Devil and his attacks.
	R	*Ben vennas, maio.*	*Welcome, May!*
6	1	Ben vennas, maio, con bõos sabores	Welcome, May, full of good things
	2	e nos roguemos e demos loores	and let us ask and praise the lady
	3	aa que sempre por nos pecadores	who always beseeches God for us,
	4	roga Deus que nos guarde de doores.	to protect us from pain.
	R	*Ben vennas, maio.*	*Welcome, May!*
7	1	Ben vennas, maio, con vacas e touros	Welcome, May, with cows and bulls
	2	e nos roguemos a que nos tesouros	and let us ask that lady who sits
	3	de Jesucristo é, que aos mouros	among Jesus's riches, to quickly confound
	4	cedo cofonda, e brancos e louros.	the Moors, both white and black.
	R	*Ben vennas, maio.*	*Welcome, May!*

Cantiga 406 (To App 1)

Linguistic notes

10.4] 'alvardão', 'rogue', is a rhyme-driven variant of 'alvardan' (see *cantiga* 401 [anthology Epilogue], 7.7) (Parkinson 1993).

12.4] 'ẽaio', 'evil, ugly, dirty', appears in two other variant forms in the *CSM* ('eanyo' in *cantiga* 2, 5.3, and 'ẽatio' in *cantiga* 34, 5.1) and in the derived form 'ẽatidade' ('d' enhatidade') usually edited as 'de maldade' in a *cantiga de escarnho* by Pero Larouco, 'De vós senhor quer' eu dizer verdade' (B612, V214). See Tavani 2010: 57 for a discussion of readings and etymology.

8 1 Ben vennas, maio, alegr' e sen sanna
2 e nos roguemos a quen nos gaanna
3 ben de seu fillo, que nos dé tamanna
4 força, que saian os mouros d' Espanna.
R *Ben vennas, maio.*

Welcome, May, glad and without wrath
and let us ask that lady who wins
her son's favour for us, to give us the strength
to drive the Moors out of Spain.
Welcome, May!

9 1 Ben vennas, maio, con muitos gãados
2 e nos roguemos a que os pecados
3 faz que nos sejan de Deus perdõados,
4 que de seu fillo nos faça privados.
R *Ben vennas, maio.*

Welcome, May, with many cattle
and we shall ask that lady who has our sins
pardoned by God,
to bring us to her son's household.
Welcome, May!

10 1 Ben vennas, maio, con bõo verão
2 e nos roguemos a Virgen de chão
3 que nos defenda d' ome mui vilão
4 e d' atrevud' e de torp' alvardão.
R *Ben vennas, maio.*

Welcome, May, with the heat of summer
and let us ask the Virgin plainly
to defend us from wicked men
and bold and vile scoundrels.
Welcome, May!

11 1 Ben vennas, maio, con pan e con vĩo
2 e nos roguemos a que Deus minĩo
3 troux' en seus braços, que nos dé camĩo
4 por que sejamos con ela festĩo.
5 *Ben vennas, maio.*

Welcome, May, with bread and wine
and we will ask the lady who bore the Christ Child
in her arms to show us the way
by which we can soon be with him.
Welcome, May!

12 1 Ben vennas, maio, mans' e non sannudo
2 e nos roguemos a que noss' escudo
3 é, que nos guarde de louc' atrevudo
4 e d' om' ẽaio e desconnoçudo.
5 *Ben vennas, maio.*

Welcome, May, calm and happy
let us ask that lady who is our shield
to protect us from bold madmen
and from villainous strangers.
Welcome, May!

13 1 Ben vennas, maio, alegr' e fremoso
2 por end' a madre do Rei grorioso
3 roguemos que nos guarde do nojoso
4 om' e de falso e de mentiroso.
5 *Ben vennas, maio.*

Welcome, May, happy and fair,
so let us ask the mother of our glorious King
to protect us from vile
men and from deceitful liars.
Welcome, May!

14 1 Ben vennas, maio, con bõos manjares
2 e nos roguemos en nossos cantares
3 a santa Virgen, ant' os seus altares,
4 que nos defenda de grandes pesares.
5 *Ben vennas, maio.*

Welcome, May, with good things to eat
let us in our songs
ask the Blessed Virgin, kneeling at her altars,
to protect us from great sorrows.
Welcome, May!

Metrics

10' 10' 10' 10' | 4'
a a a a | B

1.4] =de‿erro‿e 2.1] sa·u·de 2.3] =sempre‿ajude 2.4] =demo‿e 4.4] =guarde‿e; de‿avolezas 5.3] mer·ce·es 5.4] =demo‿e 6.1] bõ·os 6.2] lo·or·es 6.3] a·a 6.4] do·or·es 7.3] a·os 8.1] =alegre‿e 8.2] ga·a·nna 8.4] =de‿Espanna; sai·an 9.1] gã·a·dos 10.1] bõ·o 10.3] =de ome 10.4] =de‿atrevudo‿e de torpe‿alvardão 11.3] =trouxe‿en 12.1] =manso‿e 12.2] =nosso‿escudo 12.3] =louco‿atrevudo 12.4] =de‿ome‿ẽ·ai·o 13.1] =alegre‿e 13.2] =ende‿a 13.4] =ome‿e 14.1] bõ·os 14.3] =ante‿os

Editorial variants

2.2] M2 por que roguemos M1, V, RL por que loemos 3.2] M2 por que roguemos M1, V, RL por que loemos 5.3] M2 merçes M1, RL merçees V merçées 6.4] M, V rog' a Deus RL roga Deus 9.1] V ganados 11.1] V vinno 11.2] V minynno 11.3] V camynno 12.4] V enayo

Manuscript variants

2.2] To por q*ue* loemos 3.2] To por que loemos

Rubric

Esta primeira e das maias.

44. *Cantiga de loor*

R *Santa Maria | estrela do dia*
mostra-nos via | pera Deus e nos guia.

1 Ca veer faze-los errados
que perder foran per pecados
entender de que mui culpados
son, mais per ti son perdõados
da ousadia | que lles fazia
fazer folia | mui mais que non devia.
R *Santa Maria | estrela do dia …*

2 Amostrar nos deves carreira
por gãar en toda maneira
a sen par luz e verdadeira
que tu dar nos podes senlleira
ca Deus a ti a | outorgaria
e a querria | por ti dar e daria.
R *Santa Maria | estrela do dia …*

3 Guiar ben nos pod' o teu siso
mais ca ren pera paraiso
u Deus ten sempre goi' e riso
pera quen en el creer quiso
e prazer-m'-ia | se te prazia
que foss' a mia | alm' en tal compannia.
R *Santa Maria | estrela do dia …*

Cantiga 100 (To App 10b, T 100, E 100)

Note
The word profile of *(e)strela* shows that the shorter form is always the result of elision, i.e. *'strela* or *‿estrela*. For this reason we use the full form *estrela* with elision across the caesura.

Metrics

9' [4' 4']	11' [4' 6']	|	8'	8'	8'	8'	9' [4' 4']	11' [4' 6']
A	A	|	b	b	b	b	a	a

R.1] =Ma·ri·a‿e·stre·la *and subsequent refrains* 1.1] ve·er 2.5] ou·tor·ga·ri·a 3.1] =pode‿o 3.2] pa·ra·i·so 3.3] =goio‿e 3.4] cre·er 3.5] =prazer-me‿-i·a 3.6] =fosse‿a mia alma‿en

Editorial variants
R.1] **M** Strela **V, Fid** strela 1.1] **V** fázel-os 1.5] **C** que les 2.2] **V** gannar 3.4] **M** pora 3.5] **Fid** prazerm' ia

Manuscript variants
R.1] **To, T, E** strela 1.6] **T, E** folia mais que non deueria 3.4] **To, E** pora

Rubric
De loor de Santa Maria.

Captions (T)
missing

Holy Mary, star of the day,
guide us to God and show us the way.

[1] For you make those who have gone astray through their sins understand how much they are at fault, but through you they are forgiven for the presumption which made them do foolish things which they should not have done.

[2] You must show us the path to find the ways to reach the matchless light of truth which you alone can give us, for God would grant you the power, and would willingly give it for you.

[3] Your wisdom more than any other thing can show us the way to paradise, where God gives pleasure and laughter to all who have believed in him, and it would please me if you were pleased for my soul to join such a company.

45. *Cantiga de loor*

1 Virgen madre groriosa
de Deus filla e esposa
santa, nobre, preciosa
quen te loar saberia
ou podia?
Ca Deus que é lum' e dia
segund' a nossa natura
non viramos sa figura
se non por ti que fust' alva.

2 Tu es alva dos alvores
que faze los pecadores
que vejan os seus errores
e connoscan sa folia
que desvia
d' aver om' o que devia
que perdeu per sa loucura
Eva, que tu Virgen pura
cobraste porque es alva.

3 Tu es alva dos mesquĩos
que non erren os camĩos,
a grandes, a pequenĩos,
ca tu lles mostras a via
per que ia
o teu fillo todavia
que nos sacou da escura
carreira maa e dura
per ti que es nossa alva.

4 Tu es alva dos culpados,
que cegos por seus pecados
eran, mais alumeados
son per ti Santa Maria.
Quen diria,
nen quen osmar poderia
teu ben e ta gran mesura?
Ca sempre en ti atura
Deus a luz ond' es tu alva.

[1] Glorious Virgin mother,
daughter and bride of God
holy, noble and precious,
who could have the wit
or the skill to tell your praises?
For because of our sinful nature
we would never have seen the face of God,
who is our light and day,
without you, who are our dawn.

[2] You are the dawn of dawns
who makes sinners
see the error of their ways
and recognise the folly
which turns us away
from earning the reward we should,
that reward which Eve lost for us
by her rashness, and which you, pure Virgin,
regained for us because you are the dawn.

[3] You are the dawn for the wretched
both great and small,
so that they do not lose their way,
for you show them the path
which your son
always trod
when he rescued us from
the dark, hard and rough road
through you, who are our dawn.

[4] You are the dawn of the sinful
who were blinded by their sins
but are now enlightened
by you, Holy Mary.
Who could recount,
or who could tell
your goodness and your great wisdom?
For God ever keeps in you
his sight, for you are the dawn.

5 Tu es alva per que visto
foi o sol que éste Cristo
que o mund' ouve conquisto
e sacado du jazia
e jaria,
e de que non sairia
mais Deus por ti da altura
quis de ti sa creatura
nacer, e fez de ti alva.

6 Tu es alva dos que creen
e lume dos que non veen
a Deus, e que por mal tẽen
o ben per sa bavequia
d' eresia
que é maa ousadia
e Deus non á destes cura
mais pela ta gran cordura
lles dás lume come alva.

7 Tu es alva que pareces
ante Deus e escrareces
os ceos, e que mereces
d' averes sa compania
e querria
t' eu ver con el, ca seria
quito de maa ventura
e metudo na folgura
u es con Deus, u es alva.

Cantiga 340 (E 340, E Festas 2)

Notes

The order of the strophes is different in the two manuscript witnesses. For this edition, we follow **E340**, which seems to be an earlier copy; the booklet of *festas* was copied as a separate unit and appended at the beginning of the manuscript at a late stage (Avenoza 2004). Other editions follow the **EFestas** order (S1, S5, S2, S3, S4).

Both manuscripts contain false refrains (see Parkinson 1987). The incipit of strophe 1 (**E340** 'Virgen madre groriosa | de Deus filla'; **EFestas** 'Virgen madre gloriosa | de Deus filla e esposa | santa') is added at the end of the first strophe. In **E340**, 1.1 is repeated after the fifth and final lines of each strophe.

Linguistic note

2.2] 'faze los' = 'fazes os'. This type of contraction is normal in Galician-Portuguese, but is limited to combinations of verbs and object pronouns in Modern Portuguese.

Metrics

7' 7' 7' 7' 3' 7' 7' 7' 7'
a a a b b b c c d (d= alva)

1.6] =lume‿e 1.7] =segundo‿a 1.9] =fuste‿alva 2.6] =de‿aver ome‿o 3.5] i·a 3.8] ma·a 4.9] =onde‿es 5.3] =mundo‿ouve 5.6] sa·i·ri·a 6.1] cre·en 6.2] ve·en 6.3] tẽ·en 6.5] =de‿eresia 6.6] ma·a 7.3] ce·os 7.4] =de‿averes 7.6] =te‿eu 7.7] ma·a

[5] You are the dawn which brings us
the sun which is Jesus Christ
who conquered the world
and rescued it from where it lay
and would still be lying
and whence it could not escape;
but through you, God from on high
chose to be born of you, his creation,
and made you our dawn.

[6] You are the dawn for those who believe
and light for those who cannot see
God, and who think little of
virtue, in the babblings
of their heresy
which is wicked boldness indeed.
God cares nothing for such people,
but by your great wisdom
you give them light, for you are the dawn.

[7] You are the dawn who appears
before God, and lights up
the heavens, so that you deserve
to be with him.
And I would dearly wish
to see you there with him, for I would then
be free from ill fortune
and would enjoy the pleasures
of where you live with God, and where you are our dawn.

Editorial variants

1.1–5] M, V(340), A(340) *first 5 lines given as refrain* 1.1] V(412), RL gloriosa 1.16] V(340) lũa A(340) lũ-a‿et 2.3] V(412) uieam RL vejam 2.4] M connoscan V(412) conoscam RL con[h]oscam 2.7] M por 3.1] M mesqỹos V(340) mesqynnos V(412) mesquynnos **Fid**, C mesquinnos RL mesquinhos 3.2] V, **Fid**, C caminnos V(412) errem RL errem; caminhos 3.3] V(340) pequenynnos V(412), **Fid**, RL, C pequeninnos 4.2] V(412), RL per 4.3] V(412), RL eram 4.5] V(412) Quém RL Quem 4.6] V(412), **Fid**, RL quen contar 5.8] V(412), **Fid**, RL criatura 6.1] V(412), RL creem 6.2] V(412) ueem RL veem 6.3] V(412), **Fid**, RL teen 6.7] V(340) d' estos 6.8] **Fid** per la ta 7.2] V(412), RL esclareçes **Fid** esclareces 7.4] **Fid** compannia RL compan[h]ia 7.6] V ueer RL veer 7.7] V(412), **Fid**, RL quite 7.9] V(412), **Fid** ond' es RL ond' és

Manuscript variants

1.1] **EFestas** gloriosa 1.6] **E340** lũa e 2.2] E peccadores 2.3] **EFestas** veiam 2.4] **EFestas** conoscam 2.7] **E340** p*or* 3.1] **E340** mesqỹos **EFestas** mesq*uin*n*os* 3.2] **EFestas** errem; ca*min*n*os* 3.3] **EFestas** peq*ue*ueninn*os* 4.2] **EFestas** p*er*; peccados 4.3] **EFestas** eram 4.5] **EFestas** quem 4.6] **EFestas** q*ue*n co*n*tar 5.8] **EFestas** criatura 6.1] **EFestas** creem 6.2] **EFestas** veem 6.3] **EFestas** teen 6.7] **E340** destos 7.2] **EFestas** esclareçes 7.6] E ueer 7.7] **EFestas** quite 7.9] **EFestas** ond es

Rubric

De loor de Santa Maria.

E340 *missing*

BIBLIOGRAPHY

Editions

CUNNINGHAM, MARTIN (ed.). 2000. *Alfonso el Sabio. Cantigas de Loor* (Dublin: University College Dublin Press).

FIDALGO, ELVIRA (ed.). 2003. *As Cantigas de Loor de Santa María* (Santiago de Compostela: Xunta de Galicia).

LAPA, MANUEL RODRIGUES (ed.). 1933. *Afonso X, o Sábio, Cantigas de Santa Maria*, Textos de Literatura Portuguesa, 1 (Lisbon: Imprensa Nacional).

METTMANN, WALTER (ed.). 1959–72. *Afonso X o Sábio, Cantigas de Santa Maria*, 4 vols (Coimbra: Universidade; reprinted. Vigo: Edicións Xerais de Galicia, 2 vols, 1981).

—— (ed.). 1986–89. *Alfonso X el Sabio, Cantigas de Santa María*, 3 vols (Madrid: Castalia).

SCHAFFER, MARTHA E. (ed.). 2010. *Cantigas de Santa Maria. Códice de Toledo* (Santiago de Compostela: Consello da Cultura Galega).

VALMAR, LEOPOLDO DEL CUETO, MARQUÉS DE (ed). 1889. *Cantigas de Santa María de don Alonso el Sabio*, 2 vols (Madrid: Real Academia Española, 1889; reprinted Madrid: Caja de Ahorros y Monte de Piedad, 1990).

Facsimiles

CCG. 2004: *Alfonso X o Sabio. Cantigas de Santa María. O códice de Toledo*, introd. Henrique Monteagudo (Santiago de Compostela: Consello da Cultura Galega).

EDILÁN. 1979: *Alfonso X el Sabio, Las Cantigas de Santa María. Edición facsímil. El Códice Rico del Escorial (Manuscrito escurialense Tj1)*, 2 vols (Madrid: Edilán).

EDILÁN. 1989: *Alfonso X el Sabio, Cantigas de Santa María. I. Edición facsímil del códice B. R. 20 de la Biblioteca Nazionale Centrale de Florencia. Siglo XIII. II. El códice de Florencia de las cantigas de Alfonso X el Sabio. Volumen complementario de la edición facsímil del ms. B. R. 20 de la Biblioteca Nazionale Centrale de Florencia* (Madrid: Edilán).

TESTIMONIO. 2011: *Alfonso X El Sabio 1221–1284, Las Cantigas de Santa María, Códice Rico, Ms. T-I-1, Real Biblioteca del Monasterio de San Lorenzo de El Escorial,El Códice Rico de las Cantigas de Santa Maria*, coord. Laura Fernández Fernández and Juan Carlos Ruiz Sousa (Madrid: Testimonio).

Books and Articles

ANGLÉS, HIGINIO (=Higini Anglès). 1943–64. *La música de las Cantigas de Santa María del Rey Alfonso el Sabio*, 3 vols (Barcelona: Biblioteca Central).

AVENOZA, GEMMA. 2004. 'Codicología afonsí', paper given at the *Colóquio Cancioneiro da Ajuda (1904–2004)*, Faculdade de Letras de Lisboa-Biblioteca da Ajuda, 11, 12 e 13 de Novembro de 2004.

BERTOLUCCI, VALERIA PIZZORUSSO. 1995. 'Alcuni sondaggi per l'integrazzione del discorso critico su Alfonso X poeta', in Mondéjar and Montoya, eds, *Estudios Alfonsíes*, pp. 91–117.

BÉTÉROUS, PAULE V. 1984. *Les Collections des Miracles de la Vierge en Gallo et Ibéro-Roman au XIIIe Siècle*, Marian Library Series. New Series, Vols. 15–16 (Dayton, Ohio: University of Dayton).

BETTI, MARIA PIA. 1997. *Rimario e lessico in rima delle Cantigas de Santa Maria di Alfonso X de Castiglia* (Pisa: Pacini).

——. 2005. *Repertorio metrico delle 'Cantigas de Santa Maria' di Alfonso X di Castiglia* (Pisa: Pacini).

BOYNTON, SUSAN. 2011. *Silent Music: Medieval Song and the Construction of History in Eighteenth-Century Spain* (Oxford: OUP).

CLARKE, DOROTHY CLOTELLE. 1955. 'Versification in Alfonso el Sabio's Cantigas', *Hispanic Review*, 23: 83–98.

COHEN, RIP. 2009. 'The Medieval Galician-Portuguese Lyric', in Stephen Parkinson, Cláudia Pazos Alonso and T. F. Earle (eds), *A Companion to Portuguese Literature* (Woodbridge: Tamesis), pp. 25–44.

CUNHA, CELSO FERREIRA DA. 1961. *Estudos de poética trovadoresca. Versificação e ecdótica* (Rio de Janeiro, INL).

DOMÍNGUEZ RODRÍGUEZ, ANA and PILAR TREVIÑO GAJARDO. 2007. *Las 'Cantigas de Santa Maria': Formas e imágenes* (Madrid: AyN Ediciones).

DUFFELL, MARTIN J. 2007. *Syllable and Accent: Studies on Medieval Hispanic Metrics* (London: Department of Hispanic Studies, Queen Mary, University of London).

FERNÁNDEZ FERNÁNDEZ, LAURA. 2009. '*Cantigas de Santa María*: fortuna de sus manuscritos', *Alcanate*, 6: 323–48.

——. 2013a. 'Los manuscritos de las *Cantigas de Santa Maria*: Definición de un proyecto regio', *Alcanate*, 8: 81–117.

——. 2013b. *Arte y ciencia en el scriptorium de Alfonso X el Sabio* (Puerto de Santa Maria: Catedra Alfonso X el Sabio — Universidad de Sevilla).

Fernández Fernández, Laura, and Juan Carlos Ruiz Sousa (coords). 2011. *Alfonso X El Sabio 1221–1284, Las Cantigas de Santa María, Códice Rico, Ms. T-I-1, Real Biblioteca del Monasterio de San Lorenzo de El Escorial, El Códice Rico de las Cantigas de Santa Maria*, 2 vols (Madrid: Testimonio).

Ferreira, Manuel Pedro. 1998. 'The Layout of the Cantigas: A musicological overview', *Galician Review*, 2: 47–61, republished as 'A disposição gráfica das cantigas medievais: uma perspectiva musicológica', in *Aspectos da Musica Medieval*, I, 49–70.

——. 2000a. 'The Influence of Chant on the *Cantigas de Santa Maria*', *Cantigueiros*, 11–12: 29–40.

——. 2000b. 'Andalusian music and the *Cantigas de Santa Maria*', in Parkinson (ed.) *Cobras e Son*, pp. 7–19.

——. 2001. 'Afinidades musicais: as *cantigas de loor* e a lírica profana galego-portuguesa', in *Memória dos afectos. Homenagem da cultura portuguesa a Giuseppe Tavani*, ed. Manuel G. Simões, Ivo Castro, and João David Pinto Correia. (Lisbon: Colibri), pp. 187–205.

——. 2007. 'Alfonso X, compositor', *Alcanate*, 5: 117–37.

——. 2009a. *Aspectos da Musica Medieval no Ocidente Peninsular. I Musica Palaciana* (Lisbon, Imprensa Nacional-Casa da Moeda — FCG).

——. 2009b. *Antologia de Música em Portugal na Idade Média e no Renascimento*, 2 vols, 5 (Lisbon: CESEM — Arte das Musas).

Ferreiro Alemparte, Jaime. 1972. 'La ciudad mozárabe de Santa María de Faro y el milagro de la Cantiga CLXXXIII en fuentes anteriores al Rey Sabio', *Grial*, 38: 404–30.

Ferreiro, Manuel, C.P. Martínez Pereiro, and L. Tato Fontaíña (eds). 2008. *A edición da Poesía Trobadoresca en Galiza* (A Coruña: Baía).

Fidalgo, Elvira. 2002. *As Cantigas de Santa Maria* (Vigo: Edicións Xerais).

Filgueira Valverde, José, 1979. 'Introducción histórico-crítica', in *Alfonso X el Sabio, Las Cantigas de Santa María. Edición facsímil. El Códice Rico del Escorial (Manuscrito escurialense Tj1)*, 2 vols (Madrid: Edilán, 1979), II, 33–49.

González Jiménez, Manuel. 1993. *Alfonso X (1252–1284)*, Colección Corona de España (Palencia: Editorial la Olmeda).

Guerrero Lovillo, Francisco. 1949. *Las Cantigas. Estudio arqueológico de sus miniaturas* (Madrid: Consejo Superior de Investigaciones Científicas, Instituto Diego Velázquez, Sección de Sevilla).

Jensen, Frede. 1978. *The Earliest Portuguese Lyrics*, Études romanes de l'Université d'Odense, 11 (Odense: Odense University Press).

Katz, Israel. J., and John E. Keller (eds). 1987. *Studies on the 'Cantigas de Santa María': Art, Music and Poetry. Proceedings of the International Symposium on the 'Cantigas de Santa María' of Alfonso X el Sabio (1221–1284) in Commemoration of its 700th Anniversary Year - 1981, New York, November, 19–21* (Madison: Hispanic Seminary of Medieval Studies).

Keller, J. E. 1958. 'Daily Living as Presented in the Canticles of Alfonso the Learned', *Speculum*, 33: 484–89.

Kulp-Hill, Kathleen. 2000. *Songs of Holy Mary of Alfonso the Wise* (Tempe, Arizona: Arizona Center for Medieval and Renaissance Studies).

Maia, Clarinda de Azevedo. 1984. '"Ona", um arcaísmo galego-português. Breve contributo para o estudo das fórmulas de tratamento na língua medieval galego-portuguesa', *Revista de filología románica*, 2: 71–78.

Martínez, Henrique Salvador. 2003. *Alfonso X, el Sabio: una biografia* (Madrid: Polifemo); in English, *Alfonso X, the Learned: A Biography*. trans. Odile Cisneros (Leiden: Brill, 2009).

Mettmann, Walter. 1987. 'Algunas observaciones sobre la génesis de la colección de las *Cantigas de Santa María* y sobre el problema del autor', in Katz and Keller, *Studies on the 'Cantigas de Santa María'*, pp. 355–66.

Miranda, J. C. R. 2010. 'Cantar ou *cantiga*? Sobre a designação genérica da poesia galego-portuguesa', in *Aproximacións ao estudo do vocabulário trovadoresco*, ed. Mercedes Brea and Santiago Lópes Martínez-Morás (Santiago de Compostela: Centro Ramón Piñeiro), pp. 161–79.

Mondéjar, José and Jesús Montoya Martínez (eds). 1985. *Estudios Alfonsíes* (Granada: Universidad de Granada).

Montoya Martínez, Jesús. 1991. *O Cancioneiro marial de Afonso X, o Sabio* (Santiago de Compostela: Universidade).

——. 1999. *Composición, estructura y contenido del cancionero marial de Alfonso X* (Murcia: Real Academia Alfonso X el Sabio).

—— and Ana Domínguez Rodríguez (eds). 1999. *El scriptorium alfonsí: de los libros de astrología a las 'Cantigas de Santa María'* (Madrid: Editorial Complutense).

Nascimento, Aires Augusto. 1979. 'Um "mariale" alcobacense', *Didaskalia*, 9: 339–412.

Nepaulsingh, Colbert. 1986. 'Poems on a string', in *Towards a History of Literary Composition in Medieval Spain*, University of Toronto Romance Series 54 (Toronto — London: University of Toronto Press), ch. 1.
O'Callaghan, Joseph. 1998. *Alfonso X and the Cantigas de Santa Maria: A Poetic Biography* (Leiden: Brill).
Odber de Baubeta, Patricia. 1992. *Anticlerical Satire in Medieval Portuguese Literature*, (Lewiston: Mellon).
Oliveira, Antonio Resende de. 1994. *Depois do espectáculo trovadoresco. A estrutura dos cancioneiros peninsulares e as recolhas dos séculos XIII e XIV* (Coimbra: Colibri)
——. 2010. 'Na casa de Afonso X. O Rei, a Corte e os trovadores', *Revista de História das Ideias*, 31: 53–76.
Parkinson, Stephen (ed.). 2000. *Cobras e Son: Papers on the Text, Music and Manuscripts of the 'Cantigas de Santa Maria'* (Oxford: Legenda).
——. 1987. 'False Refrains in the *Cantigas de Santa Maria*', *Portuguese Studies*, 3: 21–55.
——. 1992. 'Miragres de maldizer?: Dysphemism in the *Cantigas de Santa Maria*', *Cantigueiros*, 4: 44–57.
——. 1993. 'Final Nasals in the Galician-Portuguese Cancioneros', in *Hispanic Linguistic Studies in Honour of F.W. Hodcroft*, ed. David Mackenzie and Ian Michael (Llangrannog: Dolphin), pp 51–62.
——. 1998. 'Two for the Price of One: On the Castroxeriz *Cantigas de Santa Maria*', in *Ondas do Mar de Vigo. Actas do Simposio Internacional sobre a Lírica Medieval Galego-Portuguesa, Birmingham 1997*, coord. Derek W. Flitter and Patricia Odber de Baubeta (Birmingham: Seminario de Estudios Galegos, Department of Hispanic Studies, University of Birmingham), pp. 72–88.
——. 1999. 'Meestria metrica: metrical virtuosity in the *Cantigas de Santa Maria*', *La corónica*, 27.2: 21–35; 28.1: 220–25.
——. 2000a. 'Layout in the códices ricos of the *Cantigas de Santa Maria*', *Hispanic Research Journal*, 1: 243–74.
——. 2000b. 'Phonology and Metrics: Aspects of Rhyme in the *Cantigas de Santa Maria*', in *Proceedings of the 10th Colloquium of the Medieval Hispanic Research Seminar*, ed. Alan Deyermond (London: Queen Mary and Westfield College), pp. 131–44.
——. 2000c. 'Structure and layout of the Toledo manuscript of the *Cantigas de Santa Maria*', in Parkinson (ed.) *Cobras e Son*, pp. 133–53.
——. 2001. 'Para uma nova edição das *Cantigas de Santa Maria*: duas leituras novas', in *Literatura y Cristiandad. Homenaje al prof. Jesús Montoya Martínez*, ed. Manuel José Alonso García, María Luisa Dañobeitia Fernández & Antonio Rafael Rubio Flores (Granada: Universidad), pp. 387–94.
——. 2006a. 'Concurrent patterns of verse design in the Galician-Portuguese Lyric', in *Proceedings of the Thirteenth Colloquium*, ed. Jane Whetnall and Alan Deyermond (London: Department of Hispanic Studies, Queen Mary, University of London), pp. 19–38.
——. 2006b. 'Rules of Elision and Hiatus in the Galician-Portuguese Lyric: The View from the *Cantigas de Santa Maria*', *La coronica*, 34.2: 113–33.
——. 2007. 'The Evolution of Cantiga 113: Composition, Recomposition, and Emendation in the *Cantigas de Santa Maria*', *La coronica*, 35.2: 227–72.
——. 2010a. 'Front matter or text?: prologues and tables of contents in the *Cantigas de Santa Maria*', in *"De ninguna cosa es alegre posesión sin compañía". Estudios celestinescos y medievales en honor del profesor Joseph Thomas Snow*, coord. Devid Paolini (New York: Hispanic Seminary of Medieval Studies) vol II, pp. 252–65.
——. 2010b. 'Questões de estrutura estrófica nas *Cantigas de Santa Maria*: estruturas múltiplas, assimetrias e continuações inconsistentes', in *Estudos de edición crítica e lírica galego-portuguesa*, ed. M. Arbor Aldea and A. Fernández Guiadanes (Santiago de Compostela: Universidade de Santiago de Compostela), pp 315–36.
——. 2011a. 'Alfonso X, Miracle Collector', in Fernández and Ruiz Sousa. 2011, *Códice Rico*, vol. II, pp. 79–105.
——. 2011b. 'The Miracles Came in Two by Two: Paired Narratives in the *Cantigas de Santa Maria*', in *Gaude Virgo Gloriosa: Marian Miracle Literature in the Iberian Peninsula and France in the Middle Ages*, ed. Juan-Carlos Conde and Emma Gatland (London: Queen Mary, University of London), pp. 65–85.
——. 2012. 'Cut and Shut: On the hybridity of Cantiga 173', *eHumanista*, 22: 49–64.
——. 2013. 'How to Eat a Spider: Alfonso X, *Cantiga de Santa Maria* 225', in Cláudia Pazos Alonso and Stephen Parkinson (eds), *Reading Literature in Portuguese: Commentaries in Honour of Tom Earle* (Oxford: Legenda), pp. 5–14.
—— and David Barnett. 2013. 'Linguística, codicologia e crítica textual: interpretação editorial da variação interna nas *Cantigas de Santa Maria*', in *Ao sabor do texto: Estudos dedicados a Ivo Castro*, ed. Rosario Álvarez, Ana Maria Martins, Henrique Monteagudo & Maria Ana Ramos (Santiago de Compostela: Instituto da Lingua Galega — Universidade de Santiago de Compostela), pp. 467–80.
—— and Deirdre Jackson. 2006. 'Collection, composition, and compilation in the *Cantigas de Santa Maria*', *Portuguese Studies*, 22: 159–72.
Procter, Evelyn. 1951. *Alfonso X of Castile, Patron of Literature and Learning* (Oxford: Clarendon Press).

Ramos, Maria Ana, and Luciano Rossi. 2004. 'Afonso X, un de bolonna e a abadessa prenne', *Santa Barbara Portuguese Studies*, 6: 33–76.

Ribera y Tarragó, Julián, 1922. *La música de las Cantigas. Estudio sobre su origen y naturaleza, con reproducciones fotográficas del texto y transcripción moderna* (Madrid: Real Academia Española).

Roberge, Pierre F., and Todd McComb, *Alfonso X "el Sabio" (1221–1284) — A discography of attributed works* <http://www.medieval.org/emfaq/composers/cantigas.html>.

Scarborough, Connie. 2009. *A Holy Alliance. Alfonso X's Political Use of Marian Poetry.* (Newark: Juan de la Cuesta).

Schaffer, Martha E. 1992. 'Epigraphs as a clue to the conceptualization and organization of the *Cantigas de Santa Maria*', *La corónica* 19.2: 57–88.

——. 1997. 'Questions of authorship: the *Cantigas de Santa Maria*', in *Proceedings of the Eighth Colloquium of the Medieval Hispanic Research Seminar*, ed. Andrew M. Beresford and Alan Deyermond (London: Queen Mary and Westfield College), pp. 17–30.

——. 1999. 'Los códices de las "*Cantigas de Santa Maria*": su problemática', in Montoya Martínez and Domínguez Rodríguez, *El scriptorium alfonsí*, pp. 127–58.

——. 2000. 'The "evolution" of the *Cantigas de Santa Maria*: the relationships between mss T, F, and E', in Parkinson (ed.), *Cobras e Son*, pp. 186–213.

——. 2001. '"Ben vennas mayo": A "failed" *cantiga de Santa Maria*', in *Estudos Galegos Medievais*, ed Antonio Cortijo Ocaña, Giorgio Perissinotto, and Harvey L. Sharrer (Santa Barbara: Centro de Estudos Galegos, University of California Santa Barbara), pp. 97–132.

Signori, Gabriela. 1996. 'The Miracle Kitchen and its Ingredients. A Methodical and Critical Approach to Marian Shrine Wonders (10th to 13th Century)', *Hagiographica*, 3: 277–303.

Snow, Joseph T. 1979. 'The Central Role of the Troubadour persona of Alfonso X in the *Cantigas de Santa Maria*', *Bulletin of Hispanic Studies*, 56: 305–16.

——. 1985. 'Alfonso X y/en sus Cantigas', in Mondéjar and Montoya Martínez (eds), *Estudios alfonsíes*, pp. 78–88.

——. 1987. 'Lo que nos dice la Cantiga 300 de Alfonso X' *Studia Hispanica Medievalia. II Jornadas de Literatura Española Medieval* (Buenos Aires: Universidad Catolica Argentina), pp. 99–110 .

——. 1990. 'The satirical poetry of Alfonso X: a look at its relationship to the *Cantigas de Santa Maria*', in *Alfonso X of Castile, the Learned King (1221–1284): An International Symposium, Harvard University, 17 November 1984*, ed. Francisco Márquez-Villanueva and Carlos Vega, Harvard Studies in Romance Languages, 43 (Cambridge: Department of Romance Languages and Literatures of Harvard University), pp. 110–31.

——. 1994. 'Macar poucos cantares acabei e con son': la firma de Alfonso X a sus *Cantigas de Santa Maria*', in *Actas del III Congreso de la AHLM (Salamanca, 3–6 oct. de 1989)*, ed. M. I. Toro Pascua (Salamanca: Depto de Lit. Española e Hispanoamericana), vol. II, pp. 1021–30.

——. 2009. 'El yo anónimo y las *Cantigas de Santa María* de Alfonso X', *Alcanate*, 6: 309–22.

——. 2012. *The Poetry of Alfonso X el Sabio. An Annotated Critical Bibliography (1278–2010)* (Woodbridge: Tamesis).

——. 2014. 'Alfonso X' *Oxford Bibliographies Online* <http://www.oxfordbibliographies.com>

Tavani, Giuseppe. 1969. *Poesie del duecento nella Peninsola Iberica. Problemi della lirica galego-portoghese*, Officina Romanica, 12 (Rome: Edizioni dell'Ateneo).

——. 2002. *Trovadores e Jograis. Introdução à Poesia Medieval Galego-Portuguesa* (Lisbon: Caminho).

——. 2007. *Arte de Trovar do Cancioneiro da Bibioteca Nacional de Lisboa* (Lisbon: Colibri).

——. 2010. 'Copistas, cancioneros, editores. Tres problemas para a lírica galega medieval', in *Estudos de edición crítica e lírica galego-portuguesa*, ed. Mariña Arbor Aldea and Antonio F. Guiadanes (Santiago de Compostela: Universidade), pp. 55–67.

Ward, Benedicta. 1982. *Miracles and the Medieval Mind* (London: Scolar Press).

Wilson, Evelyn Faye. 1946. *The Stella Maris of John of Garland. Edited, together with a Study of Certain Collections of Mary Legends Made in Northern France in the Twelfth and Thirteenth Centuries* (Cambridge: Medieval Academy of America — Wellesley College).

MHRA Critical Texts

This series aims to provide affordable critical editions of lesser-known literary texts that are not in print or are difficult to obtain. The texts will be taken from the following languages: English, French, German, Italian, Portuguese, Russian, and Spanish. Titles will be selected by members of the distinguished Editorial Board and edited by leading academics. The aim is to produce scholarly editions rather than teaching texts, but the potential for crossover to undergraduate reading lists is recognized. The books will appeal both to academic libraries and individual scholars.

Malcolm Cook
Chairman, Editorial Board

www.criticaltexts.mhra.org.uk

www.ingramcontent.com/pod-product-compliance
Ingram Content Group UK Ltd.
Pitfield, Milton Keynes, MK11 3LW, UK
UKHW051132260726
13967UKWH00010B/3002

9 781781 880234